DAY TRIPS IN DELMARVA

by
by Alan Fisher

RAMBLER BOOKS

Baltimore 1992

DAY TRIPS IN DELMARVA

by Alan Fisher
Maps and photographs by the author

Rambler Books
1430 Park Avenue
Baltimore, MD 21217

If you notice errors in the text or maps, please point them out in a letter to the publisher.

Printed in the United States of America

FIRST EDITION   1 2 3 4 5 6 7 8 9 10

Permission has kindly been granted to quote passages from the following books and publications:

Dize, Frances. *Smith Island, Chesapeake Bay.* Tidewater Publishers, Centreville, MD, 1990, p. 18.

Horton, Tom. *Bay Country.* The Johns Hopkins University Press, Baltimore and London, 1987, p. 113.

Wheatley, Harold. *"This Is My Island, Tangier."* National Geographic, November 1973, p. 700.

ISBN 0-9614963-2-0

CONTENTS

MAP 1 -- The Delmarva Peninsula

NOTE:

Big numbers refer to chapters.

Little numbers designate roads.

PREFACE

THE DELMARVA PENINSULA is the landmass — intriguing on a map and just as intriguing in reality — that separates Chesapeake Bay from Delaware Bay and the Atlantic Ocean. It consists of southern Delaware and the Eastern Shore of Maryland and Virginia — hence *Del-Mar-Va*, a term of commercial origin that came into use during the first quarter of this century. Although Delmarva has two cities exceeding 20,000 in population — Dover and Salisbury — and a string of popular beach resorts along the Atlantic coast, these places are not featured in this book, which deals rather with the region's chief natural attractions and its smaller towns and historic sites.

Recognizing that the Delmarva Peninsula is large and that many visitors will be coming from beyond its bounds, I have included in this book only places that I think are worth driving a considerable distance to see — in short, the best of Delmarva. I have tried to provide variety: car tours combined with short walks and longer hikes; wildlife refuges and wild beaches; historic river ports, agricultural market towns, and bayside villages. Many of the places and itineraries described here provide outstanding opportunities for bicycling as well as car touring (as, for example, along the C. & D. Canal embankment roads) and for canoeing (as at the Pocomoke River, where canoes can be rented locally). Smith and Tangier islands, of course, are not only fascinating in themselves but also provide the occasion for a pleasant ride on the mail boat or one of the tourist excursion boats.

Because it is anticipated that readers will be driving from different places to reach the sites described here, the directions outline different avenues of approach. Necessarily, there is much repetition, so focus on the set of directions that applies to you and skip the others.

Most of this book's commentary on social history and natural history is general in character. It is intended to be read ahead of time and consists of pertinent essays rather than specific observations about this or that structure or feature seen along the way — although there is that too. Each chapter stands on its own, but I hope that the cumulative effect is a fairly comprehensive introduction to Delmarva's land, history, and wildlife.

The following people helped me with this book by reviewing the text and making suggestions: Bronwen Anderson, Maggie Briggs, Paul D. Daly, Ben Hren, Michael J. Kennedy, Larry G. Points, and John D. Schroer. Joanne Doyle researched the word *Delmarva*. And Penny Firth and David Knapp posed for the cover. Many, many thanks.

Alan Fisher
Baltimore

PERSONAL COMFORT AND SAFETY

PLEASE READ THIS. It is customary, in guidebooks such as this, to include a catalog of cautions about possible nuisances and hazards. Such matters do not make for scintillating reading, but really, I think that you will be glad to have read here about a few potential problems — so that you can avoid them — rather than learn about them through uncomfortable (or even dangerous) experience.

Many of the excursions described in this book include rural walks, some fairly long. For these outings, wear shoes that you do not mind getting muddy or wet. In winter wear hiking boots or leather hiking shoes. I usually carry a small knapsack containing insect repellent, sunscreen (especially for the beach), a sandwich, a plastic water bottle, perhaps a bathing suit and towel, and an extra layer of clothing, such as a sweater or rain parka. For longer walks, you should always be prepared for bad weather, particularly during the colder part of the year, when wind, rain, or snow can introduce a risk of hypothermia. Personally, I think that late fall, winter, and early spring are the best times for exploring Delmarva's many marshy wildlife areas, because at that time of year there are no mosquitoes, no heat, no crowds, and abundant waterfowl.

Ticks can be a problem from early spring through autumn; some may even carry Lyme disease. So check your clothing occasionally while walking through woods or tall grass, and also when you return to your car. And check your body for ticks when you get home.

Hunting is sometimes allowed at the wildlife management areas described in this book. Even many of our national wildlife refuges have brief hunting periods in order to control deer populations. Where appropriate, I try to alert you to the possible risk from hunting, but for precise information on hunting schedules, call the telephone numbers provided in the introductory material to the various chapters. And if you go walking in areas where hunting is underway, wear bright orange clothing.

During winter, all too often drownings occur when people fall through the ice after venturing out onto frozen ponds, rivers, or the shelf of ice that sometimes extends from shore into Chesapeake Bay or even the ocean. I am sure that you have heard this before; everybody has. And yet each winter a few more people die in this manner. Don't be one of them; stay off the ice. And tell your kids.

Other sound advice that is ignored with puzzling regularity concerns lightning. If you are at the beach or some other exposed area and a lightning storm approaches, return to your car immediately. That is the safest place to be — safer even than a small shelter. And if a storm arrives before you get back to your car, hunker down in a low spot. Don't worry about getting wet or feeling stupid as you lie there with the rain pouring down. Clearly it is better to get wet and yet be safe than to try to stay dry by huddling under a beach umbrella, an isolated tree, or some other target for lightning.

Because the car tours in this book are too long for most bicyclists and occasionally make use of major highways, they are not intended to double as bicycle tours. Nonetheless, most of the chapters describe shorter opportunities for bicycling — but not for children. Bicycling on roads is risky enough for adults, and in my experience children lack the discipline to stay steadily as far to the right as possible and to ride single file. Two other major rules for bicycling are to get off the road before dusk and to wear a helmet.

Several of the outings described here are at the beach. Some of these beaches are lifeguarded; others are not, and clearly the latter require more vigilance and caution if you go swimming. At lifeguarded beaches you might be discouraged — or even prohibited — from using buoyant mats or floats, but at unguarded beaches there may be no one to tell you about the hazards of these devices. Briefly, they can provide a false sense of security to poor swimmers, particularly children. Some of these items can deflate suddenly, or the occupant can be knocked off by a wave or blown out to sea by a strong wind. The fact is that drownings have been associated with these devices. Also, when there is surf, be conservative in judging what you and your children can handle.

Finally, where the trails described here follow roads for short distances, walk well off the road on the shoulder to minimize the risk of being hit by a car, and use caution, especially at dusk or after dark, where the routes cross roads. Studies show that in poor light conditions, motorists typically cannot even see pedestrians in time to stop, so your safety depends entirely on you.

In sum, use good judgment and common sense to evaluate the particular circumstances that you find. Heed local regulations and signs, and do not undertake any unusual risks.

1

SOUTH CHESAPEAKE CITY
THE CHESAPEAKE AND DELAWARE CANAL
DELAWARE CITY
FORT DELAWARE STATE PARK

The Chesapeake and Delaware Canal cuts across the narrow neck of land at the northern end of the Delmarva Peninsula, linking the head of Chesapeake Bay with the Delaware River about 25 miles downstream from Wilmington. A stupendous volume of earth dredged from the waterway has been heaped along the banks, creating high bluffs that slope steeply down to the ribbon of water that parts the land. Running along the bluffs are a series of dirt roads, in some places arranged one above the other, and now and then interconnected, like the tiers and ramps of an open pit mine. Exploring these roads by car, by fat-tired all-terrain bicycle, or on foot is great fun and provides by far the best way to view the canal and to appreciate the immensity of this engineering project. The canal embankment and dirt roads are open daily from dawn until dusk, but before you go, please read the discussion starting at the bottom of page 18. The canal (and the canal museum at South Chesapeake City) are managed by the U.S. Army Corps of Engineers; telephone (410) 885-5622. Parts of the canal embankment and of the land and marsh farther back from the canal constitute the C. & D. Canal Wildlife Management Area, which is administered by the Delaware Department of Natural Resources and Environmental Control, Division of Fish and Wildlife; telephone (302) 834-8433.

Near the western end of the canal is South Chesapeake City, a small and picturesque canal town that retains much of the appearance of its nineteenth-century origins. In the few blocks of its old business district are concentrated a variety of antique shops, country stores, and restaurants. Located just outside South Chesapeake City is the outstanding C. & D. Canal Museum, which is open Monday through Saturday from 8 to 4:15. And near the eastern end of the waterway is another old canal town, Delaware City, from which a passenger ferry operates to Fort Delaware State Park on Pea Patch Island in the Delaware

River. Built immediately before the Civil War, massive Fort Delaware is open from 11 to 6 on weekends and holidays from the last weekend in April through September. The last boat that will allow you sufficient time to see the fort leaves Delaware City at 4 P.M. Pets must be leashed. The ferry and fort are managed by the Delaware Department of Natural Resources and Environmental Control, Division of Parks and Recreation; telephone (302) 834-7941. On some evenings in summer, the ferry also provides cruises on the C. & D. Canal. Call for schedule information and details.

THE CANAL ERA got underway in this country toward the end of the eighteenth century and reached its peak in the 1830s and '40s, when many hundreds of miles of waterways were built in the eastern states to transport bulk products to and from the major cities. Then canal construction and use tapered off as most of the waterways were supplanted by the newly-developed railroads. In a few cases, however, some of the most successful canals, originally built early in the last century, are still in operation today, and, indeed, have been enlarged repeatedly over the years so that they now carry infinitely more tonnage than the old canals ever did. Among these still-flourishing works is the Chesapeake and Delaware Canal, shown on Map 2 and now one of the busiest canals in the world.

The idea for such a canal goes back to the first century of European settlement in the Chesapeake region. In 1661 Augustine Herman, surveyor and maker of an excellent map of Maryland and Virginia (for which Cecilius Calvert, second Baron Baltimore and the proprietor of Maryland, granted him 4,000 acres in the "farr remote, then unknown wilderness" in 1662), outlined the possibility of a canal linking the head of Chesapeake Bay with the westernmost meander of the Delaware River. The idea was considered several times in the eighteenth century, but not surprisingly, nothing came of the proposal during the colonial period, when Great Britain was more interested in promoting trade *with* the colonies than *among* them.

After the War of Independence and more than a decade of desultory negotiations, the canal got its start in 1799, when Pennsylvania, Maryland, Delaware, and the federal government agreed to join together to purchase stock in the Chesapeake and Delaware Canal Company. Five possible routes were surveyed — the most northerly linking the Elk River with the Christiana River at Wilmington and the most

MAP 2 -- Chesapeake and Delaware Canal

southerly making use of the Chester River — before a route was finally selected. Excavation of the canal began in 1804, but funds were quickly spent and work came to a stop in 1806. Not until 1824 was a reorganized canal company able to muster financial support, in the form of new subscriptions for stock, to resume work on the waterway, which opened for navigation in 1829.

As first constructed, the canal was nearly 14 miles long, 66 feet wide at the water line, 36 feet wide at the bottom, and 10 feet deep. Near the canal's midpoint, up to 77 vertical feet of earth in a swath 366 feet wide had to be excavated by hand. Water level in the canal was 14 feet above sea level. Boats were raised to, and lowered from, the canal by locks, each measuring 100 by 22 feet. There was a high lock at Chesapeake City at the western end of the waterway and a pair of locks — one at St. Georges and another at Delaware City — near the eastern end of the canal. Barges, mostly carrying coal and lumber, were pulled by tow lines harnessed to mules or horses that followed a towpath along the canal bank. Later, steam tugs took over the task of pulling or pushing barges through the narrow waterway. Other vessels using the canal included passenger packets, floating stores, and an occasional itinerant showboat. The Baltimore and Philadelphia Steamship Company even built a fleet of narrow, shallow-draft, propeller-driven boats that closely fit the canal locks and provided through passage between the two metropolises.

Because water was constantly lost from the canal through evaporation, leakage, and locking boats in and out at each end, water in the canal had to be replenished. At first this was done exclusively from several streams that flowed into the canal and by water released from Lums Pond (a man-made reservoir north of the canal, and now a state park). But these sources proved to be inadequate, so water was pumped up to the canal from sea level. The C. & D. Canal Museum occupies the former pump house, built in 1837 and still containing a huge waterwheel and a pair of handsome rocker-beam steam engines installed in 1851.

Because passage through the canal and more particularly through the locks was limited to boats of shallow draft and narrow beam, the towns at each end of the waterway became thriving transfer points where cargo was unloaded from larger vessels, warehoused, and reloaded onto canal boats, and *vice versa*. So-called arks — large, ungainly barges used to float bulk cargo down the Delaware and Susquehanna rivers — were even dismantled at Delaware City and Chesapeake City and sold for timber because they could neither pass through the canal nor be taken back upstream.

By the beginning of the twentieth century, the canal no longer accommodated the growing commerce of the mid-Atlantic region, so in 1906 President Theodore Roosevelt (a promoter, too, of the Panama Canal) appointed a commission to study the possibility of a federal takeover and enlargement of the Chesapeake and Delaware Canal. In 1919 the canal was purchased by the federal government, which undertook the Herculean task of lowering the canal to sea level, thus eliminating the need for locks and pumps. Also, the waterway was widened to 90 feet, its depth increased to 12 feet, and its east entrance relocated to Reedy Point. This work was completed in 1927, and although the result was a much more efficient (and toll-free) canal, the improvements led to the rapid decline of Chesapeake City and Delaware City, where boats no longer had reason to stop. And, of course, a large part of Chesapeake City along the north bank was taken for the canal.

During the Great Depression of the 1930s the canal's width and depth were more than doubled as a project of the Works Progress Administration. And during the 1950s and early '60s, the canal was enlarged yet again to its present width of 450 feet (measured at the bottom) and depth of 35 feet, thus accommodating ocean-going cargo ships. Vessels as large as 958 feet long and 106 feet wide have passed through the canal. As ships have gotten bigger and bigger, there has even been talk of enlarging the canal still further.

AUTOMOBILE DIRECTIONS: Cutting across the isthmus that separates the upper end of Chesapeake Bay and the Delaware River, the Chesapeake and Delaware Canal more or less defines the northern boundary of the Delmarva Peninsula. (See Map 1 in the Table of Contents.) Go first to South Chesapeake City and the C. & D. Canal Museum, located near the western end of the canal, where Route 213 crosses the waterway.

To South Chesapeake City from Interstate 95 north of Delmarva: Interstate 95 passes about 8 miles north of the C. & D. Canal, but there is no direct exit onto Route 213. So if you are coming from the direction of Baltimore on Interstate 95, take Exit 100 for Route 272 toward the town of North East. Near the bottom of the exit ramp, fork right toward North East and follow Route 272 south 1.5 miles to Route 40. Turn left (east) onto Route 40 and go 6.6 miles, then turn right (south) onto Route 213.

If, however, you are coming from the direction of Wilmington on Interstate 95, take Exit 1A for Route 896 south toward

16

Middletown. From the bottom of the exit ramp, follow Route 896 south 3.0 miles to Route 40. Turn right (west) onto Route 40 and go 4.5 miles, then turn left (south) onto Route 213.

Once you are on Route 213, follow it south 5.8 miles to and across the C. & D. Canal. At the first opportunity after crossing the high bridge, turn right for Route 286 and Route 342 toward the Chesapeake City Historical District and C. & D. Canal Museum. Immediately bear right again, pass under the bridge, then turn left onto George Street (Route 286). Go 0.2 mile to an intersection with Second Street, then turn right and go one block to Bohemia Avenue. This is **South Chesapeake City**, shown on Map 3.

To South Chesapeake City from the Chesapeake Bay Bridge: Follow Route 50/301 across Kent Island. At the point where Route 50 and Route 301 split, continue straight on Route 301 northbound for 31.8 miles to an intersection with Route 313. Turn left and follow Route 313 for 2.5 miles to a traffic light in Galena, and from there continue straight north on Route 213 for 14.2 miles toward Elkton. Immediately before the high bridge over the C. & D. Canal, exit to the right for Route 286 toward the Chesapeake City Historical District, the C. & D. Canal Museum, and South Chesapeake City. Go 0.4 mile to an intersection with Second Street, then turn right and go one block to Bohemia Avenue. This is **South Chesapeake City**, shown on Map 3.

To South Chesapeake City from southern Delmarva and the Chesapeake Bay Bridge-Tunnel at Norfolk: After crossing the bridge-tunnel, follow Route 13 north into Maryland and past Salisbury to Dover, Delaware. (Alternatively, follow Route 113 north to Route 13 in Dover.) Then, from the junction of Route 13 and Route 113 in Dover, continue north on Route 13 for 5.8 miles to an intersection with Route 42 at a traffic light. Turn left toward Cheswold and Kenton and go 18.0 miles as Route 42 passes through Cheswold and Kenton; continue as straight as possible as the road (which loses its Delaware number designation and finally joins Maryland's Route 313) heads northwest and reaches a junction with Route 301. Cross Route 301 and follow Route 313 north 2.5 miles to a traffic light in Galena, and from there continue straight north on Route 213 for 14.2 miles toward Elkton. Immediately before the high bridge over the C. & D. Canal, exit to the right for Route 286 toward the Chesapeake City Historical District, the C. & D. Canal Museum, and South Chesapeake City. Go 0.4 mile to an intersection with Second Street, then turn right and go one block to Bohemia Avenue. This is **South Chesapeake City**, shown on Map 3.

To South Chesapeake City from Salisbury and the Delaware and Maryland seashore resorts: From the vicinity of Salisbury, take Route 13 north to Dover, Delaware. From Ocean City and Bethany Beach, go west to Route 113 and follow it north to Route 13 in Dover. And from Rehoboth Beach, follow Route 1 north to Route 113, then take 113 north to Route 13 in Dover.

Once you are at the junction of Route 13 and Route 113 in Dover, follow Route 13 north for 5.8 miles to an intersection with Route 42 at a traffic light, and there turn left (west) toward Cheswold and Kenton. Go 18.0 miles as Route 42 passes through Cheswold and Kenton; continue as straight as possible as the road (which loses its Delaware number designation and finally joins Maryland's Route 313) heads northwest and reaches a junction with Route 301. Cross Route 301 and follow Route 313 north 2.5 miles to a traffic light in Galena, and from there continue straight north on Route 213 for 14.2 miles toward Elkton. Immediately before the high bridge over the C. & D. Canal, exit to the right for Route 286 toward the Chesapeake City Historical District, the C. & D. Canal Museum, and South Chesapeake City. Go 0.4 mile to an intersection with Second Street, then turn right and go one block to Bohemia Avenue. This is **South Chesapeake City**, shown on Map 3.

FROM SOUTH CHESAPEAKE CITY TO THE C. & D. CANAL MUSEUM: The bold line on Map 3 shows the way. From the corner of Second Street (Route 286) and Bohemia Avenue in South Chesapeake City, follow Second Street downhill away from the high bridge. With the canal on the left, go 0.4 miles to the entrance to the C. & D. Canal Museum on the left.

CANAL EMBANKMENT ROADS: A system of dirt roads runs along both banks of the canal and around various plateaus and diked basins of spoil dredged from the canal. At the canal's midpoint, where the cut is deepest, as many as six tiers

MAP 3 -- South Chesapeake City

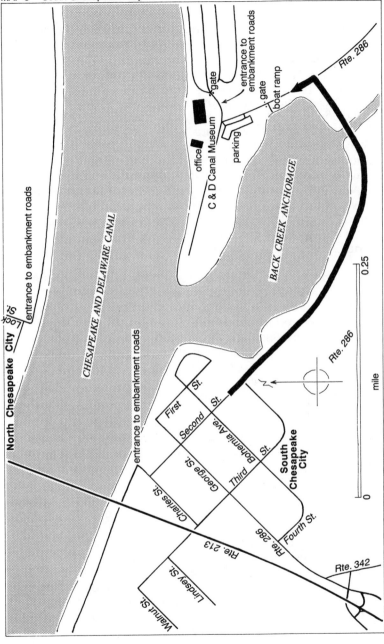

of roads rise one above the other along the north bank. The entire system of roads is shown on Map 4, which is a schematic diagram not drawn to scale. If you want to explore these roads, bear in mind two warnings.

First, the embankment roads are rough in places. Because they are unpaved, their condition varies with the weather and with the seasons, and it is impossible to say ahead of time what condition they will be in when you go there. In general, the lower roads near the canal are the best maintained, while the higher roads are sometimes little more than rutted Jeep tracks through man-made badlands. I have seen ordinary cars traveling on the low roads without difficulty at all seasons (and have often driven over them myself in the car shown on the cover of this book). But I have also seen Jeep-type vehicles mired in mud along some of the more obscure roads distant from the canal. Of course, you will have to judge for yourself whether your car or your bicycle can handle the conditions that you find.

Second, hunting is permitted along the embankments and plateaus at times during fall and winter; telephone (302) 834-8433 for the precise hunting schedule. During the hunting season, stay on the roads, out of the hunters' way. If you are bicycling or walking during this period, wear a blaze-orange vest or jacket. However, even during the hunting season, you can avoid hunters altogether by going on Sunday, when hunting is prohibited.

There are several places to enter the system of embankment roads. Focusing first on the roads along the south side of the canal, one access point (usually open only on weekdays before 3 P.M.) is by the C. & D. Canal Museum just outside South Chesapeake City. From the museum's parking lot, follow a driveway up past the stone museum and through a gate in a chainlink fence.

Another entrance (one that is always open) is at the village of Summit, which is located midway along the south bank of the canal. Summit can be reached from the C. & D. Canal Museum as follows: After exiting from the museum compound through the main gate, pass the road that leads right toward South Chesapeake City. Go 3.3 miles on Route 286, then turn left at an intersection and continue 0.8 mile to Route 896. Turn right onto Route 896, but go only 0.7 mile, then turn left toward Summit on Road 63. Go 0.8 mile to the entrance to the Delaware C. & D. Canal Wildlife Management Area, where you can descend a series of ramps to the edge of the canal.

MAP 4 -- Schematic diagram of the C & D Canal embankment roads

This schematic map is not drawn to scale and is only intended to show how the embankment roads interconnect with each other and with nearby paved roads. Entrances to the embankment roads are marked with this symbol: ▲

As shown on Map 4, the embankment roads can also be entered (or exited) at South St. Georges.

An entirely different section of dirt roads west of South Chesapeake City can be entered by descending from the corner of Second Street and Charles Street in the old canal town.

The embankment roads along the north side of the canal can be entered at several points shown on Map 4. These embankment roads are split into two sections (east and west) separated by an arm of the old canal at Summit North Marina. At North Chesapeake City, the western section of roads can be entered at the foot of Lock Street. At North St. Georges, the eastern section of roads can be entered under the Route 13 bridge where North Main Street joins the Kirkwood - St. Georges Road.

DELAWARE CITY and FORT DELAWARE STATE PARK:

As shown on Map 2, near the eastern end of the C. & D. Canal is Delaware City, formerly the waterway's terminus on the Delaware River before the canal's outlet was moved south to Reedy Point. The town is still served by the relatively narrow Delaware City Branch Canal, which follows the old route, now lowered to sea level. The canal's only surviving lock (it is not in service) is located at Delaware City, which better than any other place provides a glimpse of what the C. & D. Canal looked like during the nineteenth century. The town, too, retains much of its nineteenth-century architecture and atmosphere, particularly along Clinton Street and the adjacent streets to the north. Delaware City is also the embarkation point for the passenger ferry operating to Fort Delaware on Pea Patch Island in the middle of the Delaware River.

To reach Delaware City, use Map 2 to navigate from wherever you end up after exploring the canal's embankment roads. Go to the intersection of Route 9 and Clinton Street in Delaware City, and then follow Clinton Street to its end at the waterfront. The parking lot and ferry dock for Fort Delaware State Park are on the right near the end of Clinton Street.

Fort Delaware on Pea Patch Island was built by the federal government in order to guard the water approach to Wilmington and Philadelphia. The island was the site of earthworks during the War of 1812 and of a masonry fort built on inadequate foundations in 1819 and torn down in 1833. Work on yet another fort began in 1848, and by the time it was finished in 1859 and equipped with guns and manned at the outbreak of the Civil War, the massive pentagonal fortress was said to be the strongest bastion on the East Coast. As still seen today, its high, moated walls were sheathed in granite. On the two sides facing downstream, cannon concealed within vaulted brick chambers (or casemates) fired through openings (embrasures) arranged on two levels with yet a third tier of smaller guns atop the walls. The photograph on page 22 shows the fort's western side, with many openings for small arms.

In March of 1862 the fort's commander was warned by Secretary of War Edwin Stanton that the Confederate ironclad *Virginia*, which was based at Norfolk, might try to run passed the fort to attack Philadelphia. This threat, however, evaporated when the *Virginia* was destroyed by her commander as the Confederates abandoned Norfolk in May. Even before then, the possibility of a raid by Southern ships up the Delaware River was considered to be so remote that Fort Delaware was used to house 258 Confederate prisoners who arrived in April.

For the rest of the Civil War, Fort Delaware and Pea Patch Island served as a prison camp. Barracks were built outside the fort's walls, and by July of 1862, there were about 3,000 captured Confederate soldiers on the island guarded by fewer than 300 Union troops. Eventually, barracks for 10,000 prisoners and a hospital for 800 patients were built. Following the battle of Gettysburg in July of 1863, the prisoner population on Pea Patch Island reached a peak of 12,595, and after that fluctuated between 6,500 and 9,300 for the duration of the war. Confederate officers — at times numbering as many as 160 — were confined within the fort itself, as were some political prisoners.

In the prison camp's crowded conditions, mortality from epidemics of smallpox, dysentery, and other diseases was high, totaling about 2,700 men during the war. In just October of 1863, 12.5 percent of the prisoners died. On July 26, 1863, Dr. S. Weir Mitchell of Philadelphia visited the vermin-infested camp (which he termed an "inferno") and summarized what he saw there:

A thousand ill; twelve thousand on an island which should hold four . . . ; twenty deaths a day of dysentery and the living having more life on them than in them. Occasional lack of water and thus a Christian (!) nation treats the captives of its sword.

More than two months later the Union surgeon at the fort wrote to his superior that "the mortality to me is fearful and it is melancholy proof . . . of the unfitness of this wet island as a depot for large numbers of men." However, Confederate prisoners continued to be brought to the island in droves following each large battle and held there until they were either paroled after taking an oath of allegiance to the United States of America or exchanged for Union soldiers held by the South.

The Civil War provided the impetus for such rapid improvements in naval ordnance that by the end of the conflict Fort Delaware and other forts like it were obsolete. Their high masonry walls were intended only to protect against smoothbore guns mounted on wooded ships, which presumably would be sunk or repelled before such forts suffered much damage. But the development of rifled artillery with greater range, accuracy, and penetrating power than the old smoothbores raised the spectre that works like Fort Delaware could be reduced quickly to rubble from a great distance, as in fact occurred during the Civil War at several massive masonry forts guarding Southern seaports, albeit the damage there was inflicted by land-based siege guns. But it was not long before guns of similar power were mounted on battleships. In 1869 Major General John Gross Barnard, who during the Civil War had directed the construction of a ring of sixty-eight low, earthen forts surrounding Washington, D.C., recommended that Fort Delaware be supplemented by a modern fort on each bank of the Delaware River, as was subsequently done.

In 1897 construction began on reinforced-concrete revetments for three 12-inch coastal defense guns within the old walls of Fort Delaware. The difference between these emplacements and the older part of the fort emphasizes the tremendous changes that had occurred in the field of armaments during the prior fifty years. The new guns were mounted on carriages that allowed them to be lowered — or to "disappear" — behind the revetment walls for loading. Elevators raised the shells and powder from the ammunition chambers below. Batteries of smaller guns were built outside the walls.

Fort Delaware was garrisoned during World War I and again following the entry of the United States into World War II, but it was abandoned by all but a searchlight squad in 1943 after Fort Miles at Cape Henlopen became the main center for the defense of the Delaware. Declared surplus property, Pea Patch Island was leased in 1945, then turned over to the state of Delaware in 1948. In 1951 the fort — by then severely vandalized — was made a state park, largely as a result of lobbying by the Fort Delaware Society, a non-profit organization that maintains a museum and gift shop at the fort and which continues to work for the fort's restoration. For information on the society's programs or on how to become a member, write to the Fort Delaware Society, P.O. Box 553, Delaware City, DE 19706.

Also on Pea Patch Island is a short trail leading upriver from the fort to an observation tower overlooking one of the region's largest heron nesting areas.

2

ODESSA and vicinity

The 60-mile car tour outlined in this chapter explores some of the back roads of northeastern Delmarva, and along the way visits colonial manors, eighteenth-century merchant houses, old churches, Victorian villages, and other oases of the past scattered throughout the rich agricultural landscape that for more than three centuries has formed the foundation of most commercial activity in this region. The route starts (and ends) at the village of Odessa, Delaware, where under the auspices of Historic Houses of Odessa, two sumptuous houses, both furnished to reflect life in the late eighteenth and early nineteenth centuries, are open to the public. Historic Houses of Odessa also features the Brick Hotel Gallery, which offers exhibits of American decorative arts. The houses and gallery are open March through December, Tuesday through Saturday from 10 to 4, and Sunday from 1 to 4. They are closed Mondays, Easter, July 4, Thanksgiving, December 24 and 25, and all of January and February. Historic Houses of Odessa is administered by Winterthur Museum; telephone (302) 378-4027 or (302) 378-4069. "Christmas in Odessa" is an annual open house when many old private residences may be toured as well. Sponsored by The Women's Club of Odessa, the open house is held on the weekend that includes the first Sunday in December.

The car tour eventually leads to Smyrna, where there are many old houses, one of which is operated by the Duck Creek Historical Society as the Smyrna Museum, open on Saturdays from 1 to 4.

The car tour also passes the Allee House southeast of Smyrna at Bombay Hook (which is mentioned in Chapter 3 as well). The Allee House is a distinguished colonial farmhouse that has been restored to its eighteenth-century appearance. It is open free of charge each Saturday and Sunday from 2 to 5; telephone (302) 678-4266.

Although they are rarely open, two old churches that are discussed in this chapter are well worth visiting, even if only to view from the outside. Those who want to see the insides must plan carefully. Services are held at Old Drawyers Presbyterian

Church north of Odessa *once annually* on the first Sunday in June, and the public is welcome. Old Bohemia Church near Warwick, Maryland — one of the oldest permanent Catholic churches in the English colonies — is open from 1 to 5 on the third Sunday of April, May, September, and October. Mass is celebrated at 4 P.M. (Should Easter fall on the third Sunday of April, Old Bohemia Church is open the following Sunday.)

Finally, bicyclists may enjoy a ride of 32 miles round-trip along scenic Route 9 between Odessa and Bombay Hook, as discussed at the beginning of the tour directions on page 32.

IN THE SECOND QUARTER of the seventeenth century, the tidewater region along the Delaware River was settled by Swedes, Finns, and a few Dutchmen under the direction of the New Sweden Company, organized in 1637. By mid-century New Sweden had a European population of about 300 people concentrated at Fort Christiana (now Wilmington) and Tinicum Island (now part of Philadelphia). In 1655, however, the straggling Swedish colony was overawed by a Dutch force sailing from New Amsterdam (New York). Dutch rule, however, was brief, for in 1663 the English seized New Amsterdam, and the following year gained control of the region along the Delaware River.

Odessa (originally called Cantwell's Bridge) got its start as a small village about sixty years after the English took over the Delaware region. Among those Englishmen receiving spoils of conquest was Captain Edward Cantwell, first Sheriff of New Castle County, who in 1676 acquired a large estate on the Appoquinimink River that had been confiscated from a former Dutch official. In 1731 Cantwell's son Richard obtained permission to erect a toll bridge over the Appoquinimink, and Cantwell's Bridge evolved into a stopping place for people traveling from the Delaware River to Chesapeake Bay.

In about 1760 David Wilson opened a general store at Cantwell's Bridge, and from it he sold all manner of supplies, tools, and household goods to farmers from throughout the surrounding district. Wilson's activity did much to make Cantwell's Bridge a center of agricultural trade and a local port for shipping out grain.

In 1765 land at Cantwell's Bridge was purchased by William Corbit, a member of the third generation of a prosperous Quaker family that had lived in New Castle County since 1717. After learning the tanning trade as a young man in Philadelphia, Corbit opened a tannery at Cantwell's Bridge in 1767. Two years later his sister married David

Wilson, who had a large Georgian house built for himself and his new wife on Main Street next to his store. Wilson's master builder/architect was John May, who in turn was hired by William Corbit to build a still grander house, finished in 1774 and apparently based on the best of what Corbit had seen in Philadelphia. The house is shown in the photograph on page 26. With its generous but balanced proportions, five-bay facade, stone lintels, central hall, and interior paneling, the Corbit House is said by architectural historians to be one of the best examples of the Georgian style in Delaware.

In 1817 there were about thirty houses at Cantwell's Bridge, all on the south side of Main Street. Four years later the land to the north was laid out into lots and streets, and the following year the Brick Hotel was built at the corner of Main and Second. The Corbit House, the Wilson House, and the Brick Hotel are now all open to the public under the auspices of Historic Houses of Odessa.

Cantwell's Bridge reached its peak of prosperity during the second quarter of the nineteenth century. In his *History of Delaware* (published in 1888), J. Thomas Scharf wrote:

> In 1825 Cantwell's Bridge was a place of considerable importance. . . . At this time Cantwell's Bridge was the principal grain market for the surrounding country. Grain was conveyed here for shipment from all points within a radius of twelve or fifteen miles. Six large granaries, holding about thirty thousand bushels, standing on the bank of the Appoquinimink, were often completely filled, which delayed the purchase of grain until some of it was shipped to Philadelphia. From 1820 until 1840 there were shipped from this town four hundred thousand of bushels of grain annually. . . . During the busiest seasons, six sloops made weekly trips to Philadelphia, and three coasting schooners went to Boston and the East, besides a large number of transient vessels.

In 1855 the town's name was changed to Odessa after the large Russian grain port on the Black Sea. At about the same time, however, the newly-constructed Delaware Railroad bypassed the town by more than 3 miles to the west, a circumstance that led to a precipitous economic decline at Odessa as shippers relocated their business to be near the railroad. By the beginning of the twentieth century, Odessa's big granaries had disappeared from her rotting wharves, and the town was served by only one small steamer making two trips weekly to Philadelphia.

Compounding Odessa's difficulties was a trauma affecting the entire region. In the last quarter of the nineteenth century the "yellows" — a form of blight — ruined the extensive peach orchards that by then provided the main crop of southern Delaware (whose state flower is the peach blossom).

Odessa's decline as a mercantile center has been complete, and today it is almost wholly residential in character. Although it lies astride Route 13, it has the air of a quiet village, where dozens of handsomely restored houses, barns, and gardens provide a glimpse into a seemingly idyllic past — a scene not entirely accurate, since many of today's residences on Main Street formerly housed (at least in part) trade establishments and professional offices. Still other commercial structures, including the Corbit tannery and the Wilson store, have been removed altogether.

The leading figure in Odessa's program of architectural restoration was H. Rodney Sharp, who in 1938 bought the Corbit House from a descendant of William Corbit. Sharp restored the Corbit house, then went on to acquire and restore — or in some cases, tear down — other dilapidated structures nearby. His work included moving a house — the Collins-Sharp House, now located at the corner of Second Street and High Street — from the shore of the Delaware River near Taylors Bridge. Using material left over from some of his restoration projects, he even built a new old house, called Left Overs, next to the Brick Hotel. In 1959 Mr Sharp gave the William Corbit House (now called the Corbit-Sharp House) to Winterthur Museum, and in 1966 he gave Winterthur the Brick Hotel, after restoring its exterior. The David Wilson House (now the Wilson-Warner House) was similarly given to Winterthur by Wilson's descendants, one of whom — Mrs. E. Tatnall Warner, Wilson's great-granddaughter — had opened the house as a museum.

AUTOMOBILE DIRECTIONS: The car tour shown on Map 6 begins at Odessa, Delaware, which is located on Route 13 about 7 miles south of the Chesapeake and Delaware Canal and 23 miles north of Dover. (See Map 1 in the Table of Contents.)

To Odessa from northernmost Delmarva and Interstate 95 southwest of Wilmington: From Interstate 95 take Route 7 south, then follow the signs for Route 1 to Route 13 toward Dover. (Please note, however, that Route 7 will not be linked to Route 1 until the fall of 1992, so until then simply take Route 7 south to Route 13.) Once you are on Route 13 southbound, follow it to Odessa. At the intersection with Route 299 in Odessa, turn left (east) and go 0.3 mile to the Brick Hotel Gallery on the left.

To Odessa from the Chesapeake Bay Bridge: After crossing the bridge, follow Route 50/301 across Kent Island. At the point where Route 50 and Route 301 split, continue straight on Route 301 northbound for more than 43 miles to Middletown. At the intersection where Route 301 turns left (north) on the outskirts of Middletown, go straight (east) on Route 299 for 3.3 miles through Middletown to Odessa. From the intersection with the southbound lanes of Route 13 in Odessa, continue straight east on Route 299 for 0.4 mile to the Brick Hotel Gallery on the left.

To Odessa from southern Delmarva and the Chesapeake Bay Bridge-Tunnel at Norfolk: After crossing the bridge-tunnel, follow Route 13 north into Maryland and past Salisbury to Dover, Delaware. (Alternatively, take Route 113 north to Dover.) From the junction of Route 13 and Route 113 in Dover, continue north on Route 13 for about 23 miles to Odessa. At the intersection with Route 299 in Odessa, turn right (east) and go 0.3 mile to the Brick Hotel Gallery on the left. (Starting in 1994, you will be able to take Route 1 — a new limited-access highway — north from Dover to Smyrna, and from there continue north on Route 13 to Odessa.)

To Odessa from Salisbury and the Delaware and Maryland seashore resorts: From the vicinity of Salisbury, take Route 13 north to Dover, Delaware. From Ocean City and Bethany Beach, go west to Route 113 and follow it north to Route 13 in Dover. And from Rehoboth Beach, follow Route 1 north to Route 113, then take 113 north to Route 13 in Dover.

Once you are at the junction of Route 13 and Route 113 in Dover, follow Route 13 north for about 23 miles to Odessa. At the intersection with Route 299 in Odessa, turn right (east) and go 0.3 mile to the Brick Hotel Gallery on the left. (Starting in 1994, you will be able to take Route 1 — a new limited-access highway — north from Dover to Smyrna, and from there continue north on Route 13 to Odessa.)

HISTORIC HOUSES OF ODESSA: Start at the **Brick Hotel Gallery**, which fronts on Main Street but is entered around the corner on Second Street. At the Brick Hotel you can buy a ticket that enables you to visit not only the gallery, but also the **Corbit-Sharp House** and the **Wilson-Warner**

House, which are adjacent to each other across the street. By all means see all three.

After you have toured the houses and their gardens, you may enjoy walking up and down Main Street and High Street east of Route 13, where many other old houses have been restored. (See Map 5.)

CAR TOUR: The bold line on Map 6 shows the route followed by this 60-mile car tour, which circles to the south of Odessa. A shorter excursion for bicyclists is to follow the tour route *backwards* from Odessa along Route 9 to the Allee House at Bombay Hook, then return the way you came, for a round trip of 32 miles. Bicyclists should bear in mind, however, that although Route 9 is not a major road, it is used by cars traveling at high speeds.

From the Brick Hotel Gallery in Odessa, follow Route 299 (Main Street) west 0.3 mile to the intersection at a traffic light with the northbound lanes of Route 13, and there turn right. Follow Route 13 north only 0.9 mile, then turn left into the entrance for Old Drawyers Presbyterian Church, which overlooks (toward the back) Drawyers Creek.

The congregation that eventually built **Old Drawyers Presbyterian Church** was formed late in the seventeenth century. In 1708 the Presbytery at Philadelphia directed the minister at New Castle (at that time the site of the only Presbyterian church in Delaware) to preach "once a month on a week day" to the "persons about Apoquinimy." The next year the minister was instructed to supplement his weekday preaching with a sermon "once a quarter on Sunday." Land at Drawyers Creek was purchased in 1711 and a wooden meeting house was built. With John May serving as master builder, the present church was built in the Georgian style starting in 1773. Old Drawyers was closed in 1861 after the construction of a new Presbyterian church in Odessa, since torn down. In 1895 a nondenominational group called The Friends of Old Drawyers was organized to care for the church, which belongs to the Presbytery of New Castle.

CAR TOUR (Map 6): To continue on the car tour, leave Old Drawyers Church by turning right onto Route 13. Follow Route 13 south less than a mile to an intersection at a traffic light with Route 299 in Odessa, and there turn right (west) toward Middletown — but after only a few hundred yards turn left into the driveway of the Appoquinimink **Friends Meeting**

MAP 5 -- Odessa

Main Street

1. #2 Main Street -- January House (1770s).
2. #114 Main Street -- Frame and log house (ca. 1740).
3. #116 Main Street -- Pump House (ca. 1772).
4. #201 Main Street -- Bank of Delaware (1854).
5. #203 Main Street -- John Zelefro Crouch House (ca. 1854).
6. #205 Main Street -- Davis Store (ca. 1824).
7. #206 Main Street -- Corbit-Kabis House (ca. 1760; refaced in the 1800s).
8. #215 Main Street -- Vandyke House; an old doctor's office (ca. 1840).
9. #300 Main Street -- Mailly House (mid-section, ca. 1770).
10. #301 Main Street -- Tatman Office; Odessa's oldest bank (ca. 1840).
11. #307 Main Street -- Red Men Lodge; Appo-quinimink Lodge of the Loyal Order of Red Men (ca. 1895).
12. #309 Main Street -- Tradesman's House (ca. 1850).
13. #310 Main Street -- Starr-Lore House; built in stages (ca. 1775, 1800, 1830).
14. #314 Main Street -- (pre-1780; Victorian-ized in the 1860s).
15. West Main Street -- Zoar United Methodist Church (1881).

Numbered Streets

16. Top of Second Street -- Collins-Sharp House; moved from Taylors Bridge (ca. 1700).
17. #110 Third Street -- Enos House (1840s).
18. #111 Third Street -- Tatman House (ca. 1845).
19. East side of Fourth Street -- The Old Academy; formerly a public library and school (1844).

High Street

20. #107 High Street -- Cantwell House (ca. 1840).
21. #108 High Street -- Replica of early 18th-century house in Lincoln, Rhode Island (1987).
22. #301 High Street -- William Polk House (1846).
23. #303 High Street -- Miller-Cyrus Polk House.
24. #305 High Street -- (ca. 1845).
25. #307 High Street -- Van Ogtrop House (1903).
26. #402 High Street -- Sylvester Roe House (1840s).
27. #501 High Street -- Gilch House (ca. 1858).
28. #506 High Street -- Old St. Paul's Church (1851).
29. #513 High Street -- (pre-1840).

Drawyers Creek

Old Drawyers Church (1773-1823)

Rte. 13

N

0   0.25
mile

Rte. 299

15
Friends Meeting House (1783)

Rte. 13 southbound

Rte. 13 northbound

Main St.

High St.

4th St.

3rd St.

2nd St.

Front St.

Brick Hotel Gallery (1822)

Wilson-Warner House (1769)

Corbit-Sharp House (1774)

Appoquinimink River

Rte. 299

House. Although he was not a Quaker, David Wilson built this meeting house in 1883 for his wife's Quaker congregation. The small brick meeting house is set back about a hundred yards from Route 299 behind the Zoar United Methodist Church, which was established in 1881.

From the Friends Meeting House, follow Route 299 west about 3 miles to Middletown.

The history of **Middletown** is in some ways the obverse of Odessa's. In 1816 there were only a few houses at Middletown, but after 1855, when the Delaware Railroad was built immediately west of the village, Middletown grew fast, as reflected in its large stock of Victorian structures along Main Street. Soon the town supplanted Odessa as the center of the surrounding farming district, a role it has retained to the present day.

CAR TOUR (Map 6): From the center of Middletown, continue west on Route 299 to the intersection with Route 301 just beyond the railroad, and from there continue straight on Route 301/299 for 2.7 miles, passing, along the way, two large "peach mansions" on the left — **Cochran Grange** (built about 1840) and **Hedgelawn** (1856).

"Peach mansion" is a term used by historians of Delaware architecture to describe a number of somewhat ostentatious houses built during the middle of the nineteenth century by farmers made wealthy by growing peaches, at that time a new cash crop. Cochran Grange is basically a Georgian house with Greek Revival and Italianate features added to the exterior. The original owner of Cochran Grange was John Price Cochran, a leading farmer and fruit grower who was Delaware's governor from 1875 to 1879. Cochran eventually owned fifteen farms totaling about 4,000 acres west of Middletown, and during his life he gave a farm to each of his six sons, one of whom built the Italianate Hedgelawn. And just down the road on the right (opposite a large brick house, but not easily seen from the highway) is Summerton, built in about 1850 by another Cochran son.

CAR TOUR (Map 6): As noted above, follow Route 301/299 for only 2.7 miles, then bear right onto Route 299 west toward Warwick. Go 1.2 miles as Delaware Route 299 becomes Maryland Route 282, then turn right onto Church Road in the village of Warwick. Follow Church Road 1.8 miles to an intersection with Bohemia Church Road, and from there

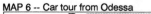
MAP 6 -- Car tour from Odessa

continue straight toward the church, visible a few hundred yards ahead. Pass in front of the church and bear right to park by the rectory museum, which is open on the same days as the church.

Old Bohemia Church, more properly called St. Francis Xavier Church, was built about 1790 as part of a Jesuit mission established here in 1704 under the leadership of the Reverend Thomas Mansell. At first Old Bohemia was the only Catholic mission in Delmarva and southeastern Pennsylvania, but its influence diminished over the following sixty years as other missions were established in Pennsylvania and at Cordova, Maryland (northeast of Easton). After the Diocese of Wilmington was established in 1868, a conventional parish structure was introduced to the Delmarva Peninsula, and in 1898 the Jesuits relinquished the Old Bohemia mission to the Bishop of Wilmington.

Old Bohemia included not just a church but also a self-sufficient plantation of 1,200 acres, complete with a gristmill and sawmill, a kiln for making bricks, a blacksmith shop, barns, and a wharf on Little Bohemia Creek. Developed by the early priests, the plantation generated income to support the Jesuits' missionary and educational activities, including an academy run at the plantation during the second half of the eighteenth century. Among the students at Bohemia Academy were John Carroll, the first American Catholic bishop and archbishop, and his cousin Charles Carroll of Carrollton, signer of the Declaration of Independence.

The interior of Old Bohemia Church burned in 1912 but was rebuilt. Presently, the church and plantation are being restored by the Old Bohemia Historical Society, Inc. in cooperation with the Diocese of Wilmington.

CAR TOUR (Map 6): Follow the driveway back to the first intersection, and there turn right onto Bohemia Church Road. Go 1.2 miles, then turn left onto Worsell Manor Road. After only 0.3 mile pass Worsell Manor on the right; it is a private residence just barely visible from the road.

In 1683 Charles Calvert, third Baron Baltimore and the proprietor of Maryland, granted Major Peter Sayer, a prominent Catholic, a tract of 1,000 acres called **Worsell Manor**. The plantation later came into the possession of James Heath, who died in 1731 and is buried on the property. On May 14, 1773, Daniel Heath had as his guest for the night George Washington, who was taking his stepson Jackie Custis to King's College, New York (now Columbia University). And why, you ask, would Washington choose a route through this remote place to go north? At that time, the main north-south road — the Upper King's Road — lay through this part of Delmarva, running from the harbor at Rock Hall (which was served by ferry from Annapolis) to Chestertown and on through Warwick and Middletown to Wilmington and Philadelphia.

CAR TOUR (Map 6): Continue on Worsell Manor Road to a T-intersection with Route 282, and there turn right. Go 1.0 mile, then turn left onto Wards Hill Road. Continue as straight as possible for 3.0 miles to a junction with Route 301. Cross Route 301 and follow Route 299 for 0.8 mile to the hamlet of **Sassafras**, site of the **Old Rehoboth Methodist Protestant Church**, built in 1859 by a black congregation but now abandoned. Turn left by the church onto the Sassafras - Caldwell Road. After only 1.2 miles, pass a large house on the left.

Called **Rich Levels**, this painted brick house was built in the middle of the eighteenth century as a two-story structure. About a century later the third story with hipped roof was added. Inside, this private residence has a central hall with a handsome stairs and paneled rooms on the first two floors. The name Rich Levels is derived from the region, locally called The Levels, and said to be among the best farmland in Delmarva.

CAR TOUR (Map 6): From Rich Levels, continue on the Sassafras - Caldwell Road for 1.0 mile to a five-way intersection called Caldwell Corners, and from there continue as straight as possible for 8.6 miles. (For most of this distance, you will be following the Vandyke - Greenspring Road.) At a T-intersection with Duck Creek Road, turn right and go 1.1 miles. This is part of the Lower King's Road, which ran south from New Castle to Smyrna and Dover, and remained the main road until the DuPont Highway (Route 13) was built in the 1920s. Cross Glenwood Avenue (Route 6/300) at a traffic light and continue straight on Main Street about 0.3 mile to the center of Smyrna at the Four Corners. Take the time to park and to walk up and down Main Street and Commerce Street, where there are many houses, stores, and a few hotels dating from the late eighteenth, nineteenth, and early twentieth centuries.

The history of **Smyrna** somewhat resembles that of Odessa. The town, which at first was called Duck Creek Cross Roads, grew up around the Four Corners of what is now Main and Commerce streets, where in 1768 Samuel Ball, a Quaker merchant from Philadelphia, purchased 15 acres and erected a general store. A combination sawmill, gristmill, and bolting mill was already located on Duck Creek a mile north of the crossroads. Immediately to the south of the crossroads was another gristmill on Mill Creek, and to the east was Duck Creek Landing, to which ships could navigate from the Delaware River.

During the second half of the eighteenth century, coastal sloops and schooners carrying grain sailed regularly from the landing for Philadelphia and New York. By 1790 large ships were being repaired and built at Duck Creek Landing. At that time the crossroads was a stage coach stop and had a post office, several taverns, a Methodist meeting house, and over fifty houses. In 1806 the name of the town was changed to Smyrna (a Turkish port and site of one of the "seven churches which are in Asia" in the Bible).

By the 1850s, when Smyrna entered its most prosperous half-century, as many as seven vessels per day sailed from Smyrna Landing during the height of the grain shipping season. At harvest time, the roads to Smyrna were clogged with teams hauling wagons loaded with grain and peaches. A substantial business district of Victorian buildings grew up around the Four Corners and new industries — principally canneries and fertilizer plants — were established.

In the twentieth century, however, Smyrna encountered a series of difficulties. As was the case at Odessa, the Delaware Railroad had bypassed the town 2 miles to the west, where Smyrna Station eventually developed into the rival town of Clayton. Grain output declined and the blighted peach crop failed utterly. Competition from the railroad, the siltation of Duck Creek, and the trend toward ever larger vessels turned Smyrna Landing into a forgotten backwater. When Route 13 reached Smyrna in 1923, it bypassed the Four Corners. Smyrna has managed to adapt, however, and today the town is a center — on a modest scale — for light manufacturing. Retailing has flourished along DuPont Highway (Route 13) so that now it too has been bypassed by the new Route 1 immediately to the east.

As already noted, there are many old houses and commercial structures in Smyrna. At 11 South Main Street is the **Smyrna Museum**, thought to have been built about 1790. The **Enoch Spruance House** at 21 East Commerce Street grew in sections, starting with the part farthest to the right, which was built late in the eighteenth century. The ground floor was used as a bank, with living quarters for one of the bank's officers above. The "simplified Regency" **John Cummins House** is across from 115 North Main Street. Cummins was Smyrna's leading merchant in the first quarter of the nineteenth century. A little annex to one side was Cummins' office. The house was built about 1820, at a time when Cummins was one of the greatest grain merchants in Delaware and a delegate to the state's General Assembly. Cummins' schooners sailed to Philadelphia, New York, and Boston loaded with grain and returned with manufactured goods, which he wholesaled to crossroads stores throughout lower Delaware and into Maryland.

CAR TOUR (Map 6): At the intersection of Main Street and Commerce Street in the center of Smyrna, turn left (east) onto Commerce Street and go 0.2 mile to the junction with Route 13. Cross Route 13 and follow Route 6 east 5.2 miles to a crossroads with Route 9, and there turn right. Follow Route 9 south 1.7 miles to the entrance to the Allee House on the left, opposite Road 83. Turn left and follow the driveway 0.6 mile to the Allee House.

The **Allee House** was built about 1753, probably by Abraham Allee, the son of John Allee, a Huguenot emigre who first acquired land at Bombay Hook in 1706. Abraham Allee was elected to the General Assembly in 1726, was appointed a Justice of the Peace in 1738, and in 1749 was Chief of the Kent County Rangers, or that is, mounted militia riflemen. Although the exterior of the Allee House is plain, the brickwork in Flemish bond includes a few decorative glazed headers. The interior of the house is surprisingly elegant, with paneling on the end wall of the main room.

CAR TOUR (Map 6): From the Allee House, turn right out the entrance and follow Route 9 north 1.7 miles back to the crossroads with Route 6. From there continue north on Route 9 for 12.9 miles; follow the route signs closely so as not to be shunted off Route 9 onto some other road. Incidentally, after 3.9 miles you will pass Flemings Landing on Duck Creek; a glimpse of the river here will perhaps make it easier to believe that coasting schooners used to ascend to Smyrna Landing farther upstream. Later you will reach Taylors Bridge, where there is a high navigational beacon for the nearby Delaware River and where the road turns sharply left. About 1.5 miles beyond this turn, Route 9 passes an old farmhouse atop a knoll on the left several hundred yards from the road (which itself bends left at this point).

This is the **Huguenot House**, built in 1711 by Elias Naudain, whose father, also named Elias, had fled from France to England when

40

the Edict of Nantes (which granted religious freedom to Protestants) was revoked in 1685. The younger Elias Naudain came to Delaware, then part of Pennsylvania, in about 1708 and acquired large landholdings. In 1715 he was recorded as being one of the elders of Old Drawyers Church. About 0.5 mile beyond the Huguenot House, also on the left, is another old house, of which the front part (built sometime between 1812 and 1835 by one of Naudain's descendants) was appended to a still older rear section.

CAR TOUR (Map 6): Finally, at an intersection where Route 9 turns abruptly right, continue straight west on Route 299. After only 0.2 mile, turn right at a T-intersection and follow Route 299 for 1.2 miles across the Appoquinimink River and back into Odessa, where the car tour ends.

About half a mile before entering Odessa, Route 299 passes a handsome Georgian house on the right called **Fairview**, built in 1773 for Captain (later Major) James Moore, who served during the Revolutionary War. Like the Corbit and Wilson houses in Odessa, Fairview is the work of master-builder John May, and shows the same elegant simplicity outside and fine woodwork and paneling inside.

3

BOMBAY HOOK NATIONAL WILDLIFE REFUGE

Containing more than 23 square miles, Bombay Hook in Delaware is one of the largest national wildlife refuges on the Atlantic coast's migratory flyway. Bird watching here is made easy by more than 11 miles of dirt roads that overlook a vast expanse of tidal marsh and large freshwater ponds. There are several short foot trails leading to observation towers or other vantage points. Walkers can also simply follow the refuge roads (but first please read the discussion starting at the bottom of page 48). If you have a fat-tired bicycle that can handle the sometimes loose, gravelly surface, the refuge roads also provide good bicycling.

The refuge is open daily from sunrise to sunset. Dogs must be leashed. Deer hunting is permitted on a few days each fall, and on those rare occasions part of the refuge is closed to non-hunters, so you may want to call ahead of time. The Allee House — a small but handsome colonial house that has been restored to its eighteenth-century appearance — is open free of charge on Saturday and Sunday afternoons from 2 to 5. The refuge is managed by the U. S. Fish and Wildlife Service; telephone (302) 653-9345.

FROM THE DIKE ROAD at Bombay Hook, salt marsh stretches east to the horizon. Sinuous tidal creeks meander through the marsh, eventually connecting with Delaware Bay, which is out of sight beyond the marshy flats. Bordering the dike road to the west is a chain of large freshwater impoundments, and inland from them are low, swampy woods and farm fields, used in part to grow food for ducks and geese. Taken altogether, the saltwater and freshwater marshes, tilled and fallow fields, woods, and ponds provide a wide diversity of habitats and the opportunity to see many bird species. A bird list showing seasonal fluctuations is available at the refuge visitor center.

The best bird watching is at the various ponds (or pools, as the management calls them). Here immense rafts of Canada geese, snow geese, and more than sixteen species of ducks and other waterfowl congregate from late September through early December, reaching a peak at the end of October and beginning of November. Particularly stirring is the sight and sound of wave upon wave of geese — at times seeming to fill the sky — returning to the refuge at dusk after feeding during daylight in farm fields. Some waterfowl stay through the winter or are present again as they pass northward late in winter.

By lowering weirs in spring, the pools are partially drained to create mud flats and shallow water suitable for migratory shorebirds and waders. Thousands of sandpipers, plovers, and larger birds such as herons, ibises, American avocets, greater and lesser yellowlegs, dunlins, and dowitchers, provide interest at a time of year when the waterfowl population is relatively sparse. Many of the shorebirds return in August, and a few species — notably black-necked stilts and willets — stay through June and July to breed in the refuge. Of course, the usual birds of forest and field are also present during summer. And in fall the weirs are raised again so that the pools slowly refill to suit migratory waterfowl.

Land at Bombay Hook was first acquired by the federal government in 1937, three years after passage of the Migratory Bird Hunting Stamp Act provided a reliable stream of funds to buy refuge land. Under the hunting stamp act, waterfowl hunters are required to buy a revenue stamp annually. As bird watching has grown in popularity, refuge entrance fees have also helped to generate funds for the purchase, maintenance, and periodic enlargement of our national wildlife refuges.

Of the approximately 15,000 acres at Bombay Hook National Wildlife Refuge, all but 20 percent are tidal salt marsh. Estuaries such as Delaware Bay are a typical setting for salt marsh formation — and, indeed, satellite images of the bay show that nearly its entire coast is lined by marshes, often extending 2 or 3 miles inland. Where rivers meet the sea — and we are talking here not just of major rivers like the Delaware but also of many small streams like the Leipsic and Smyrna rivers near Bombay Hook — the sediments that have been carried downstream settle out. As the sediments accumulate in the river mouths or farther offshore in the estuary, they form mud flats that are exposed at low tide, and here marsh grasses establish themselves. The dense, grassy carpet that spreads over the flats slows and filters the muddy tidewater that twice daily inundates the marsh, thus further contributing to the deposition of sediments. Thick layers of peaty mud develop, bound in a matrix of partially decomposed roots and leaves of marsh grasses.

As long as the marsh is flooded by the tide, upward growth of the surface continues because of the ongoing processes of sedimentation and peat formation. But as the marsh builds vertically toward the high water level, less material is washed onto the surface and upward growth slows. The limit is about a foot above average high water. At that level only storm tides or the highest tides of the year during spring and fall cover the marsh, so that there is no longer enough deposition to raise the level of the marsh appreciably. To some extent, the accumulation of dead and decaying salt grass builds up the surface. But at the same time, the underlying peat is continually decomposing, which causes the surface of the marsh to settle back toward the level of the yearly high tides. The marsh is thus in equilibrium among the processes of deposition, plant growth, compaction, and decay, which altogether produce a remarkably level surface.

There are, however, some slight differences in elevation, which are reflected in different varieties of plant life. At Bombay Hook the short *Spartina patens* (commonly called saltmeadow cordgrass or saltmarsh hay) and *Distichlis spicata* (salt grass) dominate the high marsh that is flooded only during the year's highest tides or storm surges. The far taller *Spartina alterniflora* (7 or 8 feet high and vernacularly called saltmarsh cordgrass) occupies lower areas that are inundated during every high tide.

Salt marshes are extraordinarily productive. Their shallow sunlit waters permit photosynthesis to take place at a very rapid rate. Great quantities of algae and animal microorganisms are produced. Algae are even able to grow during the winter. According to John and Mildred Teal, authors of *Life and Death of the Salt Marsh*, a tidal marsh yields more vegetable and animal matter than a comparable area of the most fertile farmland or pasture. Marsh grasses and algae capture up to 6 percent of the solar energy falling on the marsh during the year, compared to 2 percent for a corn field at its peak. The algae in turn consume only 10 percent of their energy intake, passing 90 percent along to the myriad of animals that feed on them. An acre of salt marsh yields about 10 tons of organic material yearly, compared to 1.5 tons for wheat fields (including stems and leaves) and 4 tons for the very best hay fields.

Coastal marshes are prime feeding and breeding grounds not only for migratory waterfowl but also for fish. Worms, shrimp, shellfish, and baitfish thrive on the algae and rotting vegetation. In turn, the young of larger fishes find food and protection in these rich nurseries. According to the Teals, two-thirds of the value of the commercial harvest of fish and shellfish caught on the East Coast comes from species that spend at least part of their life cycle in coastal and estuarine marshes. Such areas are about ten times as productive of fish as the coastal waters of the continental shelf, and about one hundred times more productive than the open ocean.

In recent years attention has focused also on the importance of freshwater wetlands, which in Delmarva's level terrain often occur as low, soggy woods, meadows, and farm fields lying immediately inland from coastal marshes, as, for example, in the vicinity of Bombay Hook's Finis Pool, fed by Finis Branch. Freshwater wetlands soak up immense quantities of storm runoff during periods of rain and flood, then slowly release it over a period of weeks or months. In this way they help to replenish groundwater and serve also as natural reservoirs and filters for streams that eventually flow into coastal marshes and estuaries.

AUTOMOBILE DIRECTIONS: Bombay Hook National Wildlife Refuge is located in Delaware about 7 miles northeast of Dover, where Delaware Bay narrows and becomes the Delaware River. (See Map 1 in the Table of Contents.)

To Bombay Hook from northernmost Delmarva and Interstate 95 southwest of Wilmington: From Interstate 95 take Route 7 south, then follow the signs for Route 1 to Route 13 toward Dover. (Please note, however, that Route 7 will not be linked to Route 1 until the fall of 1992, so until then simply take Route 7 south to Route 13.) Once you are on Route 13 southbound, follow it toward Dover, but go only as far as Smyrna, located 11 miles north of Dover. After going through Smyrna and passing the Odd Fellow's Cemetery on the left, turn left off Route 13 at a traffic light, where a sign points the way toward Bombay Hook National Wildlife Refuge. Follow this road (Road 12) for 4.6 miles. Curve right as Road 12 merges with Route 9, then go only 0.2 mile on Route 9 before turning left onto Road 85 toward Bombay Hook. Follow Road 85 for 2.5 miles to the refuge visitor center on the left.

To Bombay Hook from the Chesapeake Bay Bridge: After crossing the bridge, follow Route 50/301 across Kent Island. At the point where Route 50 and Route 301 split, continue straight on Route 301 northbound for 20.5 miles to an intersection with Route 300. Turn right (east) toward Sudlersville and follow Route 300 for 21.6 miles to a T-intersection with Route 13 in Smyrna. Turn right and follow Route 13 south 1.1 miles, then turn left at a traffic light, where a sign points the way toward Bombay Hook National Wildlife Refuge. Follow this road (Road 12) for 4.6 miles. Curve right

MAP 7 -- Bombay Hook National Wildlife Refuge

as Road 12 merges with Route 9, then go only 0.2 mile on Route 9 before turning left onto Road 85 toward Bombay Hook. Follow Road 85 for 2.5 miles to the refuge visitor center on the left.

To Bombay Hook from southern Delmarva and the Chesapeake Bay Bridge-Tunnel at Norfolk: After crossing the bridge-tunnel, follow Route 13 north into Maryland and past Salisbury to Dover, Delaware. (Alternatively, take Route 113 north to Dover.) From the junction of Route 13 and Route 113 in Dover, continue north on Route 13 for 5.8 miles to an intersection with Route 42 at a traffic light, and there turn right. Follow Route 42 east 4.0 miles to an intersection with Route 9 in Leipsic. Turn left (north) onto Route 9 and go 1.5 miles to an intersection with Road 85, and there turn right toward Bombay Hook National Wildlife Refuge. Follow the road 2.5 miles to the refuge visitor center on the left.

To Bombay Hook from Salisbury and the Delaware and Maryland seashore resorts: From the vicinity of Salisbury, take Route 13 north to Dover, Delaware. From Ocean City and Bethany Beach, go west to Route 113 and follow it north to Route 13 in Dover. And from Rehoboth Beach, follow Route 1 north to Route 113, then take 113 north to Route 13 in Dover.

Once you are at the junction of Route 13 and Route 113 in Dover, take Route 13 north for 5.8 miles to an intersection with Route 42 at a traffic light, and there turn right. Follow Route 42 east 4.0 miles to an intersection with Route 9 in Leipsic. Turn left (north) onto Route 9 and go 1.5 miles to an intersection with Road 85, and there turn right toward Bombay Hook National Wildlife Refuge. Follow the road 2.5 miles to the refuge visitor center on the left.

TOURING BOMBAY HOOK BY CAR OR BICYCLE: Map 7 shows the refuge roads. After paying the entrance fee at the visitor center or at the pay station on the main tour route, follow the system of dike roads around the various pools and to the western spurs at the **Allee House** and Finis Pool. Please drive slowly; note that some of the roads are one-way.

WALKING AT BOMBAY HOOK: Several short foot trails are shown on Map 7. The **Boardwalk Trail** is about 0.25 mile long, and the **Parson Point Trail** (which is sometimes closed in order to enable eagles to roost or nest undisturbed) is 1.0 mile round-trip. The other trails merely lead a few hundred yards to various observation towers.

Serious hikers may find it more satisfying to park their cars at the visitor center or one of the tower lots and then walk on the dike road. The safest place to do this is where the road is one-way; walk facing the oncoming traffic in order to minimize the risk of being hit by a car. The **road around Raymond Pool** is one-way and forms a circuit 2.0 miles long. The **road around Bear Swamp Pool** forms a 3.0-mile circuit and is less frequented by cars, but a short part of it is two-way. Walking on the road is best during late fall, winter, and early spring, when mosquitoes are absent, birds abundant, and excessive heat merely a memory.

4

CHESTERTOWN
REMINGTON FARMS
ROCK HALL
EASTERN NECK NATIONAL WILDLIFE REFUGE

The 60-mile car tour outlined in this chapter links the chief points of interest in southwestern Kent County, Maryland.
Chestertown, the county seat, is an old port far up the Chester River. Its historic district retains nearly two dozen eighteenth-century houses, and its High Street and side streets have many restaurants and specialty shops. The Geddes-Piper House, now the headquarters of the Historical Society of Kent County, is open to the public May through October on Saturday and Sunday from 1 to 4; telephone (410) 778-3499 for information. On the way from Chestertown to Rock Hall is Remington Farms, a 3,000-acre wildlife area managed by the Remington Arms Company; telephone (410) 778-1565. Rock Hall, with its several boat basins, is a center for commercial fishing and recreational yachting. It is also home port for *The Chesapeake Flyer*, a high-speed ferry operating to Baltimore, Annapolis, and St. Michaels; telephone 1 (800) 47-FERRY. And finally, south of Rock Hall is Eastern Neck Island, a major wildlife refuge providing good walking and excellent bird watching — especially for waterfowl during fall and winter. Bicyclists may enjoy riding on the 4.5 miles of roads within the refuge; other possibilities for bicycling are described at the beginning of the tour directions on page 58. The refuge is open daily from sunrise to sunset; dogs must be leashed. Eastern Neck National Wildlife Refuge is managed by the U.S. Fish and Wildlife Service; telephone (410) 639-7056.

CHESTERTOWN WAS FOUNDED in 1706, when nine port commissioners, appointed by the colonial governor, purchased 100 acres and laid out the streets of the new town (originally called, in fact, New Town) around the Kent County courthouse, which had already existed

51

there since 1698. During the eighteenth century, Chestertown became a prosperous port and one of Maryland's leading municipalities, surpassed in population only by Annapolis and, about two decades before the Revolution, by Baltimore. Chestertown's more successful merchants built substantial — and in some cases magnificent — houses fronting on the river from which the town derived its name and reason for being.

The Chester River reaches far inland to the heart of a rich agricultural region, where by the mid-1700s wheat and corn and corn-fed livestock were replacing tobacco as the chief exports. The river carried ships that sailed directly to and from Great Britain and more particularly the West Indies, where sugar so dominated the economy that most food for the Caribbean plantations was imported. During the latter 1700s, Chestertown became the center of Maryland's West Indies trade, exchanging grain and salt pork for sugar, molasses, rum, salt, and that rarest of commodities in the tidewater region: cash, chiefly in the form of Spanish coins. Either individually or in partnerships, Chestertown's leading merchants acquired locally-built ships suitable for coastal trade southward to the Caribbean or northward to New England, which was another major market for Eastern Shore grain. And through Chestertown passed one of the main roads used by travelers going up and down the Atlantic seaboard. The route led north by post road across Delmarva to Wilmington and Philadelphia, and south by packet sailing from nearby Rock Hall to Annapolis.

By the standards of eighteenth-century Maryland, Chestertown was not only a center of commerce but also a cosmopolitan center of culture. Horse races, hunts, fancy suppers, balls, amateur theatricals, and also dramatic and operatic performances by traveling companies were held there. The Kent County Free School was established in Chestertown in 1723, and in 1782 it was chartered as Washington College, with a private endowment of £10,000.

A glimpse of Society as known to one well-connected Chestertown girl is provided by a letter, dated January 2, 1787, from Molly Tilghman to her friend Polly Pearse:

> There was a Ball the night after Christmas which was much indebted to the Majors of Queen Anne's, the formidable Cleland, the woeful looking Emory and the handsome Smyth. Mrs. Galloway flashed upon them in her Muslin attended by her admiring spouse in his Rock of Gibraltar Coat. They had 16 couple and spent a very agreeable Evening. The play came next night which afforded a few unexpected incidents. Some Bucks of true spirit which was increas'd by good Liquor, broke open one of the Windows to the great dismay of the Ladies. As to the Play, it exceeded no one's expectations. However, the Eyes of the Audience were oblig'd by a vast display of fine Cloaths

and Jewels, which more than made up for any faults in the acting.
[One player] really looked very handsome, he wore Mat Tilghman's
white sattin waistcoat &c, a black star brilliant with paste and fourteen
black and white feathers. Last night it was again repeated with the
addition of the Irish Widow. The Ball gave such a spring to the Spirit
of our Beaux they have made up a Subscription for Assemblies and the
first is to be to-morrow night. . . .

Revealing a rather different perspective on these and other doings in
Chestertown is a 1786 diary entry of the Reverend Francis Asbury, the
first American Methodist bishop: "I preached . . . in the afternoon and
at night in Chestertown. I always have an enlargement in preaching in
this very wicked place."

Although not in the vanguard of Maryland's resistance to the British
taxes and coercion that led up to the Revolution, Chestertown was not
far behind, especially when viewed in the context of the conservative
Toryism that characterized much of the rural Eastern Shore. In an action modeled on the Boston Tea Party, a group of Chestertown citizens
boarded the brigantine *Geddes*, belonging to Collector of Customs
William Geddes, on May 13, 1774, and emptied its tea into the river.
(In Annapolis a tea ship was burned by a screaming mob.) At about
the same time some of the leading men of Kent County shared the cost
of sending a cargo of flour to the people of Boston, whose port had
been declared closed by act of Parliament until such time as the city
paid for the tea dumped there. During the Revolution, the Reverend
William Smith of what is now Chestertown's Emmanuel Episcopal
Church was one of a very small minority of Anglican clergymen in
Maryland who took the oath of allegiance and fidelity to the new government. In 1780 Smith organized a meeting at Chestertown to dis-
pense with the king as the head of the church and to reorganize Angli-
canism in the former colonies as the Protestant Episcopal Church of
America, a task subsequently undertaken by a state convention of which
Smith was president.

After the Revolution, the rise of Baltimore as a major international
port led to a corresponding decline at other tidewater towns of the upper
Chesapeake. Baltimore had ample waterpower for industry and for
milling flour. Its growth was fueled by proximity to a vast agricultural
hinterland to the west and north and by water access to the world. The
effect on Chestertown was the same as elsewhere in Maryland: the
town's economic horizons shrank until they extended no farther than
Baltimore, to which Kent County's agricultural products were sent by
sloop and later by steamboat. Following the Civil War, which saw a
Union garrison occupy Chestertown and men from Kent County fighting for opposing sides, the railroad reached Chestertown from the north,

and since then much of the town's commerce has been channeled through Wilmington and Philadelphia.

Today the town remains what it has been for nearly two centuries: the seat of local government, a quiet college town, a regional retailing center, and a place for transhipping farm products and supplies. It has, too, a well-to-do population of retirees and weekend residents.

AUTOMOBILE DIRECTIONS: Chestertown is located in northern Delmarva on the Chester River. (See Map 1 in the Table of Contents.) The car tour to Rock Hall and Eastern Neck shown on Map 9 starts at Chestertown, so you should go there first.

To Chestertown from northernmost Delmarva and from Interstate 95 near Newark, Delaware: From I-95 take Route 896 south across Route 40 and over the Chesapeake and Delaware Canal to an intersection with Route 301, and there continue straight south on Route 301. Just west of Middletown, turn right to follow Route 301 south 17.0 miles to the intersection with Route 544. (You will know that you are drawing near this intersection after passing Route 291.) Turn right (west) onto Route 544 toward Chestertown and go 9.2 miles to a T-intersection with Route 213. Turn right (north) onto Route 213 toward Chestertown and go 1.9 miles across the Chester River and into Chestertown itself. Turn left onto Route 289 (Cross Street) at the first traffic light. Go two blocks to the intersection with High Street next to the town square.

To Chestertown from the Chesapeake Bay Bridge: After crossing the bridge, follow Route 50/301 across Kent Island. At the point where Route 50 and Route 301 split, continue straight on Route 301 northbound for 5.8 miles to an intersection with Route 213. Turn left (north) toward Centreville and follow Route 213 for 18 miles through Centreville all the way to Chestertown. After crossing the Chester River, turn left onto Route 289 (Cross Street) at the first traffic light. Go two blocks to an intersection with High Street next to the town square.

To Chestertown from southern Delmarva and the Chesapeake Bay Bridge-Tunnel at Norfolk: After crossing the bridge-tunnel, follow Route 13 north into Maryland and past Pocomoke City and Princess Anne to the exit for Route 50 westbound near Salisbury, and from there take Route 50 west past Cambridge and Easton. After passing through the intersection with Route 404 near Wye Mills, continue on Route 50 for 1.5 miles, then turn right onto Route 213 north toward Centreville. Follow Route 213 for 22.4 miles through Centreville all the way to Chestertown. After crossing the Chester River, turn left onto Route 289 (Cross Street) at the first traffic light. Go two blocks to an intersection with High Street next to the town square.

To Chestertown from Salisbury: Take Route 50 west past Cambridge and Easton. After passing through the intersection with Route 404 near Wye Mills, continue on Route 50 for 1.5 miles, then turn right onto Route 213 north toward Centreville. Follow Route 213 for 22.4 miles through Centreville all the way to Chestertown. After crossing the Chester River, turn left onto Route 289 (Cross Street) at the first traffic light. Go two blocks to an intersection with High Street next to the town square.

To Chestertown from the Delaware and Maryland seashore resorts: From Ocean City take Route 50 west past Salisbury, Cambridge, and Easton to the intersection with Route 404 near Wye Mills. Alternatively, from the vicinity of Rehoboth Beach, follow Route 1 north to the intersection near Lewes with Route 404 westbound, then follow Route 404 west through Georgetown and across Route 113 and Route 13 to the intersection with Route 50 near Wye Mills. In either case, once you are at the intersection of Route 50 and Route 404, follow Route 50 west for 1.5 miles, then turn right onto Route 213 north toward Centreville. Follow Route 213 for 22.4 miles through Centreville all the way to Chestertown. After crossing the Chester River, turn left onto Route 289 (Cross Street) at the first traffic light. Go two blocks to an intersection with High Street next to the town square.

TOURING CHESTERTOWN ON FOOT: Use Map 8 to explore Chestertown. The most interesting part is High Street and its side streets between the town square and the river. The Historical Society of Kent County's **Geddes-Piper House** is located on Church Alley just off Queen Street.

1   Built in the 1740s, the Custom House reflects Chestertown's status as a colonial port of entry. It features Flemish bond brickwork and glazed headers on the Water Street side.
2   This 1857 house on the corner is a fine example of an"Italian villa." Popular in the mid-19th century, the Italianate style is typified by such features as a full-width porch, side- and top-lighted door, hooded windows, corner pilasters, large cornice brackets, low-pitched, projecting hip roof, roof-top lantern, and overall symmetry.
3   The front part of this imposing house on the corner was built in the 2nd quarter of the 18th century. Thomas Ringgold, a wealthy merchant, added a rear section with grand stairs in 1767.
4   Pre-revolutionary Georgian house on the corner.
5   Late 18th-century house Victorianized in 1880s.
6 & 7   Originally a single residence (ca. 1743).
8   Frame house with brick end walls for the chimneys (2nd quarter of the 18th century).
9   Originally a single residence (ca. 1776-1796), this house has brick end walls like #8.
10   Simplified Italianate store (mid-19th century).
11   The fieldstone foundation and Flemish bond main section (ca. 1735-1750) reflect the age of this old and much-altered store/dwelling.
12   Imperial Hotel (1903).
13   Chester Theater (1928).
14   This Second Empire or Beaux Arts style corner building was built in 1886 by merchant/druggist Colin Stam for his business. The upper floors had rooms for public and private gatherings.
15   Italianate commercial building (pre-1877).
16   Bank building (1929) in Neo-Classic style.
17   White Swan Tavern (mid-18th century).
18   This late 19th-century storefront was the subject of litigation upholding the power of Chestertown's Historic District Commission to regulate external changes to buildings.
19   Volunteer firehouse (ca. 1908).
20   Railroad station (ca. 1905).
21   Former Methodist Church (1859).
22   Janes Methodist Episcopal Church (1914).
23   Showing a pair of arched, 2nd-floor windows typical of the Renaissance Revival style, this commercial building was erected after 1910, when most of its block burned.
24   The exuberant Queen Anne style popular at the end of the 19th century is seen in the roof zone of this building; the rest has been refaced.
25   This Italianate style residence (mid-1800s) has a bracketed cornice, corner pendants, hooded windows, and a full-width porch.
26   A "telescope" house, built in sections at different periods (mid-section is late 18th-century).
27   Tradesman's house (1771-1783).
28   A member of the wealthy Ringgold family built this house in the 2nd quarter of the 1700s.
29   Christ Methodist Church (1887) illustrates the "High Victorian" Gothic Revival style.
30   Like the neighboring church, this late 19th-century house shows Victorian Gothic traces.
31   Symmetrical residence (1877) with various 19th-century decorative features: hooded windows, bracketed eaves, hip roof, and ironwork.
32   Originally a public school (1901), this building strains the Colonial Revival style with its Palladian (tripartite) dormer windows, gambrel roof, Flemish bond brickwork, and stone trim.
33   The U.S. Post Office (1935) is in the Federal Revival style, with keystoned lintels, an elegant portico, and only a single -- yet tall -- story.
34   Former Methodist meetinghouse (1801-03).
35   Corner house (late 1700s or early 1800s).
36   Rockwell House, formerly a tavern, shows modest Italianate features (1850s).
37   Emmanuel Episcopal Church (1772) was built in the Georgian style, with the entrance at the center of a symmetrical five-bay facade facing High Street; it was greatly altered in the 1880s.
38   Italianate courthouse (1860) facing High Street.
39   Former Masonic Temple (early 1830s).
40 & 41   Just two of many offices on Lawyer's Row (second half of the 19th century).
42   Former shop, now an office (late 19th century).
43   The Geddes-Piper House (1780s) is home of the Historical Society of Kent County. At the time this impressive townhouse was built, the land around it was vacant.
44   Italianate house (ca. 1877) with slender pilasters, bracketed cornice, side-lighted door, and full-width porch popular in the mid-1800s.
45   Brick house in Flemish bond (ca. 1735-1750).
46   Mirror image of contemporaneous #44.
47   Front section dates from 1780s; rear ca. 1740.
48   John Nicholson, commander of the Continental sloop Hornet , built this house in the 1780s.
49   Much-altered house dating from the 1770s.
50   Simplified Italianate house (ca. 1867).
51   Former parsonage for Christ Methodist Church showing subdued Gothic elements (1896).
52   Blend of Gothic and Italianate details (ca. 1880).
53   Simplified Italianate house on corner (1860s).
54   Late 19th-century residence.
55   Queen Anne style corner house (mid-1880s), with varigated colors, textures, and materials.
56   Much-altered house dating from mid-1700s.
57   Late 19th-century features on ca. 1916 house.
58   The Frisby House (ca. 1766) was originally the only house on the town side of its Water Street block. The front wall is in all-header bond.
59   The front of this house is in all-header bond; the north wall in Flemish bond with glazed headers (2nd quarter of the 18th century).
60   Late 19th-century double residence with Colonial-Revival porches and other details.
61   Known as Watkins House, the land for this particularly old house was a wedding gift from the Ringgolds to their new son-in-law, Essau Watkins, in 1739. The brickwork is Flemish bond with glazed headers.
62   River House was built just after the Revolution and shows many elegant details, such as the high, stone-capped foundation and stone belt separating the first and second stories, Flemish bond brickwork on the street front, keystoned lintels, slender pilasters at the corners, and an elaborately carved cornice.
63   Built in about 1870, this house shows conservative Italianate features, such as a side- and top-lighted door, hooded windows, and a shallowly pitched roof with heavily bracketed eaves.
64   Built about 1796, this house was modified to fit the popular Italianate style in the mid-1800s.
65   Widehall (ca. 1770) was built by Thomas Smythe, a merchant and shipbuilder whose wealth is reflected in the generous proportions, all-header bond brickwork, large windows, and other fine details of his house. The flat, five-bay Georgian facade was conservative for a period when other mansions in bigger towns featured projecting entrance pavilions.

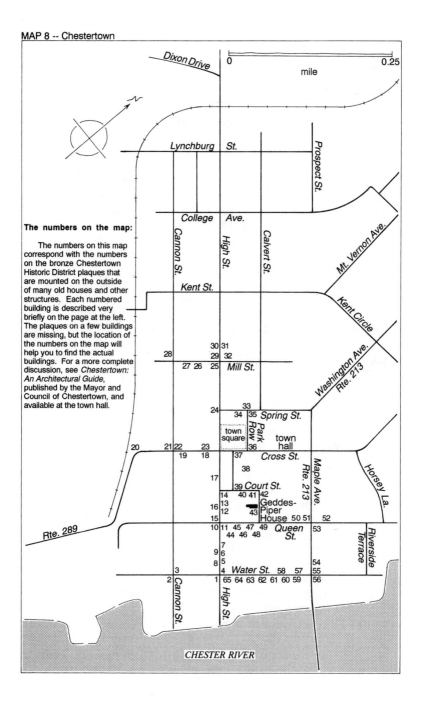

MAP 8 -- Chestertown

The numbers on the map:

The numbers on this map
correspond with the numbers
on the bronze Chestertown
Historic District plaques that
are mounted on the outside
of many old houses and other
structures. Each numbered
building is described very
briefly on the page at the left.
The plaques on a few buildings
are missing, but the location of
the numbers on the map will
help you to find the actual
buildings. For a more complete
discussion, see *Chestertown:
An Architectural Guide*,
published by the Mayor and
Council of Chestertown, and
available at the town hall.

Dixon Drive

0   mile   0.25

Lynchburg St.

Prospect St.

College Ave.

Cannon St.

High St.

Calvert St.

Mt. Vernon Ave.

Kent St.

Kent Circle

Washington Ave.
Rte. 213

28   30 31
          29 32
27 26   25   Mill St.

33
24   34 35 Spring St.
          town   Park Row
          square   36   town
                              hall
20   21 22   23   37   Cross St.
      19 18   38   Rte. 213   Maple Ave.
      17
                        39 Court St.   Horsey La.
                        14 40 41 42
                16   13   Geddes-
                        12   Piper
                15   House 50 51   52
                10 11 45 47 49 Queen   53
                   44 46 48   St.
                7   Riverside Terrace
             9 6
             8 5   54
          3   4   Water St. 58 57   55
       2   1 65 64 63 62 61 60 59 56

Cannon St.

High St.

Rte. 289

CHESTER RIVER

Nearly all of the other old houses noted on the map are private residences and so are not open to the public, but annually on the third Saturday in September many are included on a candlelight tour sponsored by the historical society. Similarly, on a Saturday in mid-December many houses are open to benefit a local educational charity; telephone the Kent County Chamber of Commerce at (410) 778-0416 for information on these and other local events.

CAR TOUR OF SOUTHWESTERN KENT COUNTY: This 60-mile car tour is shown by the bold line on Map 9. The route from Chestertown to Rock Hall is also good for bicycling, provided that you bear in mind that Route 289 at the beginning and Route 20 at the end are used by cars traveling at high speeds. Unfortunately, the side trip through Remington Farms is never open to bicyclists. I suggest that bicyclists return from Rock Hall to Chestertown on the same route along the Ricauds Branch, Langford, and Pomona roads as they took on the way to Rock Hall, for a round trip of 30 miles. A shorter bicycle excursion is to start at Rock Hall and ride down to Eastern Neck Island and back on Route 445 for a round trip of 18 miles. Again, cars here go as fast as on any other open road, but because Route 445 dead-ends at Eastern Neck Island, traffic is usually light.

From the intersection of High Street and Cross Street in Chestertown, follow Cross Street (Route 289) south. Go 4.3 miles as the road leads past the train depot, along the Chester River, and through farmland. At an intersection where Route 289 veers sharply left, turn right onto the Langford - Pomona Road. After 1.4 miles, bear left to continue on the Langford - Pomona Road where Airy Hill Road goes straight. Go 1.9 miles, then cross Langford Road (Route 446) and continue on Ricauds Branch - Langford Road. Go 2.3 miles, then turn right onto Sandy Bottom Road, which leads 100 yards to **St. Paul's Episcopal Church** on the right. The first church here was established in 1692; the present structure was built in 1713-15. Although you may find the church closed, the churchyard and cemetery are well worth visiting.

To continue toward Rock Hall on the car tour, return 100 yards to the intersection of Sandy Bottom Road and Ricauds Branch - Langford Road. Turn right and go only 0.3 mile, then turn left into **Remington Farms**, which is open daily during daylight hours. Remington Farms is a wildlife management

MAP 9 -- Car tour of southwestern Kent County

MAP 10 -- Remington Farms

MAP 11 -- Rock Hall

demonstration area operated by the Remington Arms Company. From October through March, thousands of waterfowl congregate on a pond to the right of the farm road, opposite the office. (During summer the pond is drained.) From February 1 to mid-October, a self-guided car tour leads past various habitats, each demonstrating different techniques for the management of wildlife on farmland. The 6-mile tour route is shown by the bold line on Map 10 and is further indicated by roadside signs. For an informative commentary keyed to numbered signs along the way, pick up a free tour pamphlet at the Remington Farms office.

To continue toward Rock Hall (or to take the Remington Farms tour), turn left out the farm entrance and go 0.5 mile, then turn left onto Route 20. For the Remington Farms tour, turn right immediately; at the end of the tour, you will return to this spot. For Rock Hall, continue straight 4.0 miles to the intersection of Route 20 and Route 445, and from there use Map 11 to tour Rock Hall by car. The most interesting places are the various harbors and yacht basins. The modest **Rock Hall Museum** is located in the municipal building on South Main Street (Route 445) and is open Wednesday, Thursday, Friday, and Sunday from 2 to 4:30 and on Saturday from 10 to noon. Displaying a potpourri of old photographs, tools, Indian artifacts, and other miscellaneous items, the museum has somewhat the atmosphere of the cluttered roadside curiosity shops that one sees here and there in Delmarva.

As noted above in the discussion on Chestertown, in the eighteenth century **Rock Hall** was the Eastern Shore terminus of a ferry sailing to and from Annapolis. Before the growth of Baltimore and the development of a good post road through Havre de Grace at the end of the century, the route through Rock Hall and Chestertown was a major line of travel between the North and the South. George Washington crossed the bay by the Rock Hall ferry several times, and his aide-de-camp Colonel Tench Tilghman (brother of Molly Tilghman, whose letter was quoted earlier) passed through Rock Hall on his way to Philadelphia to tell the Continental Congress of the British surrender at Yorktown. Now a passenger ferry — the *Chesapeake Flyer* — operates between Rock Hall and Baltimore, with trips also to St. Michaels and Annapolis; telephone 1 (800) 47-FERRY for information.

Ever since the Chesapeake Bay oyster fishery boomed during the decades following the Civil War, Rock Hall has been — at least until recently — a community primarily of watermen. Large fleets of skipjacks worked the deep water and crowds of tong boats moored over the shallow oyster beds off Rock Hall. Seafood factories for processing and packing oysters, rockfish, crabs, and soft clams lined the principal harbor, from which operated not only scores of independent watermen but also a charter fleet for recreational fishermen. Some people have even facetiously suggested that the town's name derives from the abundance of rockfish hauled ashore there. (More plausibly, the name is thought to be derived from a colonial manor house called Rock Hall.)

As commercial fishing in Chesapeake Bay has declined, however, Rock Hall's waterfront packing houses and workboats have in large part been replaced by harborside condominiums and by marinas filled with pleasure boats. The value of waterfront land for expensive residences, restaurants, and marinas has, in fact, become so great — and the fortunes of commercial fishing so relatively low — that in 1989 the state of Maryland felt compelled to buy one of the seafood processing plants fronting on Rock Hall's harbor in order to prevent the building from being sold for residential development. Now the state leases the building, at a rent that does not cover its costs, to a seafood processing company, so that Rock Hall's remaining watermen will still have a local market for their catch. October through March, the parade of oyster boats returning to Rock Hall harbor shortly after 3 P.M. is a fine sight.

CAR TOUR (Map 9 — from Rock Hall to Eastern Neck National Wildlife Refuge): From the intersection of Route 20 and Route 445 in Rock Hall, follow Route 445 (Main Street) south 6.0 miles to the bridge leading to Eastern Neck Island. Use Map 12 to tour the national wildlife refuge.

At 2,285 acres, **Eastern Neck National Wildlife Refuge** is relatively small compared to the other national wildlife refuges of the Delmarva Peninsula. Nonetheless, its fields and numerous coves and ponds form an important feeding and resting place for migrating and wintering waterfowl. In particular, from October through March, thousands of Canada geese, mute and tundra swans, diving ducks and puddle ducks can be seen here, reaching a peak in November. Because of the diversity of habitat, including woods, hedgerows, farm fields, marshes, swamps, and shallows, a wide variety of other birds are also present during their appropriate seasons. Nesting species include bald eagles.

May through September, picnicking and crabbing are permitted at the refuge's Ingleside Recreation Area.

As noted by an historic marker at the southern end of the refuge road, Eastern Neck Island was the site of **Wickliffe**, the home of Major Joseph Wickes, who settled here in 1658. Wickes was a member of the provincial assembly, a justice of the peace, and ultimately Chief Justice of the Kent County Court, which sometimes met at Wickliffe.

MAP 12 -- Eastern Neck National Wildlife Refuge

WALKING AT EASTERN NECK ISLAND: As shown by Map 12 and as listed below, there are several short foot trails at the national wildlife refuge. None is very long, but taken altogether, these short trails add up to a highly satisfactory excursion. Note first, however, that deer hunting is allowed at Eastern Neck Island on a few days during fall, and on these occasions the opportunities for walking are restricted. You will know that hunting is going on if a check-in station has been set up at the refuge entrance, or you can call (410) 639-7056 for information. Hunting is never permitted on Sunday.

Start at the **Tubby Cove Boardwalk**, which leads a few hundred yards to an observation tower. This and the vicinity of the bridge leading to Eastern Neck Island are the best spots from which to view waterfowl.

The Boxes Point Trail is 1.2 miles round-trip. Park in the Tubby Cove lot, then follow the refuge road 175 yards back toward the bridge. The trailhead is on the right.

The Duck Inn Trail is 1.0 mile round-trip. The trailhead is on the road leading to Bogle's Wharf. A parking lot is opposite the trailhead. The sleepy public landing at Bogle's Wharf, incidentally, was once a place where packet boats and steamboats called until as recently as 1924.

The Wildlife Trail is about 0.5 mile long. This circuit is the least interesting of the various Eastern Neck trails.

On weekends the **dirt road leading to the refuge office** makes a good walkway because it is closed to cars at that time. The round-trip distance is 2.0 miles. Park in the lot for the Wildlife Trail, then cross the main refuge road.

CAR TOUR (Map 9 — from Eastern Neck Island to Chestertown): From Eastern Neck Island, follow Route 445 for 6.0 miles back to Rock Hall. At the intersection with Route 20, turn right. Follow Route 20 for 13.0 miles to Chestertown, where the car tour ends.

DIXON'S FURNITURE AUCTION near Chestertown is so large that it is almost a place — or at least an institution. The auction (which is by no means limited to furniture) occurs every Wednesday starting at 9 A.M. on the auction house grounds located east of Chestertown on Route 544 about half way between Route 213 and Route 301. (See Map 1 in the Table of Contents.) Winning bidders must pay immediately in cash.

5

HORSEHEAD WETLANDS CENTER

Horsehead Wetlands Center in Maryland comprises 310 acres of woods, meadow, marsh, and ponds. Special features include a collection of resident North American waterfowl, a visitor center, bird blinds that overlook several ponds, observation towers, and some short trails. Apart from the resident waterfowl, about two hundred species of birds have been seen here. The Center is open daily (except Christmas) from 9 to 5. Pets are prohibited.

Horsehead Wetlands Center is managed by The Wildfowl Trust of North America, which is a private, non-profit corporation founded in 1979 and dedicated to education, conservation, and research. In 1981 the Trust purchased the Horsehead peninsula. For information about the Center and the Trust's educational programs and special events, telephone (410) 827-6694 or write to: The Wildfowl Trust of North America, P.O. Box 519, Grasonville, MD 21638.

Regarding the name "Horsehead," tilt Map 13 to the right.

THE RESIDENT WATERFOWL at Horsehead Wetlands Center provide the opportunity to see many birds up close. Under such conditions, plumage is the obvious way to tell one species from another. But in the wild, other traits are just as important, particularly when distance, haze, glare, twilight, or even molting obscure characteristic patterns of color. What follows, then, is a brief discussion of several key factors (in addition to plumage) that help to identify waterfowl in the wild. For a more comprehensive discussion of bird identification, see Chapter 7.

The distinction between dabblers and divers is basic to identifying ducks, and is in turn closely allied to habitat preference. Black ducks, gadwalls, pintails, wigeons, wood ducks, fulvous whistling ducks, shovelers, and several varieties of teal feed by dabbling at food that is floating on the surface of the water, or by upending their bodies in order to reach with their heads down to the bottom while their tails point in the air. Not surprisingly, dabblers prefer shallow marshes, ponds, and streams, and if that is the sort of environment where you are watching birds, you will know beforehand what species of ducks you are most likely to see. In contrast, redheads, canvasbacks, ring-necked ducks, scaup, goldeneyes, buffleheads, ruddy ducks, mergansers, scoters, and oldsquaws feed or escape from danger by diving, often to considerable depths. They are typically found on larger, deeper lakes, rivers, and bays. Harlequin ducks and eiders also feed by diving, and with old-squaws, scoters, and red-breasted mergansers are seen along Delmarva's seacoast in winter. To complicate matters, however, many diving ducks breed in marshes, and most surface-feeders occasionally dive. You should also keep in mind that there are some strong divers that are not strictly classified as waterfowl, including loons, grebes, and cor-morants, all of which may be seen along Delmarva's shores, particu-larly in winter. Coots both dabble and dive, and gallinules feed on the surface.

The distinction between surface-feeding ducks and diving ducks is reflected in a few physical adaptations. Since diving requires more propulsive force than does dabbling or tilting in shallow water, divers typically have bigger feet than surface-feeders, and their legs are located nearer to their tails. These adaptations make them strong swimmers but awkward on land. In contrast, the smaller feet of surface-feeders enables them to walk and run well on land, so that ducks seen feeding in farm fields are almost certainly surface-feeders (often mallards, pintails, or wigeons).

One easily observed difference between surface-feeding ducks and diving ducks has to do with the way that they take flight. Surface-feeders take off nearly vertically, seeming to jump from the water. Divers, however, are heavier in relation to their size, and in consequence they can only become airborne by first pattering along the surface for a considerable distance, like a seaplane gaining speed and taking off. An exception, however, is the bufflehead, a diver that jumps from the water like a surface-feeding duck.

In his booklet for bird watchers and hunters called *Ducks at a Distance*, naturalist Bob Hines outlines a checklist of identification traits to which observers can refer at different ranges. Even when ducks are far away, their flocking patterns on the water or in the air can be observed. For example, some species, such as wigeons, eiders, canvas-backs, redheads, and scaup, gather in large rafts on the water, especially during winter. When in flight, a few species (such as black ducks, mallards, pintails, and ring-necked ducks) are characterized by loose, random formations, while other species (such as gadwalls, wigeons, shovelers, teal, and scaup) usually fly in tight bunches. Mergansers and eiders fly in Indian file, low over the water, while canvasbacks and scoters fly in wavy lines and irregular V's, shifting back and forth between the two. During migration, many geese and swans, of course, fly in V formation.

Other characteristics of flight include various maneuvers that are typical of different species of waterfowl. For example, when descending to land, pintails zigzag down from great heights before leveling off near the surface of the water or the ground. Most ducks fly more or less straight, but flocks of wigeons, teal, scaup, and sometimes shovelers twist and turn irregularly as a unit, giving the impression of great speed as they fly low over the water or marsh. Although some species are, of course, swifter than others (canvasbacks are the fastest ducks), actual speed is hard to estimate and is not very useful in distinguishing one sort from another. But some ducks — the small ruddy duck, for example — beat their wings perceptibly faster than other species.

As with flight, idiosyncrasies of swimming distinguish certain waterfowl. The ruddy duck, which cannot walk on land, often swims with its tail cocked vertically. Mute swans typically swim with their necks held in an S-curve, whereas the posture of tundra swans tends to be more straight-necked. Among swimmers that are not strictly classified as waterfowl, coots and gallinules pump their heads back and forth while swimming. Common loons and cormorants float very low in the water, so that often it is difficult to see more than their heads, necks, and the top of their backs.

At mid-range it is sometimes possible, even in poor light conditions, to identify waterfowl simply by their silhouettes. For instance, unlike other ducks, pintails and oldsquaws have long needle-pointed tails; in addition, pintails have long, slender necks. Some profiles show highly distinctive features, like the disproportionately large, spatulated bills of shovelers or the swept-back crests of wood ducks and most mergansers. Of course, the long necks and great size of the various species of swans and geese seen in the Chesapeake region immediately distinguish them from all ducks. However, except for gross differences — as between the small ruddy ducks and teal at one extreme and the large, stocky eiders at the other — comparative size is of limited usefulness in identifying ducks.

As noted at the outset, plumage is basic to identification, but only if you have time to examine the birds in good light either up close or through binoculars or a telescope. Even then, plumage can be confusing due to the fact that nearly all ducks lose their body feathers twice each year. When drakes shed their bright plumage after mating and enter what is called eclipse, they resemble the comparatively drab females of the species for a few weeks before assuming a motley, messy look as they return to breeding plumage. After the summer molt, shovelers and blue-winged teal may remain in eclipse even into winter.

As outlined by Roger Tory Peterson in his *A Field Guide to the Birds*, patches of color on the wings are a particularly important aid to identification because ducks shed their wing feathers only once each year, and even then, wing colors remain constant. When the birds are flying, bold patterns of light and dark on either surface of the flapping wings may be conspicuous. For example, the contrasting pattern of a very dark body with flashing white wing linings helps to identify the black duck. In flight, the wigeon has a white *belly* and large white patches on each forewing, while the common eider has a white *back* and white forewings. And so on, in a manner that only much practice can master. Peterson's field guide includes a particularly good collection of black-and-white drawings showing how ducks appear in flight from below and from the side.

On a more detailed level, the upper side of a duck's wing features a great variety of smaller insignia. On most surface-feeding ducks, the speculum is a bright, often iridescent patch of color on the top trailing edge of each wing near where it joins the body. It provides a name, for example, to the green-winged teal. Unfortunately, shovelers and blue-winged teal (both of which show a pale blue patch on the *forward* edge of their wings) also have a green speculum. The speculum of black ducks is violet, gadwalls white, mallards blue, and pintails brown.

Even in pre-dawn darkness and other abysmal light conditions, some accomplished birders and hunters can identify waterfowl solely by their calls, although those of us who prefer to remain in bed may be tempted to dismiss such claims as just so much quackery. For what it is worth, I merely note here that different field guides employ an amazing variety of terms to describe duck calls, including *croak, peep, growl, grunt, twitter, purr, meow, moan, wheeze, squeak,* and *squeal.* Some authors are even given to mimicry. Hines, for example, has a rich vocabulary that starts with the basic *kwek-kwek* and goes on to *kack-kack, kaow, woh-woh, took-took, hoo-w-ett, cr-r-ek, squak, speer-speer,* and *kow-kow-kow-kow.* Clearly, however, something occasionally is lost in translation. For instance, while Hines hears oldsquaws, which are among the most vocal of ducks, say *caloo-caloo,* Peterson hears *ow-owdle-ow* and *owl-omelet* (perhaps he is just cracking a yolk). In any case, this babble of ducktalk inevitably raises the issue of what the various species are perceived to say once they migrate northward into French-speaking Quebec province and southward into Mexico. (For a relevant discussion, see Noel Perrin's suggestively-titled "Old MacBerlitz Had a Farm," which appeared in the *New Yorker* for January 27, 1962.)

Finally, for one of the ultimate niceties in the truly enjoyable pastime of bird watching and bird identification, some authorities say that a few ducks (particularly goldeneyes, also called whistlers) can be identified simply by the singing, swishing, or rushing sounds produced by their wings.

AUTOMOBILE DIRECTIONS: Horsehead Wetlands Center is located in Maryland near the village of Grasonville, 6 miles east of the Chesapeake Bay Bridge and within sight of the high bridge over the Kent Narrows. (See Map 1 in the Table of Contents.)

To Horsehead Wetlands Center from northern Delmarva and Interstate 95 near Newark, Delaware: From I-95 take Route 896 south across Route 40 and over the Chesapeake and Delaware Canal to an intersection with Route 301, and there continue straight south on Route 301. Just west of Middletown, turn right to follow Route 301 south into Maryland for about 44 miles to the merger with Route 50 west of Queenstown. After merging with Route 50, continue only 0.6 mile, then take Exit 45B. At the top of the exit ramp, turn left onto Winchester Road toward Nesbit Road, then immediately turn left onto Nesbit Road toward Route 18. Go 0.3 mile, then at a T-intersection turn right (west) onto Route 18 toward Grasonville. Follow Route 18 for 1.6 miles, then turn left onto Perry Corner Road. Go 0.5 mile, then turn right into the entrance of the Wildfowl Trust's Horsehead Wetlands Center. Follow the dirt road 1.1 miles to the parking lot.

To Horsehead Wetlands Center from the Chesapeake Bay Bridge: After crossing the Bay Bridge, follow Route 50/301 for 5.0 miles to and across the high bridge at the Kent Narrows, then take Exit 43B (the third exit after the Kent Narrows Bridge) for Chester River Beach Road. At the top of the exit ramp, turn right toward Route 18, then turn left (east) at a T-intersection onto Route 18 in Grasonville. Follow Route 18 east only 0.2 mile, then turn right onto Perry Corner Road. Go 0.5 mile, then turn right into the entrance of the Wildfowl Trust's Horsehead Wetlands Center. Follow the dirt road 1.1 miles to the parking lot.

To Horsehead Wetlands Center from southern Delmarva and the Chesapeake Bay Bridge-Tunnel at Norfolk: Follow Route 13 north into Maryland and past Pocomoke City and Princess Anne to the exit for Route 50

MAP 13 -- Horsehead Wetlands Center

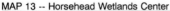

westbound near Salisbury, and from there take Route 50 west through Cambridge and Easton. After passing through the intersection with Route 404 near Wye Mills, continue on Route 50 for 6.6 miles, then turn left onto Route 18 west toward Grasonville. Go 3.1 miles, then turn left onto Perry Corner Road. Go 0.5 mile, then turn right into the entrance of the Wildfowl Trust's Horsehead Wetlands Center. Follow the dirt road 1.1 miles to the parking lot.

To Horsehead Wetlands Center from Salisbury and the Delaware and Maryland seashore resorts: Follow Route 50 or Route 404 west to the intersection of these two roads near Wye Mills. From there continue west on Route 50 for 6.6 miles, then turn left onto Route 18 westbound toward Grasonville. Go 3.1 miles, then turn left onto Perry Corner Road. Go 0.5 mile, then turn right into the entrance of the Wildfowl Trust's Horsehead Wetlands Center. Follow the dirt road 1.1 miles to the parking lot.

WALKING AT HORSEHEAD WETLANDS CENTER: After stopping by the **Visitor Center** and **Woodland Pond Observatory**, and after touring the resident **Wildfowl Exhibits**, you may want to wander farther afield. As shown on Map 13, two blinds overlook the large pond at the center of the refuge. The **J. C. White Blind** and the **Wetland Boardwalk** are reached by a wide dirt road leading west. The **East Blind** is reached by the **Marshy Creek Trail**, which terminates at an observation tower.

6

WYE ISLAND

Linked to the mainland by a short bridge, Wye Island Natural Resources Management Area in Maryland consists of 2,450 acres of farmland and woods to which the public is welcome for low-impact activities like picnicking (no fires, however), hiking, and fishing. One of the island's chief attractions is the rare opportunity to walk freely through an agricultural landscape, skirting tilled areas, cutting through woods, and passing from one field to the next. If you have a field dog, or perhaps yourself have the roving, searching instincts of a field dog, here you can have a field day. (But first please read the note about hunting on page 85). For those, however, who prefer a well-defined path, there are three trails (none longer than 1.5 miles round-trip), plus a dirt road through the western half of the island that provides up to 6 miles of excellent walking. If you have a fat-tired bicycle that can handle the sometimes loose, gravelly surface, the road is good for bicycling, too. Bicyclists may also enjoy riding on Carmichael Road, Cheston Lane, and Stagwell Road, which pass through an attractive farmscape immediately to the north of Wye Island. Although traffic on these dead-end roads is likely to be light, bicyclists should still be prepared for cars traveling at high speeds.

  Wye Island is open all day year-round; camping, however, is prohibited. The island is managed by the Maryland Department of Natural Resources, primarily to provide wildlife habitat and for agricultural experimentation in conjunction with the University of Maryland's nearby research farm called the Wye Institute. For inquiries about Wye Island, telephone (410) 827-7577.

WYE ISLAND shows the Eastern Shore of Maryland at its best. Located in an area of historic plantations and large farms, the island consists mainly of cultivated fields separated by hedgerows, woodlots, and the arms of tidal creeks. There is nothing spectacular here, just a mellow, quiet beauty that fortunately has been preserved by public acquisition of the area in 1976, just as the eastern third of the island (the part comprising William Paca's Wye Hall Farm) was being subdivided into 35 pieces ranging in size from 15 to 75 acres. Some of these parcels were in fact sold and remain in private ownership.

Along Carmichael Road on the way to Wye Island are several historic markers noting that English settlement in this area dates back to the mid-1600s. Not for a moment, however, should it be thought that the mature agricultural landscape seen today in any way resembles the Maryland of that time, when the Chesapeake region was one of the frontiers of the New World and its English inhabitants were essentially pioneers in a wilderness, all growing one crop — tobacco — for export to Great Britain.

The vast majority of tobacco planters in seventeenth-century Maryland were men of modest means, each cultivating a few acres cleared from the woods that covered all of the region's arable land to the water's edge. Every planter tried to acquire as much land as he could at his first patent, and the size of most early plantations substantially exceeded the 50-acre headright quota, but the land actually cultivated was far less. Three acres of tobacco was about the upper limit for even the hardest worker. Settlers who had capital at the time of their immigration brought with them indentured laborers (termed "servants") with whom to claim more land and to cultivate larger fields. Still other freemen who worked alone or with their sons used the profits from their first successful harvests to acquire indentured servants as quickly as possible. Some seventeenth-century writers condemned the system of indenture, but others agreed with one observer who wrote, "The work of their servants and slaves is no other than what every common freeman does." Another observer similarly noted that many masters and their sons worked alongside their bondsmen.

More than three-quarters of the immigrants to the Chesapeake region in the 1600s came as indentured servants, required by their contracts (called articles of indenture) to work for a number of years in exchange for having their passage to the New World paid by merchant recruiters, who then sold the servants to planters who could afford them. Some recruiters dealt in servants on a large scale, but most servants were transported by numerous merchants and mariners primarily engaged in other business and who had perhaps been requested by their agents and customers in the Chesapeake region to supply a few indentured laborers. Even if no such request had been received, merchants and shipmasters knew that transporting a bondservant for resale in Maryland or Virginia was a safe speculation.

In this way, even many of the smaller planters of the tidewater region acquired one or two indentured servants. Eventually, the system of indenture became so commonplace that local statutes governed the practice in cases where there were no individualized contracts. Typically, upon completion of his or her term of servitude (often five years for adults, longer for minors), each servant was paid freedom dues consisting of various items, such as new clothes, tools, and even land early on when ample land was still available. For women, the end of their indenture meant marriage to their pick of a multitude of suitors (men outnumbered women by nearly three to one) and in all probability the continuation of a workaday life not unlike what they had known as servants. For men the end of servitude meant the opportunity to set up for themselves as small tobacco planters.

The flow of indentured immigrants to Maryland and Virginia in the mid-1600s reflected depressed economic conditions in England. A variety of factors — rapid population growth, the consolidation of farms and their conversion from cultivated fields to pasture and orchards, and finally the disruption in commerce caused by the Thirty Years War and the English Civil War — all combined to create widespread unemployment in England. In consequence, many young people, mostly with family backgrounds in farming and textile manufacture, and mostly between the ages of fifteen and twenty-four, chose to go as indentured servants to the Chesapeake region, where there was at least the certainty of gainful employment and the touted prospect of becoming planters after their servitude was over.

From the 1630s through the 1650s, when tobacco prices were high and free land was available, many indentured laborers who had completed their terms of servitude did indeed manage to set up immediately as small growers on good land. By 1660, however, most land suitable for growing tobacco had already been claimed and so became something that had to be purchased from a prior owner. Under these less favorable circumstances, some newly-freed indentured servants took up less desirable land that did not offer much opportunity for economic advancement. Other former servants often got a start by tenant farming for established landowners — perhaps even their former masters — before eventually accumulating the means to become freeholders in their own right. Still others became hired workers or sharecroppers, typically living as members of a freeholder's household, but these men rarely improved their status, even after years of laboring. Toward the end of the century, economic prospects for former bondsmen dimmed still further as rising land prices and periodic slumps in the tobacco economy condemned most freed servants to the perpetual status of landless, voteless, voiceless tenants, sharecroppers, or hired hands — if, that is, they chose to stay in the tidewater region.

As economic opportunity declined in the Chesapeake region, so too did the flow of indentured servants willing to immigrate from England, where by the closing decades of the 1600s the economy was recovering and employment among the poor was rising. In consequence, the practice of importing African slaves became a way to supply labor to the tidewater plantations. Once started, the conversion to slaves was speeded by the perceived anomaly of working whites and blacks together, and also by the advantages of owning slaves, who, of course, never became free and whose children too belonged to the master. After 1698, when the African slave trade was thrown open to all English firms that wished to engage in the traffic, slaves were transported to the tidewater region in great numbers.

While the flow of English immigration to Maryland lasted, however, the population grew from somewhat more than 100 in 1634, when the *Ark* and the *Dove* arrived at St. Mary's River, to 8,000 settlers in 1660, 15,000 in 1675, and 25,000 in 1688. From freed servants and other immigrants of slender resources came the bulk of pioneer planters, each drudging with his ax and his hoe to grow tobacco, which he traded for necessary implements and for a very few luxuries — perhaps sugar and occasionally rum. Inventories of probated estates show that the typical planter made every possible article that he could with his own hands: bowls and cups from dried gourds, trenchers and plates from slabs of wood, benches and bedsteads from hewn logs, and mattresses from corn shucks. For his own use he tended also a cornfield, a vegetable garden, and possibly an orchard that he had planted. He supplemented his diet by hunting and fishing. Nearly every planter family kept a few chickens, cows, and pigs (usually allowed to roam freely in the woods) and perhaps provided board and lodging to an unmarried sharecropper or hired hand. Most planters were illiterate — they signed their names with an X or some other mark — and very few had even a single book.

Because tobacco rapidly exhausted the soil, the typical planter was always clearing new land. The best land could grow tobacco for about eight years, but poor, sandy soil would support tobacco for only three years, after which the exhausted fields might be planted in corn for a few years more and then left fallow for a decade or two. As one seventeenth-century traveler noted, "As fast as the ground is worn out with tobacco and corn, it runs up again in underwoods; and in many places of the country that which has been cleared is thicker in woods than it was before the clearing." Scattered at intervals through the forest and overgrown fields were small houses, many of them ramshackle or even abandoned by planters who had moved to be nearer to new fields.

The houses of the seventeenth-century planters were small wooden boxes. Most had only one room, shared by the master, servants, and lodgers alike. More prosperous planters might have houses of two or three rooms and perhaps a separate dwelling for servants, and a very few planters had houses with as many as six rooms. All structures were framed with wooden posts sunk into the ground. Covering the frame were boards, more often split than sawn, chinked with mud. As for the interior walls, "The best people plaster them with clay," explained two visiting Dutchmen in 1680, but some dwellings were so wretchedly constructed "that if you are not so close to the fire as almost to burn yourself, you cannot keep warm, for the wind blows through everywhere." The houses were of one story, often with an earthen floor. Windows had shutters or perhaps panes of oiled paper, but no glass. Chimneys were usually of wood daubed with mud. Roofs were at first of thatch; later shingles were used. In 1686 a visiting Frenchman observed that even the wealthier planters lived in simple structures of this kind, and added, "They build also a separate kitchen, a house for the Christian slaves [or that is, indentured servants], another for negro slaves, and several tobacco barns, so that in arriving at the plantation of a person of importance, you think you are entering a considerable village."

The larger plantations were at first the only places where more than a few people lived together. The rush to acquire land and to grow tobacco so thoroughly dispersed the population that towns did not begin to develop until the final decades of the 1600s, a half-century after the first settlement in Maryland. Even then the early towns were merely minor outposts for a few trading establishments, where tobacco was gathered together for transshipment. There might also be a courthouse, a church, and a customs house where the colonial government collected export duties, its principal form of revenue. Another reason why towns and even roads were slow to develop was that the extensive system of tidal rivers made them unnecessary. "Noe country can compare with it," reads one enthusiastic report on the Chesapeake region. "The number of navigable rivers, creeks, and inlets, render it so convenient for exporting and importing goods into any part thereof by water carriage." Early each winter or spring, ships arrived in the Chesapeake from Great Britain and ascended the rivers, sailing from one plantation to the next to trade clothing, tools, and other manufactured goods for tobacco packed in barrels called hogsheads. Along with good soil, a good waterfront location — as, for example, along the Wye River — was one of the prime considerations in picking land for settlement and cultivation. Only as good waterfront land became unavailable did planters begin to penetrate the interior.

Hard work, command of bound or hired labor, and ownership of fertile waterfront land were not the only ingredients for prosperity in the Chesapeake region. Gloria L. Main, in her book *Tobacco Colony*, points out that good health, or more precisely, a long life, was also an important factor. With its vast marshes and suffocatingly hot summers, the tidewater region was a very unhealthful climate for most English settlers. Malaria often weakened the immigrants and left them in no condition to survive the dysentery, typhoid fever, pneumonia, and influenza that were also common. In Maryland during the middle of the seventeenth century, white male immigrants who reached age twenty-two (many died earlier) could expect to remain alive only into their early forties. A mere third of the marriages in seventeenth-century Maryland lasted as long as a decade before one or the other spouse died. In southern Maryland between 1658 and 1705, 67 percent of married men and widowers who died left children who were all of minor age, while only 6 percent left all adult children. Consequently, the life of the typical planter was often cut short before he had accumulated more than very modest assets to pass on to the wife and children who may have survived him.

By living to old age, however, some planters were able to accumulate expertise and wealth over a protracted period. The first generation of successful planters eschewed spending their profits on consumption goods and instead invested in more and more land and laborers, while continuing to live in a manner that was spare, unostentatious, and frugal. In this way a few planters — perhaps one in twenty — rose to something like affluence by the standards of the time, and a still smaller number laid the foundations for major family fortunes. As the result of marriage gifts and bequests (which fathers commonly distributed well before their deaths), the children of such long-lived planters started adult life with a huge advantage over those without similar patrimony.

Gradually, however, mortality rates among settlers declined during the seventeenth century, and by way of explanation some historians have pointed to the increased consumption of cider, beer, rum, and pure water from deep wells, as opposed to the polluted and sometimes even slightly brackish surface water drunk by the early settlers. The popular notion at the time was simply that the survivors had become "seasoned," or that is, had adjusted to the new environment, but historians with a medical bent point out that the local diseases were such that no lasting immunity was possible, thus again suggesting that sanitation improved.

Some historians have gone so far as to argue that the decline in mortality diminished economic opportunity for newly-freed indentured servants. During the middle third of the seventeenth century, the lottery of longevity had favored a few, who acquired sizable and sometimes even very large landholdings. Had the likelihood of an early death continued to be the norm, such holdings would have been without long-term consequence, because much land would soon have become available for redistribution as the descendants of big landowners died young like most other people. But instead, improved sanitation and lengthening life expectancies enabled families that already had much land to retain it permanently, shutting out newcomers.

It has also been suggested that increased longevity speeded the conversion to a slave labor force, inasmuch as permanent slaves became preferable to temporary servants once it was observed that the slaves, who were more expensive to acquire than servants, were likely to survive as long-term assets. Furthermore, it became worthwhile to do with slaves what was not worthwhile with short-term bondsmen, namely to teach them a variety of valuable skills that would then remunerate the master throughout each slave's lifetime and enable the plantation to become more self-sufficient and profitable.

The stratification of society and the emergence at the top of a wealthy elite was reinforced by a pattern of wide fluctuations in the price of tobacco during the seventeenth century. At first tobacco prices were high because of the limited output, but later, as production soared and the tidewater region was wracked by periodic, precipitous drops in the price of tobacco, many growers who had not yet acquired an adequate cushion of spare capital failed, and their crops, land, and other useful assets were bought by those who were already wealthy. In particular, two periods of deep depression from 1686 to 1696 and from 1703 to 1716 eroded the holdings of the middle stratum of planters and drove away to Pennsylvania and the Carolinas (where good land was still available at low prices) the poor, the young, and the newly-freed indentured servants.

In other ways also wealth begot more wealth. Tobacco planters with adequate capital were in a position, especially after about 1680, to diversify into other fields, such as trade, moneylending, shipping, or the practice of law. Wealthy planters corresponded with English consignment houses for the sale of their tobacco, thus obtaining higher prices than did those smaller growers who simply sold their crops locally. Well-capitalized planters purchased imported goods — cloth, shoes, hats, tools, nails, salt, and other necessities — for resale at a markup of about 50 percent to the numerous smaller planters. These merchant-planters sold their goods on credit throughout the year, eventually receiving crops in payment, for tobacco served as a substitute for money. Some large planters bought shares in ships, or opened sawmills, gristmills, iron mines, tanneries, and other enterprises often manned by slaves. A few planters even began to experiment with manufacturing items, such as shoes, or with new agricultural pursuits, such as growing wheat or raising large herds of cattle, hogs, and sheep.

Finally, of course, the families of well-to-do planters intermarried, consolidating their wealth among themselves. And they came also to monopolize governmental power. For a long time the high death rate prevented the emergence of a ruling class, but after 1700, election or appointment to county and provincial offices depended increasingly on the aspiring man's family name, connections, and high economic status. Wealth enabled the patriarchs of leading families to educate their sons and grandsons in the skills necessary to assume governmental posts, judicial responsibilities, militia officerships, and church positions that were created in increasing numbers as the society expanded and matured.

In this way, a native-born tidewater aristocracy developed, epitomized by some of the families that owned plantations in the vicinity of Wye Island in the eighteenth century. For example, the plantation called Stagwell, located on Wye Neck on the way to Wye Island, was acquired in 1706 by Richard Bennett, who upon his death in 1749 was described by the *Maryland Gazette* as "the Richest Man on the Continent." By a series of marriages, Wye Island itself passed from the Lloyds to the Chews to the Bordleys and Pacas. The first three surnames rank at the forefront of colonial Maryland's merchant-planter caste, while the last is that of William Paca, a Revolutionary leader and the governor of Maryland from 1782 to 1785. Wye Plantation on the mainland was also acquired by the Pacas by marriage with yet another prominent family, the Tilghmans.

AUTOMOBILE DIRECTIONS: Wye Island is located in Maryland near Wye Mills, 8 miles southeast of the Kent Narrows and 9 miles northwest of Easton. (See Map 1 in the Table of Contents.)

To Wye Island from northern Delmarva and Interstate 95 near Newark, Delaware: From I-95 take Route 896 south across Route 40 and over the Chesapeake and Delaware Canal to an intersection with Route 301, and there continue straight south on Route 301. Just west of Middletown, turn right to follow Route 301 south into Maryland more than 37 miles. Eventually, after passing exits for Route 305 and Route 304 near Centreville, turn left at a traffic light onto Route 213 southbound. Follow Route 213 south 4.3 miles, then turn right (west) onto Route 50. Go 2.4 miles, then turn left onto Carmichael Road and follow it 5.1 miles to the bridge across Wye Narrows.

MAP 14 -- Wye Island Natural Resources Management Area

To Wye Island from the Chesapeake Bay Bridge:
After crossing the Bay Bridge, follow Route 50/301 across
Kent Island. At the point where Route 50 and Route 301 split,
fork right to follow Route 50, but go only 2.9 miles to an
intersection with Carmichael Road on the right. Turn right and
follow Carmichael Road 5.1 miles to the bridge across Wye
Narrows.

**To Wye Island from southern Delmarva and the
Chesapeake Bay Bridge-Tunnel at Norfolk:** Follow
Route 13 north into Maryland and past Pocomoke City and
Princess Anne to the exit for Route 50 westbound near
Salisbury, and from there take Route 50 west through
Cambridge and Easton. After passing through the intersection
with Route 404 near Wye Mills, continue on Route 50 for 3.9
miles, then turn left onto Carmichael Road and follow it 5.1
miles to the bridge across Wye Narrows.

**To Wye Island from Salisbury and the Delaware and
Maryland seashore resorts:** Follow Route 50 or Route
404 west to the intersection of these two roads near Wye Mills.
From there continue west on Route 50 for 3.9 miles, then turn
left onto Carmichael Road and follow it 5.1 miles to the bridge
across Wye Narrows.

EXPLORING WYE ISLAND: Once you cross the bridge at
Wye Narrows, you are on Wye Island, which for the most part is
publicly owned, but includes some private areas, including
Wye Point Farm at the extreme western end of the island and
Wye Hall at the eastern end. Map 14 shows the island's roads,
parking areas, trails, and other features. Please drive slowly
and park in designated areas only.

WALKING ON WYE ISLAND: As shown on Map 14, there
are three short foot trails on the island. **The Nature Trail**
(1.0 mile round-trip) follows a wooded belt and ends at
Grapevine Cove. **The Holly Tree Trail** is only a few
hundred yards long and leads to an exceptionally large holly
tree. **The Ferry Point Trail** (1.5 miles round-trip) follows an
arching arborway of Osage-orange trees to the site of an old
ferry landing. Note that the trail starts at a narrow gap in a fence
next to the parking area, and not at the rutted track at each end
of the fence.

Since it carries little traffic, the **dirt road** itself provides some of the best walking at Wye Island, assuming that you use extra caution. From the parking area for the Nature Trail, the distance to Ferry Point via road and footpath is 5.5 miles round-trip. Walk on the left, facing the oncoming cars, and step off the road as they pass.

You may also enjoy **wandering at large** on Wye Island, which will enable you to see more of the shoreline. The opportunity to walk freely through an agricultural landscape is a rare one, so please do not abuse the privilege by tramping across fields of standing or freshly-planted crops. Even in winter, some fields may be planted in wheat, which at that season simply resembles grass. If in doubt, follow the edges of fields and the established tracks of farm vehicles.

Finally, a note about **hunting**: Each year the area's managers decide whether to allow hunting by special permit at certain times from mid-November to mid-January. During that period, wear orange and stay on the designated trails. Or, if you want to wander through fields and woods, either do your walking on Sunday, when hunting is prohibited, or first call or stop by the office to make sure that hunting is not underway.

7

PRIME HOOK NATIONAL WILDLIFE REFUGE
BEACH PLUM ISLAND NATURE PRESERVE

Although it is located close to Delaware's popular beach resorts, Prime Hook National Wildlife Refuge is not well known. In terms of size (approximately 9,000 acres), it is in the same league with Delmarva's other major national wildlife refuges: Bombay Hook, Blackwater, and Chincoteague, all described elsewhere in this book. But unlike those places, Prime Hook lacks a system of dike-top roads and adjacent waterfowl pools that make bird watching and sightseeing easy. In short, little of interest can be seen from Prime Hook's refuge road, but for those who like to walk, there are four short trails (none longer than a mile round-trip) through areas of marsh, farm fields, hedgerows, and piny woods. And when combined with the opportunity for up to 4 miles (round-trip) of beach walking at nearby Beach Plum Island Nature Preserve, the Prime Hook area offers bird watchers and hikers a wide variety of natural habitats.

Better still, if you can bring a canoe, there is a launching ramp at the national wildlife refuge that provides access to Prime Hook Creek, which meanders for miles through the refuge. For more information about this outstanding canoe trail, see the discussion starting on page 98. Canoeing is also permitted on Turkle Pond and Fleetwood Pond within the national wildlife refuge.

Fishing and hunting are permitted at Prime Hook National Wildlife Refuge subject to the usual state and federal regulations and other special requirements. When deer hunting is in progress at the southern end of the refuge (the part described in this chapter), non-hunters are prohibited from entering. And when waterfowl hunting is underway, non-hunters are barred from Prime Hook Creek. So call beforehand during fall and early winter to make sure that your planned activity — whether bird watching, walking, or canoeing — will not run afoul of the hunting schedule. Of course, hunting is never permitted on Sunday.

Prime Hook National Wildlife Refuge is open daily from half an hour before sunrise to half an hour after sunset. Dogs must be leashed. The refuge is managed by the U.S. Fish and Wildlife Service; telephone (302) 684-8419.

Beach Plum Island Nature Preserve, which lies adjacent to the national wildlife refuge, is open all day every day from mid-March to mid-December. Vehicles with permits may drive on the beach for purposes of surf fishing. During winter the beach is accessible for hiking, but since the parking lot is closed, you must find a legitimate spot to park elsewhere. Dogs must be leashed. Beach Plum Island is managed by the Delaware Department of Natural Resources and Environmental Control, Division of Parks and Recreation; telephone (302) 645-8983.

FEATURING A BROAD RANGE OF HABITATS — sodden deciduous forest, piny (and relatively dry) woods, freshwater ponds and streams, meadows, cultivated fields, marsh, mud flats, dunes, beach, and Delaware Bay itself — Prime Hook National Wildlife Refuge and the adjacent Beach Plum Island Nature Preserve are together exceptionally good places to see a wide variety of birds at every season, although, of course, the periods of spring and fall migration are best.

Even for fledgling birders, identifying the approximately 260 species that have been seen regularly in recent years along the southern shore of Delaware Bay is easier than might at first be thought. Shape, size, plumage, and other physical characteristics are distinguishing field marks. Range, season, habitat, song, and behavior are other useful keys to identifying birds.

Range is of primary importance for the simple reason that many birds are not found throughout North America or even the eastern United States, and so can immediately be eliminated from consideration when birding in Delmarva. For example, the cedar waxwing and Bohemian waxwing closely resemble each other, so it helps to know that the latter is not seen here. A good field guide provides range maps based on years of reported sightings and bird counts. Of course, bird ranges are not static: some pioneering species, such as the glossy ibis and house finch, have extended their ranges during recent decades. Other birds, such as the ivory-billed woodpecker, have lost ground and may even have died out.

Season is related to range, since migratory birds appear in different parts of their ranges during different times of year. The five species of spot-breasted thrushes, for instance, are sometimes difficult to distinguish from each other, but usually only the hermit thrush is present in

Delmarva during winter and only the wood thrush is found here during summer. Again, the maps in most field guides reflect this sort of information.

Habitat is important in identifying birds. Even before you sight a bird, the surroundings can tell you what species you are likely to see. Within its range a species usually appears only in certain preferred habitats, although during migration some species are less particular. (In many cases, birds show a degree of physical adaptation to their preferred environment.) As its name implies, the marsh wren is seldom found far from cattails, rushes, sedges, or tall marsh grasses; if a wrenlike bird is seen in such a setting, it is unlikely to be a house wren or Carolina wren or one of the other species commonly found in thick underbrush or shrubbery. The area where two habitats join, called an *ecotone*, is a particularly good place to look for birds because species peculiar to either environment may be present. For example, both meadowlarks and wood warblers might be found where a hay field abuts a forest. All good field guides provide information on habitat preferences that can help to locate a species or to assess the likelihood of a tentative identification.

Song announces the identity (or at least the location) of birds even before they are seen. Although some species, such as the red-winged blackbird, have only a few songs, others, such as the mockingbird, have an infinite variety. (Even so, mockingbird songs tend to follow certain characteristic patterns, such as the repetition of each phrase up to a half-dozen times, before moving on to another phrase.) Some birds, most notably thrushes, sing different songs in the morning and evening. In many species the songs vary somewhat among individuals and from one area to another, giving rise to regional "dialects." Nonetheless, the vocal repertory of most songbirds is sufficiently constant in timbre and pattern to identify each species simply by its songs.

Bird songs, as distinguished from calls, can be very complex. They are sung only by the male of most species, usually in spring and summer. The male arrives first at the breeding and nesting area after migration. He stakes out a territory for courting, mating, and nesting by singing at prominent points around the area's perimeter. This wards off intrusion by other males of his species and simultaneously attracts females. On the basis of the male's display and the desirability of his territory, the female selects her mate. Experiments suggest that female birds build nests faster and lay more eggs when exposed to the songs of males with a larger vocal repertory than others of their species, and the relative volume of their songs appears to be a way for males to establish status among themselves.

In a few species, including eastern bluebirds, "Baltimore" orioles, cardinals, and white-throated sparrows, both sexes sing, although the males are more active in defending their breeding territory. Among mockingbirds, both sexes sing in fall and winter, but only males sing in spring and summer. Some birds, such as canaries, have different songs for different seasons.

Birds tend to heed the songs of their own kind and to ignore the songs of other species, which do not compete for females nor, in many cases, for the same type of nesting materials or food. In consequence, a single area might include the overlapping breeding territories of several species. From year to year such territories are bigger or smaller, depending on the food supply. Typically, most small songbirds require about half an acre from which others of their species are excluded.

Bird calls (as distinguished from songs) are short, simple, sometimes harsh, and used by both males and females at all times of year to communicate alarm, aggression, location, and existence of food. Nearly all birds have some form of call. Warning calls are often heeded by species other than the caller's. Some warning calls are thin, high-pitched whistles that are difficult to locate and so do not reveal the bird's location to predators. Birds also use mobbing calls to summon other birds, as chickadees and crows do when scolding and harassing owls and other unwanted visitors. Birds flying in flocks, like cedar waxwings, often call continuously. Such calls help birds migrating by night to stay together.

The study of bird dialects and experiments with birds that have been deafened or raised in isolation indicate that songs are genetically inherited only to a very crude extent. Although a few species, such as doves, sing well even when raised in isolation, most birds raised alone produce inferior, simplified songs. Generally, young songbirds learn their songs by listening to adult birds and by practice singing, called *sub-song*. Yet birds raised in isolation and exposed to many tape-recorded songs show an innate preference for the songs of their own species.

Probably the easiest way to learn bird songs is to listen repeatedly to recordings and to refer at the same time to a standard field guide. Most guides describe bird vocalizations with such terms as *harsh, nasal, flute-like, piercing, plaintive, wavering, twittering, buzzing, sneezy,* and *sputtering,* and although these terms are somewhat descriptive, they do not take on real meaning until you have heard the songs themselves on records or in the field. Incidentally, bird recordings that are played slowly demonstrate that the songs contain many more notes than the human ear ordinarily hears.

Shape is one of the first and most important aspects to notice once you actually see a bird. Most birds can at least be placed in the proper family and many species can be identified by shape or silhouette, without reference to other field marks. Some birds, such as kestrels, are distinctly stocky, big-headed, and powerful-looking, while others, such as catbirds and cuckoos, are elegantly long and slender. Kingfishers, blue jays, tufted titmice, Bohemian and cedar waxwings, and cardinals are among the few birds with crests.

Bird bills frequently have distinctive shapes and, more than any other body part, show adaptation to food supply. The beak can be chunky, like that of a grosbeak, to crack seeds; thin and curved, like that of a creeper, to probe bark for insects; hooked, like that of a shrike, to tear at flesh; long and slender, like that of a hummingbird, to sip nectar from tubular flowers; or some other characteristic shape depending on the bird's food. Goatsuckers, swifts, flycatchers, and swallows, all of which catch flying insects, have widely hinged bills and gaping mouths. The long, thin bills of starlings and meadowlarks are suited to probing the ground. In the Galapagos Islands west of Ecuador, Charles Darwin noted fourteen species of finches, each of which had evolved a different type of beak or style of feeding that gave it a competitive advantage for a particular type of food. Many birds are nonetheless flexible about their diet, especially from season to season when food sources change or become scarce. For example, Tennessee warblers, which ordinarily glean insects from foliage, also take large amounts of nectar from tropical flowers when wintering in South and Central America.

In addition to beaks, nearly every other part of a bird's body is adapted to help exploit its environment. Feet of passerines, or songbirds, are adapted to perching, with three toes in front and one long toe behind; waterfowl have webbed or lobed feet for swimming; and raptors have talons for grasping prey.

Other key elements of body shape are the length and form of wings, tails, and legs. The wings may be long, pointed, and developed for swift, sustained flight, like those of falcons. Or the wings may be short and rounded for abrupt bursts of speed, like those of accipiters. The tail may have a deep fork like that of a barn swallow, a shallow notch like that of a tree swallow, or a square tip like that of a cliff swallow, or a round tip like that of a blue jay.

Size is difficult to estimate and therefore not very useful in identifying birds. The best approach is to bear in mind the relative sizes of different species and to use certain well-known birds like the chickadee, sparrow, robin, kingfisher, and crow as standards for mental comparison. For example, if a bird resembles a song sparrow but looks unusually large, it might be a fox sparrow.

Plumage, whether plain or princely, muted or magnificent, is one of the most obvious keys to identification. Color can occur in remarkable

combinations of spots, stripes, streaks, patches, and other patterns that make even supposedly drab birds a pleasure to see. In some instances, like the brown streaks of American bitterns and many other species, the plumage provides camouflage. Most vireos and warblers are various shades and combinations of yellow, green, brown, gray, and black, as one would expect from their forest environment. The black and white backs of woodpeckers help them to blend in with bark dappled with sunlight. The bold patterns of killdeers and some other plovers break up their outlines in much the same manner that warships used to be camouflaged before the invention of radar. Many shore birds display countershading: they are dark above and light below, a pattern that reduces the effect of shadows and makes the birds appear an inconspicuous monotone. Even some brightly colored birds have camouflaging plumages when they are young and least able to avoid predators.

For some species, it is important *not* to be camouflaged. Many sea birds are mostly white, which in all light conditions enables them to be seen at great distances against the water. Because flocks of sea birds spread out from their colonies to search for food, it is vital that a bird that has located food be visible to others after it has landed on the water to feed.

To organize the immense variation of plumages, focus on different basic elements and ask the following types of questions. Starting with the head, is it uniformly colored like that of the red-headed woodpecker? Is there a small patch on the crown, like that of Wilson's warbler and the ruby-crowned kinglet, or a larger cap on the front and top of the head, like that of the common redpoll and American goldfinch? Is the crown striped like the ovenbird's? Does a ring surround the eye, as with a Connecticut warbler, or are the rings perhaps even joined across the top of the bill to form spectacles, like those of a yellow-breasted chat? Is there a stripe over or through the eyes, like the red-breasted nuthatch's, or a conspicuous black mask across the eyes, like that of a common yellowthroat or loggerhead shrike? Such marks are not merely peculiar to this or that individual (as is the case with a spotted horse) but rather are reliably characteristic of different bird species. From the head go on to the rest of the body, where distinctive colors and patterns can also mark a bird's bill, throat, breast, belly, back, sides, wings, rump, tail, and legs.

Finally, what a bird *does* is an important clue to its identity. Certain habits, postures, ways of searching for food, and other behavior characterize different species. Some passerines, such as larks, juncos, and towhees, are strictly ground feeders; other birds, including flycatchers and swallows, nab insects on the wing; and others, such as nuthatches and creepers, glean insects from the crevices in bark. Woodpeckers bore into the bark. Vireos and most warblers pick insects from the foliage of trees and brush.

All of these birds may be further distinguished by other habits of eating. For example, towhees scratch for insects and seeds by kicking backward with both feet together, whereas juncos rarely do, although both hop to move along the ground. Other ground feeders, such as meadowlarks, walk rather than hop. Despite the children's song, robins generally run, not hop. Swallows catch insects while swooping and skimming in continuous flight, but flycatchers dart out from a limb, grab an insect (sometimes with an audible smack), and then return to their perch. Brown creepers have the curious habit of systematically searching for food by climbing trees in spirals, then flying back to the ground to climb again. Woodpeckers tend to hop upward, bracing themselves against the tree with their stiff tails. Nuthatches walk up, down, and around tree trunks and branches, seemingly without regard for gravity. Vireos are sluggish compared to the hyperactive, flitting warblers.

Many birds divide a food source into zones, an arrangement that apparently has evolved to ensure each species its own food supply. The short-legged green heron sits at the edge of the water or on a low overhanging branch, waiting for its prey to come close to shore. Medium-sized black-crowned and yellow-crowned night herons hunt in shallow water. The long-legged great blue heron stalks fish in water up to two feet deep. Swans, geese, and many ducks graze underwater on the stems and tubers of grassy plants, but the longer necks of swans and geese enable them to reach deeper plants. Similarly, different species of shore birds take food from the same mud flat by probing with their varied bills to different depths. Species of warblers that feed in the same tree are reported to concentrate in separate areas among the trunk, twig tips, and tree top. Starlings and cowbirds feeding in flocks on the ground show another arrangement that provides an even distribution of food: those in the rear fly ahead to the front, so that the entire flock rolls slowly across the field.

Different species also have different styles of flight. Soaring is typical of some big birds. Gulls float nearly motionless in the wind. Buteos and turkey vultures soar on updrafts in wide circles, although turkey vultures may be further distinguished by wings held in a shallow V. Some other large birds, such as accipiters, rarely soar but instead interrupt their wing beats with glides. Kestrels, terns, and kingfishers can hover in one spot. Hummingbirds, like oversized dragonflies, can also hover and even fly backward. Slightly more erratic than the swooping, effortless flight of swallows is that of swifts, flitting with wing beats that appear to alternate (but do not). Still other birds, such as the American goldfinch and flickers, dip up and down in wavelike flight.

94

And now for a few practice puzzlers to illustrate and apply some of the points discussed above. All of the examples involve birds that you might see at Prime Hook or Beach Plum Island.

At a considerable distance across the hazy marsh in July, you spot a large, dark, long-legged, long-necked wading bird with a downward-curved bill. What is it? . . . . Of course, the vast majority of large, dark waders in Delmarva are great blue herons, but herons have straight bills. So your bird is probably a glossy ibis, which is also somewhat smaller than the great blue heron. The identification is confirmed when the creature flies off across the marsh with its neck outstretched. Herons and egrets fly with their necks folded back. The whimbrel, too, has a downwardly curved bill and flies with its neck outstretched, but its neck and legs are visibly shorter than those of the glossy ibis.

At the edge of Prime Hook's Turkle Pond in summer you observe a small bird that is all brown above and streaked with brown below. A long, pale-yellow stripe runs above each eye. As it walks the bird teeters and bobs. This is a . . . a . . . northern waterthrush, whose peculiar gait is shared by the somewhat larger spotted sandpiper, also seen on lakeshores.

At the edge of pine woods early in May, you hear a distinctive song: about eight buzzy notes ascending the chromatic scale, or that is, rising in a series of half tones. This song is enough to identify — what? Finally, you spot a small warbler with an olive back and yellow underparts, streaked black along the sides and having one black stripe through each eye and another below across each cheek. The bird bobs its tail. It is the misnamed prairie warbler, which is common in bushy pastures, saplings, and low pines. The palm warbler also bobs its tail, but it is brown above and in spring has a chestnut cap. Yet other birds with idiosyncratic tail tics include the eastern phoebe, which regularly jerks its tail downward while perching, and wrens, which often cock their tails vertically.

On a mud flat in spring you observe hundreds of birds probing and picking at the glistening muck. Most of them are small and brownish, so you dismiss them collectively as "peeps" — or that is, least, semi-palmated, western, Baird's, and white-rumped sandpipers. Your attention, however, is drawn by a few larger birds, as follows:

(1) A real eye-catcher is a bird whose body, neck, and head are black above and white below; it has long red legs and a needlelike bill.

(2) Another large bird has a tan head and neck and a black-and-white back; while feeding it sweeps its upwardly curved bill from side to side like a scythe.

(3) Also present are some speckled gray birds with long, thin, black bills and bright yellow legs — although some individuals appear to be distinctly larger than others.

(4) Similar in shape to #3 is a bird with bluish gray legs; when it flies its wings show a bold black-and-white pattern.

(5) Smaller than the other birds but still larger than the "peeps" is one whose breast is covered with many streaks running crosswise. It has greenish legs and a white eyebrow stripe. With its long bill it probes the mud with a rapid motion like a sewing machine.

(6) Slightly larger than #5 is a bird with a rich, rusty breast and a very long bill. It too feeds with a sewing machine motion, and when it flies, a long white wedge is visible on its back, pointing from the tail toward the head.

Answers: (1) Black-necked stilt. (2) American avocet. (3) Greater and lesser yellowlegs. (4) Willet. (5) Stilt sandpiper. (6) Short-billed dowitcher — whose bill is short only in comparison with the long-billed dowitcher.

AUTOMOBILE DIRECTIONS: Prime Hook National Wildlife Refuge and Beach Plum Island Nature Preserve are located adjacent to Delaware Bay about 27 miles southeast of Dover and 7 miles northwest of Lewes. (See Map 1 in the Table of Contents.)

To Prime Hook from northern Delmarva and Interstate 95 southwest of Wilmington: From Interstate 95 take Route 7 south, then follow the signs for Route 1 to Route 13 toward Dover. (Please note, however, that Route 7 will not be linked to Route 1 until the fall of 1992, so until then simply take Route 7 south to Route 13.) Once you are on Route 13 southbound, follow it past Smyrna to Dover, and there fork left onto Route 113 south toward Milford and the beaches. (Starting in 1994, you will be able to take Route 1 south from the vicinity of Smyrna to Route 113 below Dover.) Follow Route 113 south for 17.0 miles, then (north of Milford) fork left onto Route 1 southbound toward Rehoboth and the Delaware beaches. Follow Route 1 for 13.3 miles, then turn left onto Route 16 eastbound toward Broadkill Beach and Prime Hook National Wildlife Refuge. Follow Route 16 for only 1.2 miles, then turn left toward the refuge. Follow the refuge road to the parking lot by the office, boat ramp, and Dike and Boardwalk trails.

To Prime Hook from the Chesapeake Bay Bridge: After crossing the bridge, follow Route 50/301 across Kent Island. At the point where Route 50 and Route 301 split, fork right to follow Route 50, but after only 7.0 miles, turn left onto Route 404 east toward Denton and Rehoboth. Follow Route 404 for 20.0 miles to the intersection on the left with Route 16 (3.0 miles after Route 16 intersects from the right). Turn left and follow Route 16 east for more than 29 miles, in the process crossing Route 13, Route 113, and Route 1. After crossing Route 1, continue on Route 16 for only 1.2 miles, then turn left toward Prime Hook National Wildlife Refuge. Follow the refuge road to the parking lot by the office, boat ramp, and Dike and Boardwalk trails.

To Prime Hook from southern Delmarva and the Chesapeake Bay bridge-tunnel at Norfolk: After crossing the bridge-tunnel, follow Route 13 north into Maryland and past Salisbury. Continue on Route 13 north into Delaware and past intersections with Route 9 and Route 404, then turn right onto Route 16 eastbound. (Alternatively, from the vicinity of Snow Hill and Berlin, follow Route 113 north to Route 16, and there turn right.) Once you are on Route 16 eastbound, follow it to Route 1. After crossing Route 1, continue on Route 16 for only 1.2 miles, then turn left toward Prime Hook National Wildlife Refuge. Follow the refuge road to the parking lot by the office, boat ramp, and Dike and Boardwalk trails.

To Prime Hook from Salisbury and the Delaware and Maryland seashore resorts: From the vicinity of Salisbury, follow Route 13 north, then take Route 16 east to the intersection with Route 1. From the seaside resorts, take Route 1 north to the intersection with Route 16. In either case, once you are at the intersection of Route 16 and Route 1, follow Route 16 east for only 1.2 miles, then turn left toward Prime Hook National Wildlife Refuge. Follow the refuge road to the parking lot by the office, boat ramp, and Dike and Boardwalk trails.

WALKING AT PRIME HOOK NATIONAL WILDLIFE REFUGE: As shown on Map 15, there are several short hiking trails at Prime Hook.

The Dike Trail (1.0 mile round-trip) starts next to the boat ramp and follows the edge of a canal (the Headquarters Ditch) to a point that provides a sweeping view over the marsh behind Broadkill Beach.

The Boardwalk Trail (0.5 mile) starts opposite the parking bays at the boat ramp. It forms a short circuit through fields, marsh, and wet woods.

The Black Farm Trail (1.0 mile round-trip) starts at a yellow gate by the side of the main refuge road 0.4 mile north of the spur road that leads to Turkle and Fleetwood ponds. Park on the side of the road and follow the trail (it is an old farm road attractively bordered by hedgerows) to the edge of a marshy pond, then return the way you came.

The Pine Grove Trail (1.0 mile) forms a circuit starting at the end of the spur road that leads to Turkle Pond and Fleetwood Pond.

CANOEING ON PRIME HOOK CREEK: Map 15 shows Prime Hook Creek, which flows through the southern section of the refuge and usually is passable by canoe between Waples Mill Pond on Route 1 and the launching ramp by the refuge office. Between those two points the stream meanders for about 7 miles through forest, swamp, and marsh. Exploring this river and its various watery appendages that lead off into the marsh makes a very enjoyable day's outing.

I suggest that you launch your canoe from, and return to, the boat ramp by the refuge office. Although it is possible to canoe one-way from Waples Mill Pond to the refuge office (or vice versa) you would, of course, have to arrange for someone to shuttle your car. Besides, for a few hundred yards below Waples Mill Pond, the stream is sometimes impassable during periods of low water. Also, the marshy, easterly section of the river is more interesting, so you might as well start there.

From the launching ramp by the refuge office, paddle along the Headquarters Ditch for about half a mile, then turn left at the first opportunity. Follow the channel past bayous on either side, then bear left in order to continue on the main channel upstream toward a series of hunting blinds. Paddle upstream as far as you want (bearing in mind that you must return the same way). Once you pass Foord Landing (which is simply a small dock and a shed), the character of the river is somewhat monotonous for several miles until it broadens out into a long, sinuous pond. At the extreme western end of this pond, take the left (southern) channel — it is very small — to reach Waples Mill Pond and Route 1. Return by the way you came.

As is evident from Map 15, it is also possible to canoe in a circuit about 2.5 miles long by turning right at the end of the Headquarters Ditch, then left into Drapers Ditch, then left again

MAP 15 -- Prime Hook National Wild Wildlife Refuge

into Prime Hook Creek, and finally left once more in order to return to Headquarters Ditch.

FROM PRIME HOOK TO BEACH PLUM ISLAND: Immediately southeast of Prime Hook National Wildlife Refuge is the state of Delaware's Beach Plum Island Nature Preserve, which is not an island but rather a long spit of undeveloped beach and dunes sandwiched between the Broadkill River and Delaware Bay. The bold line on Map 16 shows the way there. As you leave the Prime Hook refuge, turn left and follow Route 16 for 2.8 miles to the community of Broadkill Beach. Within sight of Delaware Bay, turn right onto Bayshore Drive and follow it for 1.9 miles to the entrance and parking lot for Beach Plum Island Nature Preserve.

WALKING AT BEACH PLUM ISLAND NATURE PRESERVE: A hike along the shore to Roosevelt Inlet (4.0 miles round-trip; see Map 16) is a pleasant excursion, but sometimes the traffic and ruts from the vehicles of surf fishermen make the beach unattractive for walking. Vehicles are especially numerous on weekends from April through October. They are altogether barred between mid-December and mid-March.

MAP 16 -- From Prime Hook Refuge to Beach Plum Island Nature Preserve

8

LEWES
THE CAPE MAY - LEWES FERRY
CAPE HENLOPEN STATE PARK

This excursion focuses on the vicinity of Lewes (pronounced Loo-iss), site of the first European settlement in Delaware. The town is now an attractive beach resort, where many old houses and storefronts have been renovated. Antique stores, galleries, specialty shops, and restaurants occupy the small business district, which is all the more interesting for the fact that it fronts not on the beach itself but rather on the Lewes-Rehoboth Canal a half-mile inland from Delaware Bay.

Near the center of Lewes is the Zwaanendael Museum, a scaled-down replica of the town hall in Hoorn, Holland, from which the chief sponsor of the early colony came. The museum was built in 1931 to commemorate the 300th anniversary of Dutch settlement. Devoted to local history, the museum is open Tuesday through Saturday from 10 to 4:30. Telephone (302) 645-9418 for information.

Next to the Zwaanendael Museum is the restored Fisher-Martin House, built about 1728 and now an information and exhibition center run by the Lewes Chamber of Commerce; telephone (302) 645-8073. The house is usually open Monday through Saturday from 10 to 3.

A few blocks away from the Zwaanendael Museum and Fisher-Martin House is the Lewes Historic Complex, to which several old houses and other structures have been moved from nearby areas. Managed by the Lewes Historical Society, the buildings are open to the public from mid-June through the beginning of the Labor Day weekend, Tuesday through Saturday, 10 to 3 — except for the Hiram Burton House, which is open less often. On the first Saturday in December, the historic complex is open for a Christmas Fair and House Tour. Also managed by the historical society is the nearby lightship *Overfalls* and the Cannonball House Maritime Museum, which are open during summer on the same schedule (more or less) as the Lewes Historic Complex.

About a mile east of Lewes is the Delaware terminal of the Cape May - Lewes Ferry, mentioned here because of its recreational potential. For foot passengers who leave their cars in the parking lot at the Lewes terminal, a ride across Delaware Bay to New Jersey and back makes a very enjoyable ocean mini-cruise. The crossing takes about 70 minutes each way, but the duration of the round trip varies with the seasons because the boats do not run as often in winter as in summer. (During summer the round-trip time is about 3 hours.) For information about the ferry schedule and fares, telephone (302) 645-6313. Because the New Jersey terminal is located several miles from the town of Cape May, there is little reason for day-tripping foot passengers to get off the boat at the New Jersey end.

Finally, slightly east of the Lewes ferry terminal is Delaware's 3,000-acre Cape Henlopen State Park, featuring 6 miles of ocean and bay beaches (several swimming beaches are life-guarded during summer), a bathhouse and canteen, a fishing pier, a nature center, an observation tower and gun emplacements left from World War II, a campground that is open April through October, and excellent bird watching during spring and fall migrations. In addition to good beach walking, the park has trails that explore the pine forest, dunes, and marsh behind the beach. The park is open daily from 8 A.M. to sunset. Dogs must be leashed and are altogether barred from Henlopen Point and also, May through September, from swimming areas. The park is administered by the Delaware Department of Natural Resources and Environmental Control, Division of Parks and Recreation; telephone (302) 645-8983. The park's Seaside Nature Center is open year-round and provides programs, exhibits, and material on the cape's natural and cultural history; telephone (302) 645-6852.

IN 1609 THE ENGLISH NAVIGATOR Henry Hudson, at that time employed by the Dutch East India Company to search for a passage from Europe either northeast or northwest to the Orient, sailed his ship *Half Moon* into Delaware Bay before moving farther up the Atlantic coast to explore the river subsequently named for him. Although the Delaware estuary had been visited before by other Europeans, Hudson's voyage — plus later explorations by other Dutch navigators — provided Holland with a claim to the region. After New Amsterdam (later New York City) was established in 1625, Captain David Pieterszen DeVries and other promoters in Holland organized an expedition to the

Delaware in order "to plant a colony for the cultivation of grain and tobacco as well as to carry on the whale fishery in that region." Leaving the Netherlands on December 12, 1630, thirty-two men (DeVries was not among them) were transported to the vicinity of Lewes, where they arrived in April 1631 and proceeded to establish the first European settlement in what is now Delaware. At the mouth of Lewes Creek — located a mile northwest up the coast from the present-day town — the Dutchmen built a communal dwelling house and trading post surrounded by a stockade on land that had been purchased by their agents from the Indians two years earlier. The Netherlanders called the place Zwaanendael (vale of the swans). After the colonists appeared to be secure and in a position to fend for themselves, their ship returned to Holland.

In December of the following year, DeVries arrived at Zwaanendael with more men to reinforce the outpost that was supposed to generate profits for himself and the other investors. He found it, however, a total loss, and that in the starkest terms. The settlement had been burned and all the Europeans massacred by Indians. The bones of men and cattle were found lying here and there in the open. DeVries was told by a native informant that the killings were the outgrowth of an incident in which an Indian had stolen a metal sign bearing the Dutch coat of arms. After the Netherlanders complained, the thief was executed by yet other Indians who were anxious to placate ·the Europeans, whereupon the thief's friends and kin revenged themselves on the Dutchmen.

The second DeVries expedition remained at Zwaanendael only a short time, but a quarter-century later, in 1658, the site was settled once more by Netherlanders. Financed by the Dutch West India Company, a fort and trading post were again built at the site of Zwaanendael, which came to be called Hoorn on the small river Hoornkill or Horekil. In 1663 the outpost was transferred to the sponsorship of the burgomasters of Amsterdam, and that same year the colony was greatly augmented by the arrival of forty-one Mennonite emigres from Holland led by Peter Cornelius Plockhoy. The settlement benefitted too from the support of Fort Amstel at present-day New Castle, for at that time the Dutch were making a systematic effort to establish their power in Delaware Bay.

In 1664, however, during one of a series of three Anglo-Dutch wars fought between 1652 and 1678 for mercantile and maritime dominance, Great Britain seized control of the Delaware region. At Horekil an English expedition destroyed the "quaking colony of Plockhoy to a naile." ("Quaking" because the Anglicans identified the Mennonites with Quakers and other pacifist sects.)

The Netherlanders who remained at Whorekill — as the English, exercising their inimitable penchant for corrupting names, called the place — were made British citizens. This fact, however, did not deter a detachment of forty Marylanders from again attacking Whorekill on Christmas Eve, 1673, during a brief period when Holland regained control of its New York and Delaware colonies. At Whorekill the Marylanders burned the settlement, leaving only one "thatch barne" standing to provide shelter for the approximately eight families and nine single men said to live in the village at that time. By some accounts the viciousness of this raid was motivated not so much by opposition to the Dutch as by the desire of Charles Calvert, the resident governor and future proprietor of Maryland, to assert his family's ownership of the Delaware coast. In this the Calverts ultimately failed, for although the grant from King Charles I to Cecilius Calvert in 1632 delineated boundaries that included what is now Delaware, the grant covered only "land hitherto uncultivated and occupied by savages." This clause, coupled with the fact of Dutch settlement in 1631, resulted in Delaware being carved out of Maryland and joined to New York after the Netherlands permanently relinquished claim to the region by treaty with England in 1674.

In 1680 the village at Whorekill (about then renamed Deale in Deale County) was designated to be the site of the county court, a status it retained for over a hundred years until the seat of county government was moved to Georgetown in 1791. The courthouse stood in a corner of what is now the graveyard of St. Peter's Episcopal Church on Second Street in the center of Lewes. Its location there probably had something to do with the town growing up where it did rather than slightly to the northwest at the original site of Zwaanendael, for the early village was little more than a series of farms spaced at intervals along the creek and its adjacent road (now Pilot Town Road). In 1682, when the three counties of Delaware were transferred from the colony of New York to Pennsylvania (they subsequently gained their own legislature in 1704), names were again changed and the village became Lewes in the county of Sussex after the town of Lewes in Sussex, England.

The growth of Lewes — a gristmill was built in 1676 and a tannery in 1684 — did not, however, prevent the periodic despoliation of the community by raiders appearing without warning from the open ocean. In 1690 and again in 1698 the town was plundered by pirates who landed and went from house to house, taking whatever they considered of value. A pirate who came in peace, however, was Captain William Kidd; in 1700, while returning from the West Indies to New York with the intention of clearing himself of piracy charges, Kidd stood his ship off Lewes, from which some townspeople rowed out to barter for goods that had been looted from other vessels. (At his subsequent trial in

England, Kidd unsuccessfully claimed that the ships he had seized were lawful prizes of war.) Ever since Kidd's visit, the sand dunes of Cape Henlopen have been associated with legends of buried pirate treasure.

In 1709 during the War of Spanish Succession, which was fought chiefly in Europe but spilled over into the American colonies as part of a series of French and Indian wars, Lewes was again sacked by about a hundred privateersmen sent ashore from a vessel authorized by the French government to attack and plunder English ports and shipping on a for-profit basis — just as Kidd had in fact been commissioned by the governor of New York to seize French vessels. Marauding by pirates and by privateers continued in Delaware Bay until as late as the mid-1700s.

Lewes escaped damage during the Revolutionary War, although the nearby Cape Henlopen lighthouse, which had been erected in the 1760s, was burned on the interior by the English in 1776. (The lighthouse was refurbished and continued to serve until 1924; the following year the structure was toppled by erosion of the high dune on which it stood.) Also during the Revolution, several residents of Lewes had cattle stolen or extorted from them by British landing parties seeking supplies for their warships. In Lewes itself in 1776, Tories from the outlying area "cut the flagstaff down and sold the flag for 13d., and nearly did bodily injury to the Court," according to the report of a local patriot. Throughout Delmarva rural residents were often Loyalist in sympathy, while town folk usually were more radical. Lewes, in any case, supplied its share of soldiers and sailors to the revolutionary cause. Perhaps the most noteworthy patriot leader from Lewes was Colonel David Hall, a lawyer who joined the revolutionary Delaware Council of Safety in 1775. During the war, Hall was an officer in the Delaware Regiment. From 1802 to 1805 he served as the state's governor — the first of five Delaware governors from Lewes. Hall's house, built about 1790, stands opposite the front of the Zwaanendael Museum.

Lewes was yet again exposed to attack during the War of 1812. On April 6 and 7, 1813, three British ships bombarded the town after its inhabitants refused to supply the enemy with provisions. Perhaps because their view was obstructed by trees along the shore, the British inflicted only trivial damage. The Cannonball House — now a maritime museum on Front Street — was struck. Casualties of the bombardment totaled "one chicken killed, one pig wounded — leg broken," according to a contemporary account.

Not until nearly 130 years later, when Fort Miles was built at Cape Henlopen to help guard the entrance to Delaware Bay during World War II, did Lewes again see military action. German U-boats were active in the area immediately following America's entry into the war. Lewes gave succor to survivors — almost 250 in all — brought ashore from twelve vessels sunk by U-boats between January and April of 1942. During that period nearly two hundred ships were sunk off the East Coast, often within sight of land. In response, the United States eventually instituted a system of coastal convoys, while at the same time our fliers and seamen gradually gained proficiency at tracking and attacking enemy submarines. By summer the U-boats rarely came closer to the United States than the middle of the Atlantic Ocean. However, on May 14, 1945 — nearly a week after VE Day — the German submarine U-858 was surrendered by its crew and towed into Lewes' harbor. Now Fort Miles is the site of Cape Henlopen State Park. From the beach huge bunkers are visible; they formerly housed 6-inch, 12-inch, and 16-inch guns, which never had occasion to be fired at enemy warships. A spectacular view of Cape Henlopen can be had from the top of one of the fort's observation towers.

Also at Cape Henlopen, in the area to the east of the present-day fishing pier, was the Delaware Breakwater Quarantine Station, where between 1885 and 1917, immigrants thought to have contagious diseases or to have been exposed to contagious diseases were isolated for weeks or even months before being allowed to continue to Philadelphia or, as sometimes happened, being sent back to Europe.

Until tourism became the chief industry of Lewes during the second half of this century, the town's economy was based overwhelmingly on shipping (including ship building and ship chandlery), fishing, canning, and the piloting of large vessels up and down the Delaware. Although Lewes Creek may appear to be only a very minor river (it is now part of a canal linking Delaware Bay and Rehoboth Bay), in prior centuries it was a crowded roadstead that accommodated two-masted schooners and other small craft engaged in coastal trade, especially the shipping of farm products brought here from southern Delaware.

In 1828 the federal government began construction of the Delaware Breakwater just offshore from Lewes, and in consequence Lewes became an important harbor of refuge for ships entering and leaving Delaware Bay or passing up and down the coast. By 1840 about 25 vessels used the harbor daily, and over 200 when gales threatened. Despite the breakwater, however, during two extraordinary storms in 1888 and 1889, dozens of ships were wrecked in Lewes Harbor. In 1901 another breakwater was completed 2 miles farther offshore from the Delaware Breakwater, so that together the two barriers now provide a harbor of refuge totaling about 1,000 acres. However, this sheltered zone is shoaling in because of the northwestward growth of Cape Henlopen.

In 1869 a railroad spur was completed to Lewes, and by 1883 factories for drying and canning fruit and for processing menhaden into oil and fertilizer had been established near the depot. At the beginning of the twentieth century, Lewes engaged in a large trade in fruit and vegetables with northern cities. Two of the Atlantic coast's largest menhaden plants stood just east of what is now the ferry terminal. In 1953 the catch brought ashore at Lewes was approximately 360 million pounds, most of it menhaden.

Although the Delaware menhaden fishery declined during the 1950s and '60s and the fish factories closed, Lewes remains today an important center of sport fishing, as is apparent from the fleet of charter boats and head boats based in Lewes Creek. Also, another long-standing maritime tradition survives at Lewes, inasmuch as The Pilots Association for the Bay and River Delaware is still based here in the former U.S. Coast Guard station next to the ferry terminal. The largest employer in Lewes, however, is now the Beebe Medical Center, a regional hospital. One of the newest major business operating out of Lewes is the Cape May - Lewes Ferry, which made its first run in 1964.

AUTOMOBILE DIRECTIONS: Lewes and the nearby ferry terminal and Cape Henlopen State Park are located where the southern shore of Delaware Bay meets the coast of the open Atlantic. (See Map 1 in the Table of Contents.) Note, however, that as you draw within a few miles of Lewes, the many roadside signs for the ferry designate a route that bypasses the old part of town, which it would be a shame to miss. The instructions below take you first to the center of historic Lewes and then to the ferry and state park.

To Lewes from northern Delmarva and Interstate 95 southwest of Wilmington: From Interstate 95 take Route 7 south, then follow the signs for Route 1 to Route 13 toward Dover. (Please note, however, that Route 7 will not be linked to Route 1 until the fall of 1992, so until then simply take Route 7 south to Route 13.) Once you are on Route 13 southbound, follow it past Smyrna to Dover, and there fork left onto Route 113 south toward Milford and the beaches. (Starting in 1994, you will be able to take Route 1 south from the vicinity of Smyrna to Route 113 below Dover.) Follow Route 113 south for about 17 miles, then (north of Milford) fork left onto Route 1 south toward Rehoboth and the Delaware beaches. Follow Route 1 for 20.0 miles to a junction with Business Route 9, and there turn left toward Lewes. Go 2.5 miles to the Dutch-style

Zwaanendael Museum. Turn right onto Third Street and park as soon as you can in the vicinity of the museum and adjacent Fisher-Martin House.

To Lewes from the Chesapeake Bay Bridge: After crossing the bridge, follow Route 50/301 across Kent Island. At the point where Route 50 and Route 301 split, fork right to follow Route 50, but after only 7.0 miles, turn left onto Route 404 toward Denton and Rehoboth. For more than 45 miles, follow Route 404 east across Route 13 and Route 113 to Georgetown, and there go three-quarters of the way around a traffic circle and continue east on Route 9/404 for 12.3 miles. At an intersection with Route 1, continue straight ahead 2.5 miles on Business Route 9 to the Dutch-style Zwaanendael Museum. Turn right onto Third Street and park as soon as you can in the vicinity of the museum and adjacent Fisher-Martin House.

To Lewes from southern Delmarva and the Chesapeake Bay Bridge-Tunnel at Norfolk: After crossing the bridge-tunnel, follow Route 13 north about 73 miles to the intersection (near Pocomoke City, Maryland) with Route 113, and there turn right onto Route 113 north toward Berlin and Ocean City. Follow Route 113 for about 57 miles to an intersection with Route 9, and there turn right toward Georgetown and Lewes. In Georgetown, go half way around a traffic circle and continue east on Route 9/404 for 12.3 miles to an intersection with Route 1. From there continue straight ahead 2.5 miles on Business Route 9 to the Dutch-style Zwaanendael Museum. Turn right onto Third Street and park as soon as you can in the vicinity of the museum and adjacent Fisher-Martin House.

To Lewes from Salisbury and the Delaware and Maryland seashore resorts: From the vicinity of Salisbury, take Route 13 north, then Route 9 east through Georgetown to the intersection with Route 1, and there continue straight on Business Route 9 for 2.5 miles into Lewes.

From the seaside resorts, take Route 1 north to the intersection on the right — opposite Route 404 west — with Business Route 9. Turn right to follow Business Route 9 for 2.5 miles into Lewes. At the Dutch-style Zwaanendael Museum, turn right onto Third Street and park as soon as you

MAP 17 -- Lewes

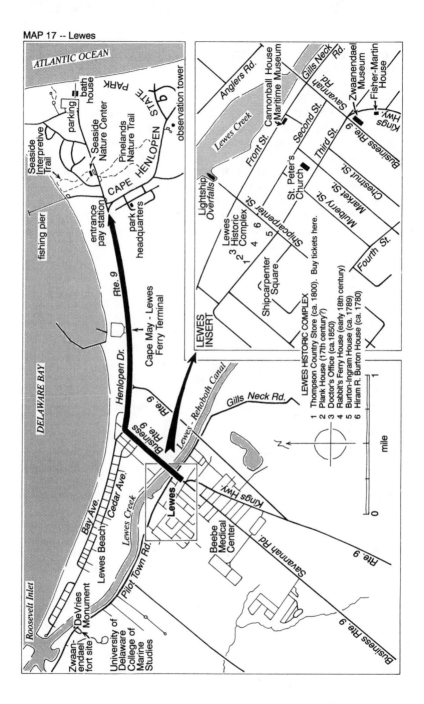

ATLANTIC OCEAN

CAPE HENLOPEN STATE PARK

bath house

parking

Seaside Nature Center

Seaside Interpretive Trail

Pinelands Nature Trail

observation tower

fishing pier

entrance pay station

park headquarters

Rte. 9

Henlopen Dr.

Cape May - Lewes Ferry Terminal

DELAWARE BAY

Roosevelt Inlet

Zwaanendael fort site

DeVries Monument

University of Delaware College of Marine Studies

Bay Ave.

Lewes Beach

Cedar Ave.

Lewes Creek

Pilot Town Rd.

Lewes

Business Rte. 9

Lewes - Rehoboth Canal

Gills Neck Rd.

Beebe Medical Center

Kings Hwy.

Savanah Rd.

Rte. 9

Business Rte. 9

N

mile

0   1

LEWES HISTORIC COMPLEX

1 Thompson Country Store (ca. 1800).
2 Plank House (17th century?)
3 Doctor's Office (ca. 1850)
4 Rabbit's Ferry House (early 18th century)
5 Burton-Ingram House (ca. 1789)
6 Hiram R. Burton House (ca. 1780)

LEWES INSERT

Anglers Rd.

Lewes Creek

Front St.

Cannonball House Maritime Museum

Gills Neck Rd.

Savanah Rd.

Zwaanendael Museum

Fisher-Martin House

Kings Hwy.

Business Rte. 9

Second St.

Third St.

Chestnut St.

St. Peter's Church

Market St.

Mulberry St.

Fourth St.

Shipcarpenter St.

Lightship Overfalls

Lewes Historic Complex

1 2
3
4 6
5

Shipcarpenter Square

Buy tickets here.

can in the vicinity of the museum and adjacent Fisher-Martin House.

TOURING LEWES BY CAR OR ON FOOT: Use Map 17 and its insert at the lower-right corner to explore Lewes. From the **Zwaanendael Museum** and adjacent **Fisher-Martin House**, drive or walk west on Third Street 0.2 mile to the **Lewes Historic Complex**, for which tickets may be purchased at the **Thompson Country Store**. Even if the historic complex is closed, the buildings are worth seeing from the outside. Also interesting is a subdivision just south of the historic complex; called **Shipcarpenter Square**, all of the houses are old structures moved here and renovated.

Within easy walking distance of the historic complex is the shopping district and **St. Peter's Episcopal Church and graveyard** on Second Street. (The present church was built in 1858 and is the third church edifice on this spot; the graves go back much further.) Within the shopping district at 118 Front Street is the **Cannonball House Maritime Museum**, and at the intersection of Front Street and Shipcarpenter Street is the **lightship *Overfalls*.** To the west, Front Street becomes Pilot Town Road, which leads 1.1 miles to a monument and cemetery at the **site of the original Zwaanendael settlement** opposite Roosevelt Inlet, as the mouth of Lewes Creek is now called.

FROM LEWES TO THE CAPE MAY - LEWES FERRY TERMINAL and CAPE HENLOPEN STATE PARK: The long bold line on Map 17 shows the way. From the intersection of Business Route 9 (Savannah Road) and Front Street at the center of Lewes, drive east on Business Route 9 across the canal. Continue 0.4 mile to an intersection with Henlopen Drive, and there turn right and go 0.7 mile to the ferry terminal's foot-passenger parking lot on the left.

For Cape Henlopen State Park, continue straight past the ferry terminal for another 0.8 mile. From the park entrance, the main **ocean swimming beach** is straight ahead.

WALKING AT CAPE HENLOPEN STATE PARK: Map 18 shows the various trails and other features that make Cape Henlopen the Delaware shore's best place for walking.

The beach provides an opportunity for a short stroll or a round-trip hike of up to 10 miles. Because vehicles are

MAP 18 -- Cape Henlopen State Park

DELAWARE BAY

ATLANTIC OCEAN

Henlopen Point

point parking lot

tower

parking

vehicle crossing

Seaside Interpretive Trail

fishing pier

parking — bath house

entrance pay station

Seaside Nature Center

Rte. 9
Henlopen Dr.

Pinelands Nature Trail

Cape May - Lewes Ferry Terminal

park headquarters

campground

observation tower

"walking dune" sand hill

Walking Dune Hiking Trails

A
vehicle crossing

CAPE

water tank

youth group camping

HENLOPEN

Battery Herring (T Building)

STATE PARK

N

Lewes - Rehoboth Canal

Gordons Pond

0   1
mile

towers

sometimes permitted on some sections of the beach for purposes of surf fishing, walking along the shore is best from November through March, when fishing is poor and few vehicles are present. But even during the warmer months, hikers can avoid vehicles on the beach by going walking on an even date of the month and staying north of the vehicle crossing at the point marked A on Map 18. Of course, in summer vehicles are always barred from lifeguarded swimming areas during daylight hours.

The western beach and sandy tidal flats of **Henlopen Point** are a particularly interesting place to walk, but from approximately mid-April through mid-July, the area is closed in order not to disturb endangered piping plovers and other beach-nesting birds. During the rest of the year, an outstanding walk is to start at the **point parking lot** and follow the point's western flank north 0.7 mile, then continue around the point and down the ocean beach for as far as you care to go. To return to the point parking lot, use the pedestrian crossover straight from the ocean beach.

Another good place to start walking is at the southernmost oceanfront parking lot by **Battery Herring** (also called the T Building), and from there hike north along the beach to Henlopen Point and back, for a round-trip distance of 6.0 miles. From the same lot south along the beach to a pair of observation towers is 2.0 miles round-trip.

The **Seaside Interpretive Trail** starts behind the west (left) end of the **Seaside Nature Center** and forms a circuit of 0.7 mile to the beach and back. A flyer discussing sights along the trail is available at the nature center.

The **Pinelands Nature Trail** starts across the road from the Seaside Nature Center and forms a circuit leading 1.6 miles through a sandy pine forest. Again, a pamphlet discussing sights along the trail is available at the nature center.

The **Walking Dune Hiking Trails** provide the best walking inland at Cape Henlopen State Park. One spur leads to a high migrating dune (a "walking dune"). Other spurs follow low, wooded ridges that project into a large marsh. These ridges are old dunes that once trailed west from Cape Henlopen before the spit extended itself farther north. Fed by material swept northward by the longshore current from the vicinity of Rehoboth Beach and Dewey Beach, Cape Henlopen continues to build into Delaware Bay.

The trailhead for the Walking Dune Hiking Trails is a small

114

parking lot located 0.4 mile southeast along the road from an observation tower that is sometimes open to the public. From the parking lot the trail starts as an old asphalt road (closed to motor vehicles). Follow this road 0.5 mile to an intersection by a small chainlink enclosure on the left opposite a concrete bunker on the right. For the "walking dune," continue straight; for the marsh spurs, turn left and go 0.5 mile to a four-way trail junction, and there turn right. As shown on Map 18, there is another less frequented spur into the marsh farther south.

Return by the way you came. Or, for a slightly longer walk, continue southeast, then east to the park road and Battery Herring (the T Building) overlooking the ocean. Follow the path down to the beach, then walk north along the shore for half a mile to the vehicle crossing at the point marked A on Map 18. Follow the rutted automobile trail back west though the dunes to your starting point.

9

EASTON
ST. MICHAELS
TILGHMAN ISLAND
OXFORD via ferry

The 60-mile car tour outlined in this chapter links the chief towns of Talbot County, Maryland. Easton, the county seat, features an historic district containing many attractive specialty shops, as well as the Historical Society of Talbot County's museum and the nearby James Neall and Joseph Neall houses and garden. The museum, which changes exhibits several times each year, is open Tuesday through Saturday from 10 to 4 and on Sunday from 1 to 4. The Neall houses are usually open at the same time. Across the street is the historical society's museum shop. For information on the historical society's various programs — including guided walking tours of Easton, for which reservations are required three days in advance — telephone (410) 822-0773. For a self-guided tour, simply pick up the historical society's pamphlet at the museum. Also in Easton is the Academy of the Arts, offering exhibits of paintings, drawings, photographs, and sculpture, and a wide variety of other programs, including lectures, concerts, and classes. For information, telephone (410) 822-0455. The Academy of the Arts is open Monday through Saturday from 10 to 4 and Wednesday and Thursday evening from 4 to 9.

Like Easton, St. Michaels has numerous shops for crafts, gifts, and antiques, as well as several outstanding restaurants overlooking its attractive harbor, where the Chesapeake Bay Maritime Museum is located. The museum includes a comprehensive collection of bay boats and maritime artifacts. It is open daily from 10 to 5 during summer and from 10 to 4 during winter, with the proviso that during January, February, and early March, the museum is open only on weekends. For information telephone (410) 745-2916. From April through October or early November, the excursion boat *Patriot* operates from the bulkhead in front of the Maritime Museum's administration buildings, departing at 11, 1 and 3 for 1.5-hour cruises on the Miles River. Telephone (410) 745-3100 for information. Also in

St. Michaels is the St. Mary's Square Museum, which is devoted chiefly to local history. It is open May through October on Saturdays and Sundays from 10 to 4.

Tilghman Island, linked to the mainland by a drawbridge, is the next port-of-call on our car cruise. A large fleet of commercial fishing craft, including several skipjacks, operates from the island. During the summer season, excursions are sometimes offered by the skipjack skippers.

Oxford is a quiet yachting village fronting on the Tred Avon River. During most of the year, it is served by the Oxford-Bellevue Ferry. However, the ferry does not operate from mid-December through February, so at that time of year you must drive the long way around to reach Oxford. In spring and fall, the ferry stops running at sunset; from June through Labor Day, the ferry stops running at 9 P.M.

ANYONE FAMILIAR WITH A MAP of the Chesapeake region has surely regarded with fascination the winglike landform that projects into Chesapeake Bay between the Miles River to the north and the Choptank and Tred Avon rivers to the south. (See Map 20 on page 123.) Here, in Maryland's Talbot County, are several interesting towns, each with its own flavor.

Easton grew up around the Talbot County Courthouse, established in 1711. Throughout most of the eighteenth century, the place was merely a tiny cluster of taverns and houses with a nearby race course where sometimes large crowds gathered — as in 1754, when about a thousand people came on horseback and in carriages to watch a race for a purse of £20 donated by Governor Horatio Sharpe. Not until after the Revolution was the town incorporated and formally laid out. Then in 1788 it was designated Maryland's administrative center for the Eastern Shore, and business boomed. (Incidentally, promotional literature for Easton often touts the town as the *colonial* capital of the Eastern Shore, which is false.) In 1790 the Eastern Shore's first newspaper was founded at Easton, and during the next four years the paper carried advertisements for 10 general merchants at Easton, plus hatters, tailors, tavernkeepers, private schoolmasters, physicians, clockmakers, and other artisans and professionals, including a barber and bleeder, a dancing master, and a portrait artist. A new courthouse, paid for largely by the state, was built in 1794 (it still stands as the middle section of the present-day courthouse) and in it were located branch offices of the

Annapolis government. Sessions of what is now the Maryland Court of Appeals were held alternately in Annapolis and in Easton, and even the federal circuit court sometimes convened at Easton from 1790 to 1796. In 1798 the *American Gazetteer* described Easton as the "chief town of Talbot County, Maryland," with "a handsome courthouse, a market house, about 150 dwelling houses, and several stores for the supply of the adjoining county."

During the nineteenth century, Easton was the most populous and important town on Maryland's Eastern Shore. As the century began, the town had two weekly newspapers. In 1805 the Eastern Shore's first bank was established at Easton, and starting in 1817 the first steamboat line linking Baltimore and the Eastern Shore ran to Easton Point (formerly sleepy Cow Landing) located a mile west of town at the head of the Tred Avon River.

After suffering from a long agricultural depression in the second quarter of the nineteenth century, the economy of Maryland's Eastern Shore began to revive in the years leading up to the Civil War as the region turned increasingly to supplying vegetables, fruit, and seafood to northern cities. Nonetheless, political sympathies among Talbot County's plantation-owning elite — descendants of the wealthy, powerful, and proud colonial gentry — were distinctly Southern. Although Talbot County voted 847 to 666 against secession in 1861, and although four times as many Talbot men served with the Union as with the Confederacy, the Civil War memorial in front of the courthouse in Easton is "To the Talbot Boys 1861-1865 CSA."

Easton's economy benefitted from the arrival of the railroad in 1869, but other towns prospered still more. Toward the end of the century, Easton was outstripped by Cambridge and Salisbury as those towns became major packing and shipping points for the Eastern Shore's farm products. Cambridge also did a large business in oysters and other seafood. During the heyday of oystering in the 1880s, even Crisfield was more populous than Easton. It was at about this time that a trend began in Talbot County that continued through the early twentieth century and the Depression years of the 1930s. Rich Northerners started buying waterfront plantations, and urban folk started coming by train and by steamboat for quiet vacations at local boarding houses.

Although Easton today has lost its former primacy among Maryland's Eastern Shore towns, it is still the commercial, financial, medical, and cultural center of an area that extends well beyond the limits of Talbot County. There is some light manufacturing at Easton, but the tone of the older part of town around the courthouse and along Washington, Harrison, and Dover streets is set by the concentration of fashionable shops, antique stores, fine restaurants, stock brokerages, banks, and real estate brokers', accountants', and lawyers' offices that serve a disproportionately well-to-do population, including a large and ever-growing number of wealthy retirees and second-home owners whose properties are arrayed along Talbot County's 600 miles of convoluted shore. Increasingly, too, expensive waterfront subdivisions are being occupied by those willing to commute long distances to jobs elsewhere in Delmarva and even on the Chesapeake's Western Shore.

Although Easton is by no means a tourist town, it has not neglected the tourist trade. In particular, the town hosts the annual Waterfowl Festival held on the second weekend in November. The festival is devoted largely to waterfowl art and artifacts, including prints, photographs, carved decoys, old guns, and other collectibles. All net proceeds from sales by the festival's vendors are donated to various conservation organizations. For information telephone (410) 822-4567.

AUTOMOBILE DIRECTIONS: Easton is located on Route 50 about 15 miles north of Cambridge and 20 miles southeast of the Chesapeake Bay Bridge. (See Map 1 in the Table of Contents.) The car tour to St. Michaels, Tilghman Island, and Oxford shown on Map 20 starts at Easton, so you should go there first.

To Easton from northern Delmarva and Interstate 95 near Newark, Delaware: From I-95 take Route 896 south across Route 40 and over the Chesapeake and Delaware Canal to an intersection with Route 301, and there continue straight south on Route 301. Just west of Middletown, turn right to follow Route 301 south into Maryland slightly more than 37 miles. Eventually, after passing exits for Route 305 and Route 304 near Centreville, turn left at a traffic light onto Route 213 southbound. Follow Route 213 south 4.3 miles, then turn left (east) onto Route 50 and go 11.0 miles to a junction with Route 322 (Easton Parkway). Bear right onto Route 322, but follow it only 0.4 mile, then turn left onto Washington Street. Follow Washington Street 1.5 miles to the county courthouse at the center of Easton.

To Easton from the Chesapeake Bay Bridge: After crossing the bridge, follow Route 50/301 across Kent Island. At the point where Route 50 and Route 301 split, fork right to follow Route 50 for 16.4 miles to the junction with Route 322 (Easton Parkway). Bear right onto Route 322, but follow it only 0.4 mile, then turn left onto Washington Street. Follow

MAP 19 -- Easton

1　Mary Jenkins House (1780)
2　Former Brick Hotel (1812)
3　Thomas Perrin Smith House -- now the Chesapeake Bay Yacht Club at 119-121 North Washington Street (1759)
4　131 North Washington Street (pre-Revolutionary tavern)
5　Old Frame Hotel at Washington and Goldsborough streets (ca. 1830)
6　The Grymes Building at Harrison and Dover streets (1794)
7　The Bullitt House (1790)
8　Talbot County Women's Club at 18 Talbot Lane (1790s)
9　Christ Episcopal Church (1842)
10　Benjamin Stevens House at 28 South Harrison Street (ca. 1790)

Washington Street 1.5 miles to the county courthouse at the center of Easton.

To Easton from southern Delmarva and the Chesapeake Bay Bridge-Tunnel at Norfolk: After crossing the bridge-tunnel, follow Route 13 north into Maryland and past Pocomoke City and Princess Anne to the exit for Route 50 westbound near Salisbury, and from there take Route 50 west past Cambridge. From the northern end of the long bridge over the Choptank River, follow Route 50 for 10.5 miles to the junction with Route 322 (Easton Parkway). Bear left onto Route 322, but follow it only 0.5 mile, then turn right onto Route 565 toward Easton. Follow Route 565 (Washington Street) 2.0 miles to the county courthouse at the center of Easton.

To Easton from Salisbury: Take Route 50 west past Cambridge. From the northern end of the long bridge over the Choptank River, follow Route 50 for 10.5 miles to the junction with Route 322 (Easton Parkway). Bear left onto Route 322, but follow it only 0.5 mile, then turn right onto Route 565 toward Easton. Follow Route 565 (Washington Street) 2.0 miles to the county courthouse at the center of Easton.

To Easton from the Delaware and Maryland seashore resorts: From Ocean City take Route 50 west past Salisbury and Cambridge, then follow the directions in the previous paragraph.

From the vicinity of Rehoboth Beach, follow Route 1 north to the intersection near Lewes with Route 404 westbound, then follow Route 404 west through Georgetown and across Route 113 and Route 13 to the intersection with Route 50 near Wye Mills. Turn left onto Route 50 toward Easton and go 9.7 miles to the junction with Route 322 (Easton Parkway). Bear right onto Route 322, but follow it only 0.4 mile, then turn left onto Washington Street. Follow Washington Street 1.5 miles to the county courthouse at the center of Easton.

TOURING EASTON ON FOOT: Use Map 19 to explore Easton's historic district, which has many structures dating from the late eighteenth, nineteenth, and early twentieth centuries. The most interesting part of town is along Washington Street, Harrison Street, and some of the cross streets between the

MAP 20 -- Car tour from Easton to St. Michaels, Tilghman Island, and Oxford two. The **Museum of the Historical Society of Talbot County** is located at 25 South Washington Street, one block below the **Talbot County Courthouse.** The front part of the museum occupies a store built in the 1850s. Next door is the **James Neall House**, built between 1804 and 1810, and behind it at the far end of a federal-style garden is the **Joseph Neall House**, built in 1795. The Neall brothers were both Quaker cabinet makers. Across the street from the museum is the **Historical Society Museum Shop**, which occupies the Tharpe House, built in 1810. · A block south and a block east of the historical society complex is the **Academy of the Arts** at 106 South Street. About 0.6 mile south of the courthouse (off the bottom edge of the map and situated at the end of a long driveway entered from Washington Street) is the frame **Society of Friends Third Haven Meeting House**. It was started in 1682 and finished two years later — long before there was any town in the vicinity — and has now been meticulously restored. Many notable Quakers, including William Penn, have worshipped in this building. The nearby brick meeting house was built in 1880 and is used in winter.

CAR TOUR TO ST. MICHAELS, TILGHMAN ISLAND, and OXFORD: This 60-mile car tour is shown by the bold line on Map 20.

From the county courthouse in Easton, follow Washington Street north about 0.1 mile, then turn left onto Bay Street. (On Map 19 the small arrow near the upper left shows the way out of town.) Follow Bay Street 0.5 mile to an intersection with Route 322 (Easton Parkway). Cross Route 322 and follow Route 33 west 9.5 miles to St. Michaels. After passing most of the way through St. Michaels, turn right onto Mill Street toward the Chesapeake Bay Maritime Museum. After visiting the museum, use Map 21 to explore St. Michaels on foot.

St. Michaels is located midway along the crooked peninsula that projects from Easton into Chesapeake Bay. Named for the Episcopal parish of St. Michael the Archangel formed here in 1672, the town itself was not established until about a century later, nor incorporated until 1805. Shipyards, however, were located at St. Michaels' harbor from the latter 1600s onward. Shipbuilding reached a peak in about 1810, when all kinds of bay boats, coastal craft, and ocean-going vessels were constructed and fitted out at more than a dozen shipyards in or near the town. Shipwrights from St. Michaels were active also at other

MAP 21 -- St. Michaels

1   Tarr House (ca. 1667)
2   Christ Episcopal Church (1878)
3   St. Luke's Methodist Church (1871)
4   The Old Inn at 401 Talbot St. (ca. 1816)
5   Cannonball House at 200 Mulberry Street (ca.1805).
      This was one of the few houses hit during the
      British bombardment of 1813.
6   Amelia Welby House at 209 Mulberry Street (1700s).
      Amelia Welby was a poet of some distinction in the
      mid-1800s.
7   St. Mary's Square Museum (front section pre-Revolutionary;
      rear section 1860s). St. Mary's Square was the original
      town square when St. Michael's was laid out in the 1770s.

leading Chesapeake shipyards, particularly at Fells Point in Baltimore. In terms of the numbers of boat built, Chesapeake Bay at that time ranked behind New England, but the average tonnage of Chesapeake craft greatly exceeded that of boats built in New England.

Although the Revolution and the War of 1812 were depressed times for maritime trade, some ships built at St. Michaels served as highly profitable blockade runners and privateers — or that is, as privately operated warships fitted out on speculation and authorized by the governor to seize and sell enemy merchant vessels and their cargoes. Sleek two-masted clipper schooners — termed Baltimore clippers but built at other bay ports also — were among the ships constructed at St. Michaels during the early 1800s. Faster than any other ships afloat, these vessels made ideal privateers. Armed with a few cannons, they could chase down weaker boats or sail away from stronger craft.

Exasperated by the glaring success of American privateers during the War of 1812, when 28 schooners from Talbot County alone operated against English shipping, a British squadron spent the spring and summer of 1813 in a tour of destruction up Chesapeake Bay, which the British blockaded throughout most of the war. After burning Havre de Grace on the Susquehanna and Georgetown and Fredericktown on the Sassafras, the British attacked St. Michaels early on the morning of August 10. In the dark they sent ashore a landing party of about 300 soldiers who stormed an earthwork fort southeast of the town. The defenders fled but the British nonetheless suffered nineteen killed when the last militiaman to leave the fort fired a cannon into their ranks. Disheartened, the British spiked the fort's guns and reembarked without taking the town. Then eleven British barges bombarded St. Michaels for a period of hours but failed to damage the town or the ships under construction there.

Following the war St. Michaels suffered from the same loss of commerce that affected all small and middling Chesapeake ports as Baltimore and Norfolk became the main centers of trade. St. Michaels' shipyards were reduced to turning out brogans and log canoes from which local watermen tonged for oysters, plus an occasional bay schooner or pungy for carrying cargo among local ports. Frederick Douglass, who worked as a slave on a large plantation near St. Michaels, described the town in 1833 as "an unsaintly as well as unsightly place," where every oyster boat carried a jug of rum against the cold. But after dredging for oysters was legalized in 1865, St. Michaels' shipyards prospered by building two-masted, beamy, shallow-draft dredge boats called bugeyes and smaller single-masted dredge boats called skipjacks. (Examples of a wide variety of bay boats can be seen at the maritime museum.) In this century, of course, the Chesapeake seafood industry has steadily declined, but the economic loss to St. Michaels has been counterbalanced by a rise in pleasure boating and tourism.

CAR TOUR (Map 20 — from St. Michaels to Tilghman Island): From St. Michaels, follow Route 33 west toward Tilghman Island. Go more than 12 miles to the drawbridge at Knapps Narrows, then continue south 3 miles through Tilghman to the end of the road at Blackwalnut Point.

Because **Tilghman Island** provides immediate access to Chesapeake Bay to the west and the Choptank River to the east, it has for generations been a watermen's community. A fleet of workboats is based at Knapps Narrows, and a few sail-powered skipjacks and even a two-masted bugeye still operate from Dogwood Harbor a half-mile south of the drawbridge. However, new yachting-oriented developments along the shore indicate that leisure activities and tourism may soon join commercial fishing as mainstays of the island's economy.

CAR TOUR (MAP 20 — from Tilghman Island to Oxford via ferry): Remember, the Oxford-Bellevue Ferry does not operate from mid-December through March, so at that time of year, simply return to Route 322 (the Easton Parkway) and from there follow Route 322 south to Route 333 and Oxford. But during the rest of the year, proceed as follows:
   Return on Route 33 from Tilghman Island to St. Michaels. From the intersection with Mill Street in St. Michaels, continue on Route 33 for 3.1 miles, then turn right onto Route 329. Follow Route 329 east for 1.0 mile to the village of Royal Oak, and there turn right onto Bellevue Road toward the ferry. Follow Bellevue Road 3.3 miles to the ferry landing. After crossing to Oxford, use Map 22 to explore the town by car or on foot.
   The **Oxford Customs House**, a small structure near the ferry landing, is a replica of the first federal customs house built in the 1790s, when Oxford no longer had any international trade to speak of. The **Oxford Museum**, located on Market Street near the corner with Morris Street, is open Friday, Saturday, and Sunday, 2 to 5, from mid-April through mid-October.

Oxford is one of Maryland's oldest towns. It appears on Augustine Herman's 1673 Map of Virginia and Maryland and was repeatedly men-

128

MAP 22 -- Oxford

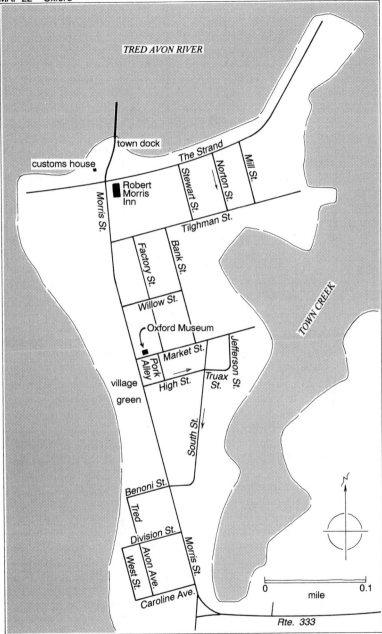

TRED AVON RIVER

town dock

customs house

The Strand

Stewart St.

Norton St.

Mill St.

Robert
Morris
Inn

Morris St.

Tilghman St.

Factory St.

Bank St.

Willow St.

Oxford Museum

Market St.

Jefferson St.

Pork
Alley

High St.

Truax
St.

village

green

South St.

TOWN CREEK

Benoni St.

Tred

Division St.

Avon Ave.

West St.

Morris St.

Caroline Ave.

N

0   0.1
mile

Rte. 333

tioned as an official port in legislation of the period designed to consolidate trade at designated sites. Cecilius Calvert — second Baron Baltimore and proprietor of Maryland — and his son and resident governor, Charles Calvert, thought that the growth of towns was desirable for a number of reasons: to make commerce more efficient, to promote education, religion, and culture, and — not least — to facilitate the collection of the province's export tax on tobacco, half of which helped to pay the expenses of government, while the rest went to the Calverts.

Directives to establish port towns — including a town at what is now Oxford — were issued in 1669 and 1671. According to the Act for the Advancement of Trade passed by the General Assembly in 1683, "Noe merchant Factor or Mariner or other person whatsoever tradeing in this province" was to import or export goods except at designated ports; people who traded elsewhere were subject to "forfeiting all such goods & merchandizes." Oxford was one of four port towns that were to be established in Talbot County, and one of thirty in the colony. The following year 100 lots were laid out at Oxford, but fewer than a third were sold, and even many of those sales were later nullified because no houses were built, as required by law. Oxford was platted again in 1694, when it was briefly called Williamstadt in honor of the current king, William III. A collector of customs was installed there, and another one at Annapolis, so that all ships from abroad had first to report to one or the other port before proceeding to trade elsewhere in Maryland. In 1695 the high sheriff of Talbot County was required to reside at Oxford as a condition of office. In 1696 merchants who brought their families to live at Oxford were granted special trading concessions. In 1707 the town was platted yet again. Still the collection point for a very large customs district (though not as large as before), Oxford finally began to grow.

For about seventy years tobacco was exported directly from Oxford to Great Britain, and all manner of manufactured goods arrived from overseas. Commercial establishments in London, Liverpool, and Bristol established stores at Oxford that were headed by local agents or factors who traded merchandise for tobacco. At one time as many as eight British firms and an equal number of local merchants operated at Oxford. In addition to the merchants' private storehouses, there was a public warehouse for tobacco. In the first half of the eighteenth century, Oxford was second only to Annapolis in terms of the number of ships that stopped there. According to Jerimiah Banning, a Talbot County man of affairs and for twenty-two years a sea captain who sailed out of Oxford, "The storekeepers and other retailers both on the western and the eastern side of the Chesapeake repaired there to lay in their supplies. . . . Seven or eight large ships at the same time were frequently seen at Oxford delivering goods and completing their lading; nor was it uncommon to despatch a ship with 500 hogsheads of tobacco within twelve days of its arrival." Hides, wheat, salt pork, and lumber were also exported from Oxford. And yet the place never amounted to more than a small village of two or three hundred people perched on the edge of a uniformly rural hinterland, throughout which most of the colonists were scattered on their small plantations or farms growing tobacco and a few other cash crops.

The fact that the colonial government tried so hard and so persistently to legislate towns into existence shows only too clearly that such places were regarded as unnecessary by those who were to be required to do business in them. In the early years of the colony, ships from England traded directly with the tobacco growers by ascending the rivers, sailing from one plantation landing to the next. At first tobacco was simply sold to the ship's captains in exchange for goods, but as some growers prospered and acquired larger plantations, they sought to get a higher price for their crops by corresponding directly with British consignment houses, which sold the tobacco on commission. These large planters also bartered for the crops of the many small farmers in their vicinity, giving in exchange essential goods ordered from England and imported directly to their plantations, where the big growers set up their own stores. As a consequence of buying goods on credit, the smaller farmers became obligated to bring their crops to the larger planters, some of whom eventually acquired ships of their own, or at least chartered them.

Because of the comprehensive dealings of the large planters, a separate merchant class was slow to develop in the tidewater region, and so too were towns. Far more often than not, the official ports designated by law never came into being or were never more than trading outposts and warehouse landings were tobacco was gathered, inspected, and stored prior to shipment. Only at a few places like Oxford, where numbers of enterprising, well-financed, and well-connected merchants took the lead, did actual villages develop on the Eastern Shore. At Oxford the merchants gradually acquired the business of the larger planters by pitching their trade directly to them, buying tobacco outright in huge quantities, and supplying a broad range of merchandise and chattels, including not only items from Great Britain, but also indentured servants, convict laborers (particularly rebels from Ireland and Scotland), slaves from Africa, wine from Madeira and the Canary Islands, and salt, sugar, molasses, and rum from the West Indies.

One Oxford merchant who rose to prominence in the eighteenth century was Robert Morris, the father of the financier of the American Revolution. The elder Morris arrived in Oxford in 1738 and proceeded to accumulate a fortune as chief factor for the large Liverpool trading house of Foster Cunliffe & Sons, which had branches throughout the Eastern Shore. Morris also engaged widely in trade on his own account. He had his residence and warehouse at the water end of Oxford's main street, now called Morris Street. A part of the house is incorporated into the present-day **Robert Morris Inn.**

Morris's influence extended throughout Maryland's tidewater region, where he introduced reforms that helped to improve and streamline the province's trade. Because the reputation and price of Maryland's tobacco suffered from the practice of adulterating good leaf with trash growth, Morris pressed for a tobacco inspection law, which finally was adopted in 1747, after Morris had already instituted a system of inspection in his own business and had gone a long way toward making other merchants do likewise. And in place of the old bookkeeping system by which debts and credits were expressed in terms of pounds of tobacco (so that entries constantly fluctuated in value with the price of the commodity), Morris introduced account keeping based on real money.

Jerimiah Banning has left a description of Morris:

His great natural abilities o'erleaped every other deficiency. As a mercantile genius, twas thought he had not his equal in this land. As a companion and bon vivant, he was incomparable. If he had any public point to carry he defeated all opposition. . . . He was a steady, sincere and warm friend . . . and had a hand ever open to relieve real distress. At repartee, he bore down all before him. [But he had also] a haughty and overbearing carriage, perhaps a too vindictive spirit, and . . . an extreme severity to his servants.

So great a role did the elder Morris play in Oxford's commercial affairs that some contemporaries regarded his death by accident in 1750 as precipitating a loss of trade at Oxford, although probably more significant were disruptions caused by the Seven Years War starting in 1756 and the Eastern Shore's shift from growing tobacco to growing wheat, which was a commodity that could not be traded to England because of prohibitive duties there. One after another, the English merchant firms sold their businesses at Oxford or moved them to Baltimore, which was emerging as the chief transshipment point for products of the Chesapeake region. The interruption in commerce caused by the War of Independence and the continued growth of Baltimore afterwards left Oxford with almost no international trade. In 1793 Jeremiah Banning, who served as Oxford's first United States customs collector during a period when very few ships arrived from foreign ports, described the town in elegiac terms:

The poor, drooping, and forsaken Oxford, bereft of almost every comfort in life, hath nothing remaining to console it except its salubrious situation and fine navigation which may anticipate better times. Oxford, whose street and strands were once covered with busy, noisy crowds, ushering in commerce from almost every quarter of the Globe, and whose rich, blooming lots echoed with fat, glowing kine — alas, now is shaded by wheat, corn and tobacco. The once well worn streets are now grown up with grass, save a few tracks made by the sheep and swine; and the strands have more the appearance of an uninhabited island than where human feet have ever trod.

During the first two-thirds of the nineteenth century, Oxford quietly stagnated. Its population dropped to less than a hundred. But the boom in oystering that followed the Civil War revived shipbuilding at Oxford and provided business for scores of boats based in the town's harbor. Packing houses sprang up, and at the beginning of each year's oyster season, hundreds of blacks and immigrants arrived by steamboat and by train (the railroad reached Oxford in 1871) to work during the winter at shucking, pickling, and canning oysters. A tomato cannery was also established and provided seasonal employment. By 1880 the population of Oxford had reached 750 and in 1890 the Oxford Saving Bank was opened. But Oxford's economy declined yet again at the beginning of the twentieth century as oyster harvests dwindled. Since then the town has experienced a gradual and almost complete cessation of commercial fishing and a corresponding reincarnation as a village in large part populated by well-heeled retirees and weekenders, with an emphasis on yachting.

CAR TOUR (Map 20 — from Oxford to Easton):
Follow Morris Street away from Oxford's ferry landing, then continue on Route 333 for 10 miles to Easton, where the car tour ends.

10

CAMBRIDGE
BLACKWATER NATIONAL WILDLIFE
REFUGE
DORCHESTER "EVERGLADES"
HOOPER ISLAND

The excursion outlined in this chapter starts in Cambridge, Maryland, which fronts on the Choptank River and is the seat of Dorchester County. Workboats and pleasure craft crowd the riverfront boat basin and Cambridge Creek, and distinguished old houses line High Street between the river and the courthouse square. Within a few minutes drive of High Street is the Dorchester County Historical Society's Meredith House (circa 1760) and adjoining Neild Museum. The former has been meticulously restored and the latter contains an outstanding collection of old tools and artifacts from everyday life. The house and museum are open Thursday, Friday, and Saturday from 10 to 4 and by appointment; telephone (410) 228-7953 on Tuesday through Saturday between 9 and 5.

Also in Cambridge is the Brannock Maritime Museum, devoted to the maritime history of Chesapeake Bay. The museum displays many old photographs and large models of locally built schooners, pungies, bugeyes, skipjacks, and other craft. The museum is open Saturday from 10 to 4, Sunday from 1 to 4, and by appointment; telephone (410) 228-6938.

From Cambridge the 90-mile car tour shown on Map 24 heads south to the 17,700-acre Blackwater National Wildlife Refuge, which is probably the best place in Delmarva to appreciate the immense number of migratory waterfowl that winter in the Chesapeake region. At any season the Blackwater refuge is also an excellent place to see bald eagles and a wide variety of other birds. The refuge has two short hiking trails and a paved road for cars and bicycles that follows a dike overlooking marshes and freshwater impoundments. The road and trails are open daily from dawn until dusk. The refuge is managed by the U.S. Fish and Wildlife Service; telephone (410) 228-2677. Bicyclists may also enjoy other local roads that cut through the refuge, as discussed at the beginning of the tour directions on page 148.

From Blackwater National Wildlife Refuge, the excursion circles south through a marshy region that somewhat resembles the Florida everglades: so flat, so low, so wet, so broad, so *different* that at times traveling through this area has the quality of navigating in some substance intermediate between land and water. A drive here in southern Dorchester County is worthwhile at any time of year just to see the landscape. If you have the time and inclination, you can also tour Hooper Island (actually several islands, now linked to the mainland by bridges) before returning north to the vicinity of Cambridge.

IMAGES PRODUCED BY LANDSAT SATELLITE show the Delmarva Peninsula to be densely speckled with farm fields interspersed with relatively little forest. An exception, however, is southern Dorchester County, which even from outer space is visibly different from most of Delmarva. From on high, southern Dorchester lacks the freckled appearance produced by numerous, irregularly-shaped fields. Instead, the region resembles rumpled, blotchy velvet. Similar material occupies the coast of Delaware Bay, the area behind the Atlantic barrier islands, and the Chesapeake shore of Somerset and Accomack counties. In Chesapeake Bay itself, large, amoeba-like islands — Bloodsworth and Smith islands, for example — appear to be made of nothing but this amorphous stuff, across which, in some places, spread dark, snaky tentacles.

The "stuff," of course, is marsh. When you travel south from Cambridge into the region drained by the Blackwater River, farmland gradually gives way to forests of loblolly pine and then to an immense and utterly flat expanse of marsh grass that is interlaced by sinuous, sluggish creeks and dotted with occasional timber islands. It is more than just a big marsh; it is a region. In fact, according to the Dorchester County Office of Soil Conservation, as much as 46 percent of the entire county — and Dorchester is the largest county on Maryland's Eastern Shore — is non-tidal wetlands, including all hydric (that is, very wet) soils, some of which are farmed or used for growing trees. When tidal wetlands are added, Dorchester's wetlands area (almost 400 square miles) reaches 66 percent of the county.

Moreover, the region is very slowly getting wetter still as the level of the sea rises at a rate which, since the time of European settlement, has been about a foot per century. Simultaneously, the land is sinking as the region's soft, thick mantle of silty, peaty soil compacts under its own weight. In southern Dorchester County some areas that once had villages — Lower Hoopers Island, for example — are no longer habitable.

Counteracting and somewhat retarding the effects of the rising ocean and the sinking land are other forces tending to build up the marsh surface. Silt eroded from higher areas is carried downstream by the region's rivers and deposited over the whole marsh during periods of flood caused by extraordinary rains or exceptionally high tides. The leaves and roots of marsh grasses help to catch and hold the silt, producing a landscape as flat as the surface of the silt-bearing floodwater. And, of course, the decaying stems and leaves of the marsh plants add bulk to the land surface, building it upward.

The predominant marsh plant of southern Dorchester is Olney three-square, also called American three-cornered sedge. It grows about 2 feet high and is easily identified by its stiff, spiky stems, which are triangular in cross-section. The prevalence of three-square reflects its ability to tolerate wide fluctuations in salinity, which in the marshes bordering the Blackwater River ranges from 2 percent to 42 percent of average sea salinity, depending on rainfall and the incursion of tides. Because of its importance as food for geese and other animals, three-square is maintained at Blackwater National Wildlife Refuge by annual burning in the fall. Burning is not harmful to the three-square roots and rhizomes (which, after all, are buried in sodden earth), yet helps to prevent intrusion by other plants. Burning also produces fresh growth on which geese can graze during late winter and early spring, when other food is scarce.

Wild rice is another important marshland food plant, attracting blue-winged teals, red-winged blackbirds, soras, and bobolinks. In Maryland its seeds mature in early September. Wild rice is often found next to streams, so long as the salinity does not exceed one-fifth that of sea water. The appearance and disappearance of stands of wild rice from one year to the next provides a local clue to the relative balance of fresh water and salt water.

Other marsh plants are similarly indicative of salinity. Narrowleaf cattail prefers standing fresh water. Saltmeadow cordgrass, which is fairly short, dense, and soft-textured in appearance (but actually rather coarse to the touch) occupies brackish flats that are a little higher and drier than the extensive areas of three-square and narrowleaf cattail. Expanses of saltmeadow cordgrass are only rarely flooded by the tide, whereas the similar sounding saltmarsh cordgrass, which grows 7 or 8 feet high, is found along the lower reaches of tidal rivers.

Although today the Blackwater marshes accommodate huge numbers of wintering Canada geese, it was not always so. According to Brooke Meanley, author of *Blackwater*, the winter population of Canada geese (identified by their large size, black heads and necks, and white cheeks) grew from about 5,000 at Blackwater National Wildlife Refuge in the 1940s to more than 100,000 in the 1970s. A similar phenomenal increase occurred simultaneously in other areas of Maryland's Eastern Shore, mainly in the vicinity of the Lower Choptank River, the Wye River, and the lower Chester River, where Canada geese congregate in immense numbers. The increase in wintering geese is thought to have been fostered not only by the establishment of national and state wildlife refuges — as at Blackwater in 1932 and Eastern Neck Island in 1962 — but also by changes in local agriculture, principally the planting of more corn and soybeans. The mechanical reapers used to harvest these crops leave as much as 10 percent of the crop on the ground, where it is eaten by geese that graze in the stubble fields. The result has been so-called "short-stopping," meaning the tendency for goose populations that formerly wintered farther south (mainly in North Carolina) to stop and stay for the winter in the Chesapeake region, as most Canada geese migrating southward along the Atlantic flyway now do. (Incidentally, the "Atlantic flyway" is somewhat of a misnomer, actually designating a wide variety of indefinite migration routes that together funnel birds from the whole breadth of northern Canada to their wintering grounds along the Atlantic seaboard and in other eastern states. The U.S. Fish and Wildlife Service uses the phrase chiefly as a jurisdictional or administrative term.)

After reaching a peak population of about 600,000 in the early 1980s, the number of Canada geese wintering in Maryland has declined by more than half (as of 1991), mostly, it is thought, because of over-hunting. Hunting, in fact, is estimated to cause 85 to 90 percent of deaths among Canada geese. In particular, hunting early in the season, before the geese settle in, not only kills off a disproportionately large number of unwary juvenile birds, but also causes those that survive to leave the region altogether. Studies show that from 1962 to 1974, when the winter population of Canada geese was increasing, the adult survival rate from one year to the next was 82 percent; but during the mid-1980s, the survival rate dropped to about 70 percent as Maryland attracted large numbers of hunters from other states. A survival rate of 76 percent is needed to maintain the winter population at a constant size. To help achieve this rate, Maryland has shortened the hunting season, set lower bag limits, and started a program (funded by revenues from non-resident hunting licenses) to pay farmers in areas that are not presently popular with hunters to leave crops standing unharvested in order to attract geese to relatively safe places.

Although Canada geese are fairly common in the Blackwater region even during summer, they do not begin to arrive in great numbers until late September, reaching a peak in November. Some continue farther south for the winter or scatter to other areas bordering Chesapeake Bay. There is, in fact, a good deal of movement throughout the winter, as flocks exhaust one food source and move to another.

Northward migration begins as early as the second week of February, and the vast majority of Canada geese are gone by the end of March. The path of migration is more or less straight north to the Ungava Peninsula east of Hudson and James bays, where the birds nest and breed. The number of young that hatch and survive depends greatly on how early the snow and ice melt on the breeding grounds, where the geese stay until August, when they begin to mass along the shores of the bays for the flight south.

The recovery of banded birds has shown that the Canada geese that summer in Ungava and winter in the Chesapeake region form a subgroup (or subspecies or geographic race) among all those Canada geese that breed across the whole width of the continent. According to ornithologists, there are at least ten, perhaps twelve, distinct populations of Canada geese. For the most part, they do not intermix, and each population has its own breeding and wintering grounds and migration route between the two. So persistent is this behavior that it has led to substantial differences in the size of birds belonging to the different groups. Mid-continental Canada geese weigh up to 18 pounds, while those seen in Chesapeake Bay weigh up to 9 pounds, and those found along the Pacific coast weigh just 3 pounds. The differences between subspecies underscores the fact that young Canada geese adhere to family groups and learn from parent birds where to breed, where to winter, and where to migrate. Even so, the geese are adaptable enough to react to changed circumstances, as demonstrated by the previously-mentioned fact that the geese of the Atlantic flyway have shifted their wintering grounds northward during the mid-1900s.

A more recent phenomenon has been the tendency for a growing number of Canada geese to spend the entire year in the Chesapeake region, often grazing on golf courses, landscaped office parks, public watershed areas, and other places where they are safe from hunters. In Maryland alone, the non-migrating population of Canada geese, which are sometimes called "street geese" because of the frequency with which they show up even in suburban residential areas, was estimated at 10,000 in 1991, and their numbers are growing.

Far less numerous than the Canada geese that winter in Delmarva — and perhaps summer here too — are snow geese, of which there are two subspecies: greater and lesser. The entire national population of greater snow goose (estimated at nearly 200,000 in January 1991) winters along the Atlantic coast, mainly between Chincoteague, Virginia and Albemarle Sound, North Carolina. In contrast, the lesser snow goose has a national population exceeding two million, of which less than 1 percent winter in Delmarva, mainly in the vicinity of Blackwater National Wildlife Refuge.

Somewhat confusingly, there are two color phases of the lesser snow goose. One is nearly all white, except for black wing tips, and thus resembles the greater snow goose. The other color phase of the lesser snow goose has a white head and neck and dark body; it is sometimes termed the blue goose. Both color phases of the lesser snow goose are usually seen together, and they interbreed on their Arctic tundra nesting grounds, located mainly on Baffin Island and Southampton Island. In contrast, greater snow geese and lesser snow geese frequent different areas and do not interbreed.

The lesser snow geese that winter in the Blackwater region congregate in September at staging areas in James Bay and southern Hudson Bay. They start their overland flight south early in October and arrive at the Blackwater refuge in October. In the Blackwater marshes they grub for rhizomes of three-square and, along with Canada geese and muskrats, are capable of denuding and digging up broad areas termed eatouts. With Canada geese and tundra swans, they also graze in stubble fields of corn and soybeans or in fields of freshly-sprouted winter wheat. Within the refuge, pastures of fescue and other grasses are planted for the lesser snow geese, partly in an effort to avoid damage to neighboring farm fields. Compared to the number of lesser snow geese wintering in the Chesapeake region, far more winter along the coast of Louisiana and Texas, where one of their main foods is waste rice gleaned from commercial rice fields.

Even more remarkable than the migratory movements of Canada geese and snow geese are the prodigious flights of tundra swans (formerly called whistling swans). During fall migration, these large, long-necked, white birds sometimes fly nonstop, night and day, for a thousand miles (compared to an average of 50 miles daily for migrating Canada geese). Tundra swans breed in the northwest Arctic, and some of the tundra swans seen in winter at Blackwater National Wildlife Refuge and Eastern Neck Island have come from as far as the north coast of Alaska, having migrated across northern Canada, Alberta, Saskatchewan, North Dakota, and the Great Lakes to the mid-Atlantic coast, for a total distance of about 3,700 miles — the same as between New York and Paris. (I note that in England the word "swanning" is now used as a slang verb synonymous with "jetsetting" — as in "swanning around the world.") There are other birds — Arctic terns, for instance — that migrate farther than tundra swans, but nothing beats the heavy swans for the amount of work performed in migrating to and from the mid-Atlantic coast. In January 1991, the Chesapeake population of tundra swans was estimated at 26,000 out of a continental population of 137,000. Other wintering grounds for tundra swans include the coastal bays of Virginia and North Carolina and the Pacific coast in the vicinity of San Francisco Bay.

Arriving in the Chesapeake region during October and November and remaining here into March, the swans favor open water up to 5 feet deep, where, using their long necks, they can feed off submerged aquatic plants and thin-shelled mollusks. In fresh water, the swans browse on wild celery, and in brackish water they eat widgeongrass, sago pondweed, muskgrass, long clams, and Baltic macoma clams. As turbidity and pollution have reduced the supply of submerged aquatic plants, tundra swans have increasingly turned to grazing (along with Canada geese and snow geese) in fields of corn and soybean stubble and winter wheat.

Incidentally, also seen in the Chesapeake region is the mute swan, a European species introduced here. It does not migrate and is the only swan that breeds in the eastern United States or that is likely to be seen here in summer. The adult has an orange bill with a black knob. When swimming, it holds its neck in an S-curve, as compared to the straight-necked posture of our native tundra swan.

In contrast to the waterfowl that winter in the Blackwater marshes are those that breed here in spring and summer. For most of these birds, the height of the nesting season is the last week of May and the first week of June. Chief among breeding waterfowl is the black duck, so-called because of its dark, mottled body (although in flight the undersides of the wings are seen to be white). These important game birds most often nest in areas of saltmeadow cordgrass, although other sites, sometimes far from water, are not unusual. Their nesting season is long, starting in March and extending through August. Another duck that breeds at Blackwater is the blue-winged teal. (Males are more easily identified by the white crescent on their cheeks than by the blue wing patches that give these birds their name.) Like black ducks, blue-winged teal prefer to nest in the salt meadow, which — since it is slightly higher than other areas of the marsh — is less likely to be flooded. Finally, mallards (males, of course, have green heads and white neck bands) also breed in large numbers in the Blackwater marshes, and like black ducks are common year round.

More often heard than seen, bitterns and various rails (black, clapper, king, and Virginia) also nest in the Blackwater marshes. Several species of herons and egrets are common as well (in some cases year-round), but only the green heron and black-crowned night heron breed in the refuge. The most abundant breeding birds in the marshlands, however, are neither waterfowl nor waders, but rather the seaside sparrow, long-billed marsh wren, and — most numerous of all — the red-winged blackbird.

Among the most dramatic breeding birds of the Blackwater region is the bald eagle, easily identified by its white head, white tail, and large, dark body. From February through May, one to three eggs (which take almost a month and a half to hatch) are laid in huge nests that are nearly always located in the upper branches of loblolly pines that overlook the marsh or open water where the eagles hunt or scavenge. It takes both parents about 30 days to build a new nest, which typically measures 5 feet across. Some reports even assert that nests that have been in use for many years measure as much as 8 feet across and 15 feet from top to bottom and weigh in the vicinity of 2 tons. (Much of the weight is from water, since at the core of the nest is a sodden mass of decaying compost.) The debris recovered from fallen eagle nests consists mainly of sticks (some up to 6 feet long), clumps of sod, stalks of corn and cattails, marsh grass (with which the birds line their nests), and undigested food fragments such as muskrat bones, duck feet, and fish heads. There may also be such odd items as furnace clinkers and muskrat traps. One nest is reported to have contained the remains of 35 muskrats, 8 waterfowl, miscellaneous fish, and one turtle.

Bald eagles pick up most of these animals dead. Fish is their main food, and although most fish are scavenged dead, eagles also catch live fish by swooping close to the surface of the water and snatching them out with their talons. This manner of fishing is distinctly different from that of ospreys, which are slightly smaller than eagles and far more common; ospreys circle at a height of 50 to 150 feet, hover, then dive feet first into the water, sometimes completely submerging themselves. Like ospreys, however, both eagle parents care for their fledglings, and by the twelfth week after hatching, the young eagles are ready to fly.

Other large birds of prey of the Blackwater marshes are harriers (also called marsh hawks) and short-eared owls, both of which breed and feed in the salt meadows. They eat voles, shrews, and other small animals. Like eagles, harriers also sometimes eat muskrats that have been caught in traps; they are not known to capture muskrats on their own. The harrier is identified by its long tail with a white patch on top at the rump. It hunts by day, flying low over the marsh, veering from side to side with wings held in a shallow V. The short-eared owl similarly scours the marsh at dusk and at night, its wings tilted upward like the harrier's.

There are yet other large predatory birds that hunt in the marsh, but that nest in nearby woods. These include the red-tailed hawk (whose unbanded tail is dark red on the upper side and light pink on the lower side), the red-shouldered hawk (narrow white bands on the dark tail), and great horned, barred, barn, and screech owls. These owls are all night hunters, but (with the exception of the strictly nocturnal barn owl) are sometimes seen perched in woods during the day or perhaps even gliding over the marsh at dusk. Red-tailed hawks and great horned owls nest in pine woods, and red-shouldered hawks and barred owls nest in hardwood swamps.

The Blackwater marshes and bordering woods are also home to numerous mammals, including muskrats, nutria, raccoons, otters, foxes, deer, meadow voles, and rice rats, but of chief interest to visitors is the endangered Delmarva Peninsula fox squirrel, so-called for its disproportionately large tail. The body, too, of the fox squirrel is bigger than that of the common gray squirrel, and its coat is more silvery. In its movements, the fox squirrel is slower and more deliberate than the gray squirrel, and it spends more time foraging on the ground. Fox squirrels usually build their nests far out on a branch, and their preferred habitat is mature piny woods, where they eat pine seeds. Piles of pine-cone cores at the foot of trees is a sign of fox squirrels, which used to live throughout Delmarva, but now are found only in the Blackwater region, at Eastern Neck Island (Chapter 4), at Chincoteague National Wildlife Refuge (Chapter 16), and a few other places.

In economic terms, the most important mammal of the Dorchester marshes is the lowly muskrat, which is trapped for fur and for food. It is sometimes termed "marsh rabbit" when set on the table. In the mid-1960s, about 280,000 muskrats were caught annually in Maryland, but the number has declined drastically since then as the market for animal fur has declined. The coastal or Virginia muskrat found in the Blackwater region measures about 2 feet long, but it is nearly half tail and weighs only 2 pounds. It has two color phases: one black (and more valuable) and the other either red or brown. Although muskrats sometimes live in burrows dug in stream banks and entered through underwater tunnels, they more usually nest in dome-shaped houses or lodges scattered throughout the marsh and made of leaves, stalks, roots, and grass piled up to 6 feet in diameter and 4 feet high. Most muskrat houses are in areas of three-square sedge, which is a prime muskrat food. Muskrats have at least two litters a year, with an average of five kits to a litter. If not kept in check by trappers and by other predators — chiefly raccoons and foxes, which break into muskrat houses to seize the kits — muskrat populations sometimes rise to the point where the animals denude large areas of the marsh.

Nutria are dark-brown rodents the size of beavers. Weighing about 10 pounds (sometimes twice that much), they look like giant hamsters. They were introduced from Argentina to Louisiana in the 1930s and from there to the Blackwater region in the 1940s. Wildlife managers say that they have adapted all too well. Their numbers have soared, and by browsing on the roots of marsh grasses, they are capable of digging up annually hundreds of acres of marsh that then degenerate into relatively barren mud flats or even sink to become brackish pools. Nutria formerly were valued for their fur, but not at present. Blackwater National Wildlife Refuge now has a program to pay muskrat trappers — who must first bid to trap within the refuge — a rebate for each nutria caught. The chief natural enemy of nutria is severe cold, for unlike muskrats, they nest in the open and in winter will form large huddles to try to stay warm.

AUTOMOBILE DIRECTIONS: Cambridge is located where Route 50 crosses the Choptank River 30 miles northwest of Salisbury. (See Map 1 in the Table of Contents.) South of Cambridge is the immense Blackwater National Wildlife Refuge, and still farther south is Hooper Island, separating the Honga River from Chesapeake Bay. The car tour of southern Dorchester County shown on Map 24 starts at Cambridge, so you should go there first.

To Cambridge from northern Delmarva and Interstate 95 near Newark, Delaware: From I-95 take Route 896 south across Route 40 and over the Chesapeake and Delaware Canal to an intersection with Route 301, and there continue straight south on Route 301. Just west of Middletown, turn right to follow Route 301 south into Maryland slightly more than 37 miles. Eventually, after passing exits for Route 305 and Route 304 near Centreville, turn left at a traffic light onto Route 213 southbound. Follow Route 213 south 4.3 miles, then turn left (east) onto Route 50 and follow it for 28 miles. After crossing the Choptank River, turn right at the first traffic light onto Maryland Avenue (toward downtown Cambridge). Follow Maryland Avenue 0.6 mile, then turn right toward the historic area. In a few hundred yards, turn right onto brick-paved High Street.

To Cambridge from the Chesapeake Bay Bridge: After crossing the Bay Bridge, follow Route 50/301 across Kent Island. At the point where Route 50 and Route 301 split, fork right and follow Route 50 past Easton and across the Choptank River to Cambridge. At the first traffic light south of the Choptank River Bridge, turn right onto Maryland Avenue (toward downtown Cambridge). Follow Maryland Avenue 0.6 mile, then turn right toward the historic area. In a few hundred yards, turn right onto brick-paved High Street.

To Cambridge from southern Delmarva and the Chesapeake Bay Bridge-Tunnel at Norfolk: After crossing the bridge-tunnel, follow Route 13 north into Maryland and past Pocomoke City and Princess Anne to the exit for Route 50 westbound near Salisbury, and from there take Route 50 west to Cambridge. After Route 50 curves right in Cambridge, watch carefully for Maryland Avenue, and there turn left toward downtown Cambridge. Follow Maryland Avenue 0.6 mile, then turn right toward the historic area. In a few hundred yards, turn right onto brick-paved High Street.

To Cambridge from Salisbury and the Delaware and Maryland seashore resorts: From the vicinity of Salisbury or from Ocean City, follow Route 50 west to Cambridge. From the vicinity of Rehoboth Beach, follow Route 1 north to the intersection with Route 9 westbound near Lewes, and from there follow Route 9 west through Georgetown and across Route 113 to Route 13 southbound. Follow Route 13 south to Route 50, and then take Route 50 west to Cambridge.

As you enter Cambridge and Route 50 curves right, watch carefully for Maryland Avenue, and there turn left toward downtown Cambridge. Follow Maryland Avenue 0.6 mile, then turn right toward the historic area. In a few hundred yards, turn right onto brick-paved High Street.

Cambridge was established in 1684, when Maryland's General Assembly authorized a port town "in Dorchester County Att Daniell Joansis plantation on the south side of Great Choptancke." This legislation, and other directives like it designating sundry ports, was intended to implement the prior year's Act for the Advancement of Trade. Taken together, the measures were supposed to promote the growth of centers of commerce and to facilitate the collection of tobacco taxes and custom duties by requiring that all trade in the colony be conducted at designated towns — most of which did not yet exist and, in fact, never came into being. Cambridge (like nearby Oxford) was one of the few specified sites that grew into a real town and (again like Oxford) was named for one of England's two great university cities.

In 1686 a courthouse was built at Cambridge, and the town has been the seat of Dorchester County ever since. Cambridge, however, still had few, if any, structures other than the courthouse and an Anglican church in 1706, when the oldest part of the town was laid out along High Street in accordance with procedures akin to present-day exercises in eminent domain. Land was taken for the town, lots were sold, and the prior owners were compensated. Buyers of lots — and these tracts might each contain a dozen or more acres — were required to build houses at least 20 feet on each side within one year, or forfeit their claim. Lots not improved with a house within seven years reverted to the original owners of the land.

From the time of the founding of Cambridge until the mid-1700s, tobacco was, of course, the main article of commerce there, as it was throughout the tidewater region. But by the late 1700s, a more diversified economy had evolved. Grain (wheat, corn, flax), livestock, salt-meat (primarily pork), and timber became the main exports of the Eastern Shore, shipped out from Cambridge and other river towns. However, as Baltimore boomed following the American Revolution, trade declined in Maryland's smaller ports, although shipbuilding continued to be an important industry at Cambridge. Throughout the nineteenth century, shipyards in Cambridge built many vessels that became active in coastal trading as far south as the Caribbean. Even several whaling ships were built at Cambridge for the New Bedford, Connecticut whaling industry.

After the Civil War, prosperity returned to Cambridge as the oyster trade flourished. Throughout the late 1800s and early 1900s, Cambridge was home port to a large fleet of sail-powered oyster dredgers, and even today a few are still based in Cambridge Creek. Seafood processing plants were built to handle the haul of shellfish and finfish caught in Chesapeake Bay and brought to Cambridge. Also during the late nineteenth and early twentieth centuries, Cambridge acquired a substantial canning industry for vegetables grown on the Delmarva Peninsula.

In recent decades, however, seafood processing and vegetable canning have fallen off at Cambridge, and during the 1960s in particular the area was economically depressed. But Cambridge has slowly recovered, and today the town (the second largest after Salisbury on Maryland's Eastern Shore) has a fairly diversified economy emphasizing publishing, the manufacturing of electronic circuitry, wire conveyor belting, fertilizer, and garments, and the processing of seafood, poultry, and vegetables.

CAR TOUR OF CAMBRIDGE: The bold line on Map 23 shows the route of a car tour that provides a quick overview of

MAP 23 -- Car tour of Cambridge

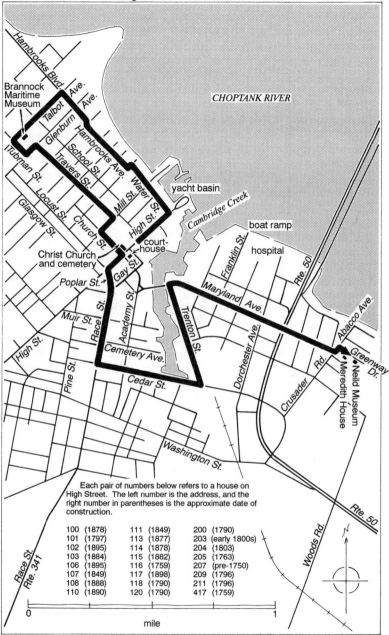

Brannock Maritime Museum

CHOPTANK RIVER

Hambrooks Blvd.

Talbot Ave.

Glenburn Ave.

Tubman St.

Hambrooks Ave.

School St.

Travers St.

Locust St.

Glasgow St.

Church St.

Mill St.

Water St.

High St.

yacht basin

Cambridge Creek

boat ramp

hospital

Christ Church and cemetery

court-house

Gay St.

Poplar St.

Academy St.

Franklin St.

Maryland Ave.

Muir St.

Race St.

Trenton St.

Dorchester Ave.

Rte. 50

Abacco Ave.

High St.

Pine St.

Cemetery Ave.

Cedar St.

Crusader Rd.

Greenway Dr.

Neild Museum

Meredith House

Washington St.

Rte. 50

Woods Rd.

Race St.
Rte. 341

Each pair of numbers below refers to a house on High Street. The left number is the address, and the right number in parentheses is the approximate date of construction.

100 (1878)	111 (1849)	200 (1790)
101 (1797)	113 (1877)	203 (early 1800s)
102 (1895)	114 (1878)	204 (1803)
103 (1884)	115 (1882)	205 (1763)
106 (1895)	116 (1759)	207 (pre-1750)
107 (1849)	117 (1898)	209 (1796)
108 (1888)	118 (1790)	211 (1796)
110 (1890)	120 (1790)	417 (1759)

0   mile   1

Cambridge. The tour starts on High Street, where between the courthouse and the Choptank River, there are many handsome old houses. (Dates of construction are noted on the map.) From the riverfront area the route leads to the **Brannock Maritime Museum**, located on Talbot Avenue. From there the tour returns to the center of town at Church Street and High Street, where you may enjoy strolling in the old **cemetery of Christ Church**, burial place of five Maryland governors. The current church dates from 1883, but its site has belonged to the parish since about 1696, when the first church was built here. From Christ Church the tour route follows High Street south, then turns left onto upper Race Street, which retains much of the flavor of the early twentieth century, when many of the buildings were constructed following a fire in 1910. After turning left onto Cedar Street and left again onto Trenton Street, the route passes **Cambridge Creek**; the harbor here was once the site of numerous packing houses but is now being developed with vacation condominiums and slips for pleasure boats. After turning right onto Maryland Avenue, the tour ends at the **Meredith House** and **Neild Museum**, located east of Route 50.

CAR TOUR OF SOUTHERN DORCHESTER COUNTY:
The bold line on Map 24 shows the route followed by this 90-mile car tour, which leads first to Blackwater National Wildlife Refuge. A shorter alternative for bicyclists is to start at the refuge and, after touring its Wildlife Drive, follow Maple Dam Road south to the Blackwater River and back for a total of about 22 very scenic miles. For a longer excursion of about 30 miles, bicyclists can follow the car tour clockwise from the refuge, but then cut northeast on Route 335 in order to return to their starting point. Bicyclists should bear in mind, however, that Route 336 and Route 335 are used by cars traveling at high speeds.

From the intersection of Maryland Avenue and Route 50 in Cambridge, follow Route 50 south (that is, away from the Choptank River) 1.4 miles, then turn right onto Route 16 toward the Blackwater refuge. Follow Route 16 for 7.3 miles (passing at 3.2 miles the **Stanley Institute**, an old one-room school house), then turn left onto Route 335 toward the Blackwater refuge. Follow Route 335 for 3.8 miles, then turn left onto Key Wallace Drive and go 0.9 mile to the refuge visitor center on the right.

MAP 24 -- Car tour of southern Dorchester County

BLACKWATER NATIONAL WILDLIFE REFUGE: The bold line on Map 25 shows the refuge's tour route for cars and bicycles, for which there is a small admission fee payable at the entrance to **Wildlife Drive**. The route leads past two short foot trails.

For Wildlife Drive, turn right out the visitor center driveway and follow Key Wallace Drive east 1.5 miles, then turn right onto Wildlife Drive just beyond the refuge headquarters. After 0.3 mile, Wildlife Drive passes a spur road leading left to the **Marsh Edge Trail** (0.3 mile in length and well worthwhile) and an overlook at the end of the road.

Continue on Wildlife Drive to the **Woods Trail** (0.5 mile in length). Eventually, turn left in order to continue 1.0 mile before exiting from Wildlife Drive onto Route 355.

CAR TOUR (Map 24 — from the Blackwater refuge south to Hooper Island, then back to Cambridge): Turn right out the exit from Wildlife Drive onto Route 335. Go 0.2 mile, then turn right onto Key Wallace Drive. Follow Key Wallace Drive 3.6 miles to a T-intersection, and there turn right. (This unmarked road is Maple Dam Road, but eventually it changes name to Robbins Road.) Follow the winding road for a total of 10.2 miles across the marsh, over the Blackwater River, and through the hamlets of Robbins and Andrews to a T-intersection with Route 336, and there turn right. Follow Route 336 for 4.8 miles to an intersection with Route 335.

At the intersection of Route 336 and Route 335, continue straight ahead on Route 335 toward Hooper Island. You are soon, however, faced with a choice. If you do not want to see Hooper Island and its several fishing communities, go only 1.8 miles, then turn right onto Smithville Road and skip the next two paragraphs.

But if you *do* want to see Hooper Island (and of course you do), stay on Route 335 southbound. After 1.3 miles, pass **Tubman Chapel** on the right; it was built in 1769 and is the oldest surviving Catholic Church on the lower Eastern Shore; the parish now meets at the nearby St. Mary's Star of the Sea Catholic Church. Continue south across the bridge to **Upper Hooper Island** and the town of **Honga**; the name is derived from the Honga River, previously known as the Hunger River. As for the name *Hooper*, Henry Hooper and his family settled on these islands from Calvert County in 1667 and at one time owned 2,300 acres. With the Hoopers came other Catholic

MAP 25 -- Blackwater National Wildlife Refuge

families, including the Meekins (whose name survives in Meekins Neck, north of Hooper Island) and the Tubmans of Tubman Chapel.

From Honga continue south on the main road, at one point turning sharply right (so as *not* to go to Old House Point). Continue through the strung-out village of **Fishing Creek** (the island's main settlement) and across the long, high bridge to **Middle Hooper Island**. Follow the road until it simply peters out in the watermen's village of **Hoopersville**, then return the way you came. After leaving Upper Hooper Island, go 4.2 miles, then turn left onto Smithville Road.

To return to the vicinity of Cambridge, follow Smithville Road north 7.1 miles to a T-intersection with Route 16, and there turn right and go 15.8 miles to Route 50; however, I strongly recommend that you stop by at **Old Trinity Church**, located off Route 16 just beyond the village of Woolford; watch for a sign on the left at the entrance to a long lane that leads to the church.

Built between 1670 and 1680 and meticulously restored in the 1950s, **Old Trinity Church** is said to be the oldest Episcopal Church in continuous use in the United States It is beautifully situated on the shore of Church Creek. In its shady churchyard cemetery is buried Thomas King Carroll, elected governor of Maryland in 1829. Even if you cannot get into the church to see its intimate interior, which has box pews and a pulpit at the side (as was the case at many early churches), the diminutive size of the church serves to remind us of the small scale of society at the time it was built.

11

DEAL ISLAND
DAMES QUARTER MARSH
WHITEHAVEN via ferry
PRINCESS ANNE

The 60-mile car tour outlined in this chapter explores northwestern Somerset County, Maryland, with a brief amphibious incursion into neighboring Wicomico County.

Deal Island, projecting into Tangier Sound but linked to the mainland by a high bridge, is a center of commercial fishing. The island's two harbors are home port for several skipjacks, such as those shown on the facing page.

Inland from Deal Island is the immense Dames Quarter Marsh, where good vantage points for birding are accessible by car. Also, a dirt road and dike that are closed to cars provide an outstanding opportunity to walk comfortably for up to 10 miles through a sea of grass. However, because waterfowl hunting is permitted here in season, please read carefully the information on page 166 before walking across the marsh. Dames Quarter Marsh is part of the Deal Island Wildlife Management Area, which is administered by the Maryland Department of Natural Resources; telephone (410) 651-2320.

Finally, after a digression via toll-free public ferry to the village of Whitehaven on the Wicomico River, the car tour ends at Princess Anne, seat of Somerset County and site of the Teackle Mansion, which is open on Sundays from 2 to 4 under the auspices of an organization called Olde Princess Anne Days, Inc.; telephone (410) 651-1705. Olde Princess Anne Days sponsors an event of the same name held annually (it may become biennial) on the second weekend in October, during which many old private houses are open to the public. Behind the Teackle Mansion is a handsome boxwood garden that is always open.

DEAL ISLAND WAS FORMERLY KNOWN as Devil's Island, supposedly because this low, marshy outpost at the head of Tangier Sound was considered by its earliest English settlers to be fit habitation only for the devil. The diabolic name, however, eventually was suppressed as incompatible with the new spirit of Methodism that spread throughout the Eastern Shore following the American Revolution. According to the Reverend Adam Wallace (writing in the middle of the nineteenth century), "Deal Island" came into use because the presiding Methodist elder of the district "used to insist on spelling the name in this way, lest there should seem to be a recognition of Satan's having some right to, or property in" the place.

Until the advent of Methodism, many of the remote island communities of watermen, shipwrights, and small farmers in the vicinity of Tangier Sound had been virtually without organized religion, and each family had worshipped (if at all) according to its own lights and traditions, frequently without the benefit of prayer books, bibles, or even literacy. Methodism filled the void. With its emotionally powerful meetings, its opportunities for all — even the unschooled and ineloquent — to testify, and its emphasis on a direct, personal relationship between each individual and God, Methodism appealed to the fiercely independent and traditionally undocile islanders, whose villages converted virtually to a man.

The eagerness with which the islanders embraced Methodism may also have been a reaction against the Episcopalianism of the ruling class that had led Maryland and Virginia into the Revolution, of which many of the communities of Tangier Sound had never approved. During the war, Maryland's revolutionary government had even oppressed the islanders, often confiscating their boats and their livestock and threatening the people with forced relocation because some of them actively aided the British by brokering supplies to their warships and by attacking and looting the landings, plantations, and vessels of patriot merchants and planters. One militia commander wrote that the freebooters based on the islands of Tangier Sound were "a set of Poor, Ignorant, Illitorate People, Yet they are Artful and Cunning as Foxes." Referring to the islanders, Colonel Joseph Dashiel of the Somerset Militia wrote to Governor Thomas Lee of Maryland, "I consider them . . . the most Dangerous Enemy we have to watch the motions of — and am Certain if they Can do us no other Damage they will rob & Plunder all they Can before they are removed." Although never carried out because of lack of means, the directive to forcibly remove the populations of Deal, Smith, and other nearby islands was in fact issued by the governor.

It is not surprising, then, that following the war Methodism became attractive to the much-reviled islanders, who saw that, like themselves, the Methodists were widely spoken against and yet seemed to care not a

156

whit and to gain rapidly in strength. As Joshua Thomas, a locally-renowned Methodist leader explained long after his conversion, he had wanted to know more of the religion that so obviously comforted a people so widely and so unjustly disparaged as were the early Methodists.

In 1825 Joshua Thomas became a deacon of the Methodist church on Deal Island. Thomas was a waterman who had been converted to Methodism on the mainland at Annemessex (now Crisfield) in 1807 and had thereafter organized a series of very successful camp meetings on Tangier Island, where he lived until moving to Deal Island. Eventually he was dubbed "the Parson of the Islands," which is the title of Adam Wallace's famous biography of him. Rough, awkward, and stammering in ordinary life, Thomas nonetheless was capable of a remarkable flow of words when the spirit came over him. While continuing as a waterman, Thomas also served as a ferryman for visiting preachers, conveying them to and from the various island communities in his large log sailing canoe, *The Methodist*. At the services and camp meetings he attended, Thomas invariably testified, and soon he became a highly effective lay preacher, exhorting the residents of isolated villages up and down the Eastern Shore with parables drawn from fishing and oystering.

In 1828 Joshua Thomas was among those who spoke at the first annual camp meeting on Deal Island, which Thomas's biographer says became the site of "many of the most powerful meetings that perhaps have ever been witnessed since the day of Pentecost" — or that is (according to Acts 2) since the apostles first received from the Holy Ghost the power of speaking in diverse tongues of fire. For the occasion of these camp meetings on Deal Island, hundreds of sailing vessels plus various chartered steamships would converge on the place, carrying not only the faithful but also the curious and those who came merely to sell provisions and other goods to the assembled throng. Scores of permanent shelters were built in concentric semicircles facing the elevated outdoor pulpit. When Thomas spoke, "the multitude, congregated under the sound of his voice, would sometimes heave like the ocean in time of storm, before the power of Divine truth falling from his lips. . . ."

Thomas preached at Deal Island's annual camp meeting until almost the last year of his life in 1853. A chapel built in 1850 still stands on Deal Island behind the larger, present-day St. John's United Methodist Church, and immediately adjacent to it is Thomas's grave.

In its life and economy, Deal Island today resembles in many ways the nearby communities of watermen at Smith Island and Tangier Island (discussed in chapters 12 and 13). There is, however, at least one difference, and that is the fact that Deal Island is home port for a few skip-jacks, Maryland's traditional sail-powered oyster dredgers. The dredge itself which these vessels pull is a triangular iron frame with teeth to loosen the oysters from their bed and a bag of rope-and-chain netting to catch them. Each skipjack pulls two dredges — one on each side — and each dredge is attended by two crewmen who alternately pull in their dredge with a power winch and cull through the catch for oysters of legal size (3 inches as of the 1991/92 season).

The survival of the skipjacks, which are the only sailing craft in North America still used for commercial fishing, is entirely the result of a state law dating from 1865. Oyster dredging had been introduced to Chesapeake Bay by New Englanders about 1800, but the practice was soon outlawed on the grounds that the dredges tore up the oyster beds. Many oyster beds, however, were too deep for traditional hand tongs, so in 1865 oyster dredging (or "drudging," as local usage has it) was again permitted, but only in deep water and from boats without motors. This was considered a compromise, but the new law set off a virtual gold rush as large fleets of sail-powered dredge boats were built.

Over the course of the following century, oyster harvests that at first were immense gradually became so relatively meager that in 1967 the law was amended to allow dredging on Monday and Tuesday while powered by an auxiliary "yawl" or pushboat, which is nothing more than a small skiff equipped with a large inboard motor, usually a converted automobile engine. Cinched into place with its bow wedged against a bracket at the stern of the skipjack, the yawl propels its mother vessel from behind, like a little tugboat. When not in use, the yawl is suspended like a lifeboat from davits at the skipjack's stern. Because of the vagaries of wind, the skipjack captains have come to depend heavily on the two days of power dredging allowed them each week, but even so their catches never approach the daily limit of 150 bushels, and are often merely 25 or 30 bushels. A yawl may also be used at any time to push its skipjack from port to open water and back, provided the dredge is not overboard.

This somewhat bizarre system of restrictions and exceptions is intended as a conservation measure, not only to protect the depleted oyster beds from utter ruin by more efficient motorized dredgers, but also to preserve the skipjacks themselves, for which the captains and most Marylanders have a certain attachment. Ever since the law was changed to permit skipjacks to dredge under power on Monday and Tuesday, there has been talk of allowing conventional motorized workboats to dredge also, subject to daily catch limits. But except for the opening of one small area near Smith Island to motorized dredgers, the law has not been liberalized further, in recognition of the fact that the skipjacks would be abandoned immediately if they did not retain their virtual monopoly on oyster dredging in Maryland waters.

Despite their favored status, however, the skipjacks are an endangered species. Most are old. They are, of course, expensive to maintain, and in recent years they have been only marginally profitable. As a result of pollution, poor reproduction, oyster disease, and a history of over-harvesting, the annual oyster crop in Maryland's portion of Chesapeake Bay fell below 1 million bushels for the first time during the 1986/87 season. As of the 1990/91 season, the oyster harvest had still failed to recover and was, in fact, below half a million bushels. There has even been talk of a moratorium on oystering.

In the 1880s, when the Chesapeake oyster fishery was at its peak of prosperity, 2,576 dredge boats were licensed on the bay, and these craft were not mere skipjack but typically larger, two-masted, beamy bugeyes. Cheaper to build than bugeyes, skipjacks did not appear until oyster harvests began to decline in the 1890s, after the gross overharvesting of the previous decade, when 15 million bushels were dredged up annually. During the early twentieth century, nearly a thousand skipjacks were in operation, but as of January 1992, only fifteen or so skipjacks were still used as working boats during the oyster season, which for dredgers lasts from November through March. During summer a few skipjacks are operated as tourist boats, and others are maintained as pleasure craft.

Apart from dredging, there are others ways to harvest oysters, and the most time-honored among these is tonging, a practice dating back to the mid-1600s. Hand tongs (also called shaft tongs) consist of a pair of long rakes with handles 12 to 30 feet long, hinged together like scissors a quarter of the overall length above the iron tines. After anchoring above a shallow oyster bed (or "rock," as the beds are called) and lowering the tongs over the side of his boat, the tonger pulls the handles apart and pushes them together so as to open and shut the tines resting on the oyster bed. When the tonger feels a number of oysters clamped between the tines, he raises the tongs into the boat hand over hand — or perhaps hand *under* hand would be more accurate — and empties the catch onto his culling board, where he picks over the oysters and throws out those that are undersize. Done for hours on end, the work is very strenuous, so some tongers now tie a cord to the tines and attach the other end to a power-winder that helps them to pull up the tongs.

Another form of tonging uses patent tongs, in which iron jaws without any long wooden shafts attached are suspended by a cable from a derrick-like mast and boom; the jaws are raised and lowered by a power winch. Obviously, patent tongs enable an oysterman to work in deeper water than do shaft tongs. A variation on patent tongs are hydraulic tongs, in which the jaws are opened and closed by hydraulic power. A full-fledged hydraulic rig consists of two sets of jaws, one on each side of the boat, and each suspended from its own boom.

Because shaft tongers can operate only in shallow water where their tongs reach the bottom, oyster dredging has long been prohibited in Maryland on rivers (such as the Chester, Choptank, and Potomac) where most shallow oyster rocks are located. This restriction has never sat well with Maryland's dredgers, and starting in the late 1860s, some dredgers organized poaching fleets that from time to time invaded the tongers' rocks. Soon tongers and dredgers were shooting at each other. During some particularly violent seasons, deaths were not uncommon. Often the dredgers engaged in all-out attacks on the tongers, ramming their small boats and driving them off. In some places, the tongers built forts armed with a few cannons on shore near the oyster rocks or at the river mouths, but these deterrents failed, as the dredge fleets slipped in at night or even seized the forts and carried off the guns.

Such lawlessness is scarcely believable today, but for poachers (who were said by most dredgers to be a minority) defiance of the law meant huge profits, especially after oyster catches from the open bay began to decline because of overharvesting. Self-righteous and willful, the dredge boat captains regarded the law as unwarranted and meddlesome interference with their traditional, God-given right to make a living on the water as they saw fit. Besides, during the oyster boom of the 1870s and '80s, the dredgers — who altogether accounted for the vast bulk of the oyster harvest — were economically and politically powerful, whereas the tongers, although more numerous, were poor folk and of relatively little account.

In 1868 Maryland's General Assembly created the Oyster Navy, precursor of the present-day Natural Resources Police, but for decades the small and underfunded Oyster Navy had little effect on the poachers, who simply sailed off when a police vessel was spotted. Often one dredge boat was stationed as a sentinel at a river mouth. Using lights or flags at the mast top, the sentinel signaled to the fleet of poachers when a police boat approached. Since the sentinel boat could not itself dredge, the other boats each contributed to it a set number of bushels of oysters.

Some hardened poachers (termed *oyster pirates* in their day) even took to shooting at the police, and there were occasions when the police refused to interfere with poachers because of fear of gunfire, or were even beaten or kidnapped by poachers, whose idea of a joke was to make the police work as crews on the dredge boats for a few days. In 1888, however, the police steamer *McLane* scored a notable success when it rammed and sank two poaching dredge boats and captured two more during a nighttime battle on the Chester River. Eastern Bay was soon subdued also. But on the Choptank and Potomac rivers, violence continued through the 1890s and into the twentieth century until gradually, as the oyster economy declined and the dredge fleets shrank, poachers simply became clandestine pilferers.

During the last three decades of the nineteenth century, some dredge boat captains operated outside the law in other ways also. At that time the crews included four men on each of the two hand-powered windlasses that were used to pull in the dredges. But these large crews were difficult to come by because the work was hard and living conditions on board the boats were poor. Blacks who at first did this work soon refused to sign on as crews because of the hardships, and so skippers turned to using immigrant laborers, mainly Irish, Germans, and some Italians, whom the captains indiscriminately termed Paddies. Agents in New York engaged these immigrants straight off the boat at Ellis Island by promising them jobs, ample food, and good pay. Most received tolerable treatment, as measured by the somewhat harsh standards of the time, but some were exploited mercilessly. Once underway, these hapless men were worked relentlessly all winter, despite common occupational maladies, such as lacerated and infected hands. For the entire season the crew might be kept on the boats and often even locked up at night to prevent their escaping. Many were subjected to a "company-store" system of charges by which they were said to be indebted to the skippers for the clothing, boots, food, and tobacco issued to them at exorbitant prices. Men who finally refused to work were beaten or put ashore in remote places without pay, and a few were even shot on the slightest provocation, afterward said to have constituted mutiny. Sometimes, especially as unpaid wages accumulated, men were murdered in a manner made to look like an accident — as by being knocked overboard by the boom, in which case the victim was said to have been "paid off with the boom."

It is hard to know how often such abuses occurred, but they were common enough so that eventually the Hiberian (or Irish) Society and German Society posted placards in the waterfront districts of New York, Philadelphia, and Baltimore warning their compatriots away from the dredge boats. In response, crimps — people whose business it is to lure or entrap men into shipping as sailors — resorted to shanghai methods, and victims were delivered to the dredge boat captains in a drunken stupor. In 1886 a federal marshal and his deputies destroyed several "Paddy shacks" on Hoopers Island, where crewmen, presumably by then sobered up and wanting to leave, were imprisoned before being distributed to the boats. In 1908 the federal Shanghaiing Act was passed, but by then systematic abuse was waning. The development of

161

small gasoline engines for winding in the heavy dredges greatly reduced the need for laborers, as did also the decline in the number of dredge boats themselves.

Every once in awhile, however, present-day allegations of abuses echo the past. For example, in July 1991, the American Civil Liberties Union of Maryland, acting of behalf of fifteen Mexican crab pickers, filed a suit in U.S. District Court in Baltimore describing a system of virtual peonage at a packing house in an Eastern Shore fishing town. Named as defendants, the owners of the packing house were said to have held the workers in a sort of bondage at a one-bedroom house by confiscating their passports, visas, and work permits and threatening to tear up these documents if the workers broke the company rules, which included a prohibition on leaving the house without permission or talking to local residents. The Mexicans were said to have been paid $15 each for a workweek of fifty hours on the night shift, after their boss charged them for food and rent. Since the time this suit was filed, at least one other, similar case has been brought against another Eastern Shore seafood packer.

AUTOMOBILE DIRECTIONS: Princess Anne is located on Route 13 about 14 miles south of Salisbury. (See Map 1 in the Table of Contents.) The car tour to Deal Island, Dames Quarter Marsh, and Whitehaven shown on Map 26 starts just west of Princess Anne, so you should go there first.

To Princess Anne from northern Delmarva and Interstate 95 southwest of Wilmington: From Interstate 95 take Route 7 south, then follow the signs for Route 1 to Route 13 toward Dover. (Please note, however, that Route 7 will not be linked to Route 1 until the fall of 1992, so until then simply take Route 7 south to Route 13.) Once you are on Route 13 southbound, follow it down through Delaware and into Maryland. After passing east of Salisbury, continue south on Route 13 to the intersection with Route 363 (Deal Island Road) just west of the town of Princess Anne.

To Princess Anne from the Chesapeake Bay Bridge: After crossing the bridge, follow Route 50/301 across Kent Island. At the point where Route 50 and Route 301 split, fork right to follow Route 50 past Easton, Cambridge, and Salisbury. East of Salisbury, take Route 13 south toward Norfolk, but go only to the intersection with Route 363 (Deal Island Road) just west of the town of Princess Anne.

MAP 26 -- Car tour of northwestern Somerset County

To Princess Anne from southern Delmarva and the Chesapeake Bay Bridge-Tunnel at Norfolk: After crossing the bridge-tunnel, follow Route 13 north into Maryland and past Pocomoke City to the intersection with Route 363 (Deal Island Road) just west of the town of Princess Anne.

To Princess Anne from Salisbury and the Delaware and Maryland seashore resorts: From the vicinity of Salisbury, follow Route 13 south to the intersection with Route 363 (Deal Island Road) just west of the town of Princess Anne.

From the vicinity of Rehoboth Beach, follow Route 1 north to the intersection with Route 9 westbound, then take Route 9 west through Georgetown and across Route 113 to Route 13 southbound. Alternatively, from the vicinity of Ocean City, follow Route 50 west to Route 13 southbound. In either case, once you are on Route 13, follow it south around Salisbury to the intersection with Route 363 (Deal Island Road) just west of the town of Princess Anne.

CAR TOUR OF NORTHWESTERN SOMERSET COUNTY: The bold line on Map 26 shows the route of this 60-mile car tour, which leads first to Deal Island.

From the intersection of Route 13 and Route 363 just outside Princess Anne, follow Route 363 west 14.3 miles to and across the high bridge leading to Deal Island. Continue 3.6 miles on the main road as it twists and turns through the town of **Deal Island** to the end of the road in the village of **Wenona**, where, as at many other fishing towns of the Eastern Shore, packing houses are being replaced by vacation town houses and workboats by pleasure craft. On the outskirts of the town of Deal Island is St. Johns United Methodist Church, and behind it are the **grave of Joshua Thomas and a small chapel** built toward the end of his life.

Return from Deal Island the way you came. From the high bridge, follow Route 363 east 5.1 miles to a dirt and asphalt road on the right, marked by a wooden sign saying (among other things) "Deal Island — Maryland Department of Natural Resources." Turn sharply right onto this road and follow it (slowly) 1.4 miles to a boat ramp. Park in the small lot overlooking Dames Quarter Marsh, which is shown on Map 27. You are at point A near the center of the map.

MAP 27 -- Walking at Dames Quarter Marsh

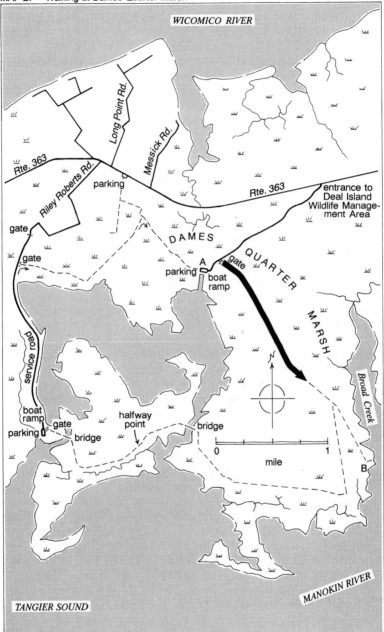

The marshy peninsula of **Dames Quarter** was formerly called Damned Quarter (as it appears on early maps), perhaps because it lies adjacent to Devil's Island, now Deal Island.

During the colder months, large congregations of waterfowl frequently are visible from the service road shown at the western (left) edge of Map 27. However, the service road, which is reached via Riley Roberts Road off Route 363, is sometimes closed to vehicles. If you wish to watch waterfowl from your car, you can drive to Riley Roberts Road and take your chances at finding the service road open (as it usually is). Or you can simply walk to the service road by heading west 2 miles from point A on the map. Yet another alternative for walking — one that I recommend — is described below.

WALKING AT DAMES QUARTER MARSH: First, bear in mind that much of this vast marsh is a public hunting area where shooting for waterfowl is permitted occasionally during fall and winter. For more precise information about specified hunting days, call the Maryland Department of Natural Resources at (410) 651-2320. If hunting is underway, you are likely to know it from the coming and going of the hunters and the popping of their guns in the distance. For your own safety and in order to show courtesy to the hunters, you should stay off the marsh's trails when hunting is underway. But even during the hunting season, you can have the marsh virtually to yourself if you go on a Sunday, when hunting is prohibited.

The bold line on Map 27 shows the start of a walk that leads either to the water's edge at **Broad Creek** (Point B; 5 miles round-trip) or in a **circuit around the entire impoundment** (10 miles). Of course, before reaching the halfway point (which is shown on the map) you can turn back for a shorter excursion. The best time of year for a walk here is late fall, winter, and early spring, when heat and mosquitoes are not a problem and when waterfowl are abundant.

Start at the parking lot by the boat ramp (point A) and follow the road for 350 yards back toward Route 363, then turn right past a gate onto a rutted dirt track. Follow this rutted road south across the marsh. Be alert for holes or places where the dike is eroded. After about 1.7 miles (and just before a slight bend in the road) there is an opportunity to turn right between two posts onto a less worn track. By turning here, it is possible to follow the dike nearly a mile south, then 3 miles west to a parking lot at the end of the dirt service road. From there, follow the service road north 1.5 miles; walk on the left facing the oncoming traffic in order to minimize the risk of being hit by a car approaching from behind. At the first opportunity, turn right onto another dike path marked by a steel gate and two wooden posts. Follow the dike 2 miles as it zigzags across the marsh; turn right at the only trail intersection in order to return to your starting point.

CAR TOUR (Map 26 — from Dames Quarter Marsh to Whitehaven): To continue on the car tour, return to Route 363 and follow it east 2.2 miles to the town of Monie (or at least, a sign announcing Monie), then turn left onto Fitzgerald Road. Follow Fitzgerald Road 2.6 miles, then turn left at a T-intersection. Go 0.8 mile, then bear right onto Black Road. Follow Black Road 2.2 miles to a T-intersection with Route 362, and there turn left and go 2.2 miles. Where Route 362 curves left, continue straight toward the Whitehaven Ferry on Fitzbounds Road. Go 2.2 miles to the ferry, which operates year-round and is free of charge. Now a rarity, such cable-guided ferries were once far more numerous on the tidal rivers of the Eastern Shore. After crossing the Wicomico River, turn left to explore the village of Whitehaven.

Whitehaven, located on the Wicomico County (or north) side of the Wicomico River, was named for a port on the Cumberland coast of northwest England, from which came Colonel George Gale, leader of a group of settlers in 1701. Gale's three ships traded regularly between England and Maryland. Just south of the Wicomico River is Monie Creek, site of Gale's plantation called Tusculum, where he lived and is buried. Gale's first wife, incidentally, was the widowed Mildred Warner Washington, whose children included Augustine Washington, the father of George Washington. During the steamboat era, Whitehaven was an oyster landing and stop for boats plying between Salisbury and Baltimore. The village had its own fishing fleet, packing houses, a substantial shipyard, a hotel, and several popular saloons.

CAR TOUR (Map 26 — from Whitehaven to Princess Anne): From Whitehaven take the ferry back across the river and return 1.5 miles to the intersection with Fitzbounds and Polks roads. Turn left and follow Polks Road 5.0 miles to a T-intersection. Turn right and go 0.8 mile to and across Route 13, then continue on Route 529 for 2.5 miles. At a stop sign, merge with the main road leading into Princess Anne and continue to the center of town.

Princess Anne, the seat of Somerset County, is named not for Queen Anne (who reigned from 1702 to 1707 and was the namesake of Queen Anne's County and of Annapolis) but rather for the daughter of King George II, the monarch when the town was founded in 1733.

As first established, the town of Princess Anne was a local port at the head of the Manokin River, which is now unnavigable because of sedimentation. Some aspects of life in Princess Anne during the 1830s and '40s are described in *The Entailed Hat*, a novel published in 1884 by George Alfred Townshend (or GATH, as he called himself). Today the town is, as ever, a rather still place where business focuses mainly on agriculture, lumber, poultry, and regional services. In addition to the various agencies of county government, the University of Maryland, Eastern Shore is located here, and nearby is the Eastern Shore Correctional Facility.

The town's Federal and Victorian houses give Princess Anne's residential streets a predominantly nineteenth-century appearance, but a few structures are older, and it is these that are most often open to the public. The **Manokin Presbyterian Church**, located on the main road (called Somerset Avenue or Alternate Route 13) two blocks north of Princess Anne's business district, has walls built in 1765; other features are more recent. The parish was organized by the Reverend Francis Makemie in 1683, and a church was built on this site by 1692. The **Washington Hotel** in the center of town was built in 1744. Its bar and old, beamed dining room are a favorite local gathering place, especially on Friday evening and on Saturday. A formal **boxwood garden**, thought to have been laid out by General George Handy in the first half of the nineteenth century, occupies the corner of Somerset Avenue and Washington Street one block south of the 1904 **courthouse**. The **Teackle Mansion**, located on Prince William Street three blocks west of the courthouse, was built in 1801 by Littleton Teackle, Princess Anne's leading citizen and first banker (and ultimately a bankrupt). The mansion is modeled after a Scottish manor house and shows a rigorous and imposing symmetry, at least on the outside and in the central drawing room. **St. Andrew's Episcopal Church** is on Church Street one block south of Prince William Street. Its walls date from about 1770; the interior was remodeled in the nineteenth century.

CAR TOUR (Map 26 — from Princess Anne back to your starting point on Route 13): From the courthouse at the corner of Prince William Street and Somerset Avenue, follow Prince William Street west to the Teackle Mansion, and there turn right onto Mansion Street, then left onto Route 363. Go 0.1 mile to the intersection with Route 13.

SMITH ISLAND
JANES ISLAND STATE PARK

Smith Island, which actually is a cluster of several islands 10 miles west of Crisfield, Maryland, lies about as low in the water as an inhabited place can be. From a distance, the trees and houses of its three villages — Ewell, Rhodes Point, and Tylerton — appear to rise directly out of Chesapeake Bay, and, in fact, some streets and yards are often awash. Even from the vantage point of the island itself, dry land is a relatively minor component of the landscape, which consists overwhelmingly of tidal salt marsh, sky, and water. Although Smith Island has a couple of miles of open road linking Ewell and Rhodes Point, the island's many channels are its main streets, and boats are far more numerous than cars. The waterfront villages consist of narrow lanes bordered by frame houses and a few larger community structures, such as fire houses, churches, recreation halls, and elementary schools. For high school, the students commute daily to Crisfield via school boat.

A visit to Smith Island combines a pleasant excursion by passenger boat, perhaps a seafood lunch, and a chance to explore the island's villages, home to generations of watermen. Passenger boats to Smith Island operate daily, leaving Crisfield at 12:30 P.M. and returning late in the afternoon. Because there are several boats to choose from, please see the discussion starting on page 177 for more precise information. Also, I recommend that you bring a bicycle for touring the island, as discussed starting on page 178.

Just outside Crisfield immediately adjacent to the mainland is Janes Island State Park, where there are miles of narrow, wild beach fronting Tangier Sound. The park is open daily from 8 A.M. to sunset. The trick, however, is getting to the island, which is separated from the mainland by a narrow channel. If you will be relying on the pontoon ferry that sometimes operates during summer, always call beforehand to make sure that it will in fact be running on the day that you plan to be there. Because of budget constraints, the ferry often does not operate, in which case you may be able to rent a canoe. Or you can use your own boat or canoe to reach the island at any time of year. (Strong winds, however, can sometimes make canoeing difficult, even in the narrow, protected channel leading to the island.) The park, which also has a campground and rental cabins, is managed by the Maryland Park Service. Pets are altogether prohibited. Telephone (410) 968-1565.

ALTHOUGH THE CHESAPEAKE REGION was settled starting early in the seventeenth century, not until the middle of the nineteenth century did industrialization and rapid urban growth in the northern states, plus improved transportation by steamboat and rail, create major markets for all that the bay could be made to yield. Among the most productive areas for seafood since then has been Tangier Sound, where the watermen of Smith Island and other nearby communities have harvested (and in some instances, grossly overharvested) immense quantities of fish, eels, terrapin, oysters, clams, crabs, and waterfowl during the last century and a half, sometimes specializing in certain activities, such as catching and shedding soft crabs (as do Smith Islanders today) or switching from one animal crop to another, depending on what is most abundant or profitable.

Despite a historic pattern of large fluctuations in crab catches from one year to the next, and a steady decline in oyster harvests, the main way of making a living on Smith Island remains crabbing from late spring through early autumn and oystering during fall and winter. To earn a good income, the watermen must go out every day that the weather permits, usually beginning an hour or two before dawn and staying out until early afternoon, six days a week. To maximize their individual profit, many men work alone, lifting oysters off the bottom with tongs, or pulling up, emptying, and rebaiting several hundred wire-mesh crab pots, or hauling in and repeatedly emptying a crab scrape (which is nothing more than a lightweight dredge with a steel frame and twine bag pulled from a shallow-draft boat). For people who do not like the physical labor, perseverance, exposure to the weather, and long hours that this manner of life requires, or the unpredictable income that it provides, there is little alternative on the island, and so they move to the mainland, leaving behind those who, perhaps more tenacious and mindful of tradition, prefer to work the water or to raise a family on the island, as did their ancestors. As one elderly waterman told Francis W. Dize, author of *Smith Island, Chesapeake Bay*, "God gave us this island. He brought us here. He took care of our granddaddies and showed 'em how to use the water and the creatures in it, and this is where we belong."

Residents of Smith Island scoff, or even take offense, at some accounts in newspapers and magazines that have portrayed their way of life as "quaint" or "old-fashioned." After all, they say, don't their villages have sewers, electricity, and running water; don't their homes, or at least those of the younger folk, have all the usual household appliances; don't they watch the same television shows as the rest of America; don't they often shop and sometimes take vacations on the mainland like anyone else; don't their women follow the fashions; and don't their teenagers like rock music? And if their cars sometimes are rattletraps, that is because it does not make much sense to bring a new car to the island, where there are only two miles of road. The place for a good car is on the mainland, and most island families keep one there.

Certainly it is true that the island is not quaint in the sense of being artificially preserved or prettified. Its great visual interest is provided by the ongoing business of making a living from Chesapeake Bay. Along the waterfront, the paraphernalia and cast-off scrap of commercial crabbing and oystering are everywhere. Lining the island's channels are the watermen's spindly docks, cluttered packing shanties, and crab floats — long, table-like rows of shallow basins through which bay water is constantly circulated by pumps. Because soft crabs fetch a far higher price than hard ones, many of the islanders keep the crabs they catch — or sell them to someone else who will keep them — until the crustaceans molt. First the crabs are sorted according to their stage in shedding their hard shells, then placed in the floats. From early morning until late evening during the summer shedding season, the crabs are periodically inspected and transferred from one basin to the next as they approach molting, when they are pulled out and packed alive on beds of eel grass and ice in waxed cardboard cartons. Smith Island and some of the other fishing communities of Tangier Sound supply the market with tens of millions of soft crabs annually.

Although the main role of island women is that of homemakers, much of the work of sorting, shedding, and packing crabs is done by housewives, either together with their husbands when the catch is brought in, or while the men are out in their boats. Nearly every household is in business for itself, and family members help out in whatever way is necessary to make the family business go.

In addition to their specialized line of work, Smith Islanders show a remarkable homogeneity in other respects also. Nearly all are of English descent, and the majority share just four surnames — Tyler, Evans, Bradshaw, and Marshall — that go back hundreds of years on the island, which was settled in the second half of the seventeenth century.

173

In addition, ever since the Great Revival swept the Eastern Shore at the beginning of the nineteenth century, virtually all the residents of Smith Island have adhered to a fervent Methodism, which provides the community with a touchstone of shared values and mutual support.

Methodism is more than a source of moral guidance and religious inspiration within this tightly knit community. The island's three churches are also the center of community life. The week-long camp meeting each July is not only a time of religious rededication but also the year's chief social event, when friends and family members who have left the island return for a visit. Christmas week too is a time of daily church-related programs, including dances.

The churches are also the center of local government, although strictly speaking, there is no government here below the county level — no mayors or town councils. Instead, it is through the Methodist churches that most community projects on the island are conceived and supported, including streetlights, water supply, medical services, maintenance of public buildings and grounds, and other traditional municipal services. (There are no police, however, because crime is almost nonexistent.) Door-to-door collections sponsored by each village's church are the principal form of "taxation," which is sometimes problematic because of the perception that not everybody contributes a fair share. And apart from money raised for local projects are the occasional special collections to help families who have suffered a death or a fire or some other misfortune.

Some visitors who have written about Smith Island speculate that the central role of religion in island life in part derives from the fact that the watermen rely so heavily on the bounty of nature or even on the mercy of nature. "Government won't save you from that big wave, won't make more crabs," the island's minister told Tom Horton, author of *Bay Country*. Horton quotes another islander as saying, "You've got to be thankful to someone. In the water business we never plant anything. We just harvest. Oysters, crabs, fish . . . it is just reap, steady reap. But you know, somebody's got to be doing some planting . . . there's got to be some system to it all somewhere."

To some extent, however, Smith Island's single-minded pursuit of oysters, crabs, and fish is changing. Since the 1920s, when the island had about 800 residents, the population has declined to less than 500 as increasing numbers of young people have left and as older folk have died. In recent years, there has been an influx of part-time residents — retirees and owners of vacation homes — who, together with tourists, represent an increasingly important element in the island's economy.

Although the excursion outlined in this chapter concentrates on

Smith Island, it may also be appropriate to say a few words about Crisfield, the principal mainland town of Tangier Sound and the port from which the boats to Smith Island run. Most watermen in the vicinity of Tangier Sound send their catch of crabs, oysters, and fish to Crisfield for processing or transshipment, and yet even so the town is only a shadow of what it was a hundred years ago.

Previously called Annemessex and then Somers Cove, Crisfield was renamed in honor of John W. Crisfield, chief promoter and president of the Eastern Shore Railroad, which reached Crisfield in 1868. Arrival of the railroad ushered in an era of great prosperity and growth as scores of packing houses sprang up at Crisfield to handle the oysters that were brought ashore there, canned, and shipped throughout the country. Extraordinary hauls of oysters during the 1870s and '80s, when the bay's oyster beds were virtually strip mined by large dredge fleets, enabled the southern end of Crisfield, where the municipal wharf is located, to expand on a foundation of oyster shells into what was once marsh and water. By 1872 Crisfield was the center of the largest oyster trade in Maryland and was served by over six hundred sailing vessels harvesting several million bushels of oysters annually. Twenty to thirty railroad cars loaded with oysters left the town daily. The port was also served by three steamboats daily. After machines for making ice were invented, the harvesting, picking, and shipping of highly perishable crabs became another major industry.

In Crisfield's boomtown atmosphere, lowlife flourished. Saloons and brothels sprang up, and in some establishments and in some streets, brawling was common. In 1875 the town commissioners voted Crisfield dry in order to curb drunken lawlessness, and in response speakeasies proliferated.

The decline in oyster catches during the twentieth century, however, has led to a corresponding falling off of seafood processing at Crisfield. Even as early as the 1890s, packing houses and shucking operations started closing, as did burlesque houses and bars. The railroad into Crisfield was torn out in the late 1950s. (The tracks ran parallel to Route 413, where there are still a few old grain elevators and other structures left over from the railroad.) Somers Cove, formerly the site of many packing houses, was redeveloped as a yacht basin for pleasure boats starting in the 1960s.

Every Labor Day weekend, Crisfield holds its famous National Hard Crab Derby and Fair at Somers Cove. Also located at Somers Cove is the J. Millard Tawes Visitor Center and Museum, where the exhibits document the life of the governor from Crisfield, plus the history of the area's fisheries. For information about tourist events in Crisfield, call the visitor center at (410) 968-2500.

AUTOMOBILE DIRECTIONS: Smith Island lies in Chesapeake Bay on the state line between Maryland and Virginia — although all of the island's three villages are in Maryland. (See Map 1 in the Table of Contents.) The island is reached by commercial passenger boats from Crisfield, which is located about 40 miles south-southwest of Salisbury. And just north of Crisfield is Janes Island State Park (discussed starting on page 180).

During summer a tourist boat runs to Smith Island from Point Lookout, Maryland, located at the mouth of the Potomac River; telephone (410) 425-2771 for information. The instructions below, however, take you to Crisfield, where there is year-round boat service to Smith Island.

To Crisfield from northern Delmarva and Interstate 95 southwest of Wilmington: From Interstate 95 take Route 7 south, then follow the signs for Route 1 to Route 13 toward Dover. (Please note, however, that Route 7 will not be linked to Route 1 until the fall of 1992, so until then simply take Route 7 south to Route 13.) Once you are on Route 13 southbound, follow it down through Delaware and into Maryland. After passing east of Salisbury and west of Princess Anne, turn right onto Route 413 toward Crisfield and go 14.6 miles to the end of the road at Crisfield's municipal dock.

To Crisfield from the Chesapeake Bay Bridge: After crossing the bridge, follow Route 50/301 across Kent Island. At the point where Route 50 and Route 301 split, fork right to follow Route 50 past Easton, Cambridge, and Salisbury. East of Salisbury, take Route 13 south toward Norfolk. Follow Route 13 past Princess Anne to the junction with Route 413, and there turn right toward Crisfield. Follow Route 413 for 14.6 miles to the end of the road at Crisfield's municipal dock.

To Crisfield from southern Delmarva and the Chesapeake Bay Bridge-Tunnel at Norfolk: After crossing the bridge-tunnel, follow Route 13 north into Maryland. From the intersection with Route 113 near Pocomoke City, continue straight on Route 13 for 3.8 miles to the intersection with Route 667 west toward Crisfield. Turn left onto Route 667 and follow it 11.5 miles to an intersection with Route 413. Turn left onto Route 413 and follow it 6.0 miles to the end of the road at Crisfield's municipal dock.

To Crisfield from Salisbury and the Delaware and Maryland seashore resorts: From the vicinity of Salisbury, follow Route 13 south past Princess Anne to the junction with Route 413, and there turn right toward Crisfield. Follow Route 413 for 14.6 miles to the end of the road at Crisfield's municipal dock.

From the vicinity of Rehoboth Beach, follow Route 1 north to the intersection with Route 9 westbound, then take Route 9 west through Georgetown and across Route 113 to Route 13 southbound. Alternatively, from the vicinity of Ocean City, follow Route 50 west to Route 13 southbound. In either case, once you are on Route 13, follow it south around Salisbury and past Princess Anne to the junction with Route 413, and there turn right toward Crisfield. Follow Route 413 for 14.6 miles to the end of the road at Crisfield's municipal dock.

BOATS TO SMITH ISLAND: There are several different passenger boats from Crisfield to the island. Most of them leave from the municipal dock, and of these the largest and fastest is the *Island Princess*, which goes to Ewell, the island's main town. To make a reservation on the *Island Princess* (recommended on weekends in summer), telephone Captain Otis Tyler at (410) 968-3206 or the Harborside Restaurant at (410) 425-2201. During winter, when there is less traffic, the *Island Princess* is sometimes replaced by the smaller *Island Belle II*.

Other boats also depart from the municipal dock for Ewell and Tylerton; simply ask the captains which boat goes where, what the fare is, and where you should park your car. The boats to Ewell offer more scope for exploration, since Ewell is connected by road to the village of Rhodes Point. Tylerton, which is on a separate island within the Smith Island archipelago, is very small, which is both its special charm and its limitation. You may want to inquire if one of the the smaller boats to Ewell plans to stop at Tylerton on the way back to Crisfield, as is sometimes done.

The boats that run from the Crisfield municipal dock to Smith Island operate daily year-round, except during stormy weather or when ice obstructs the channel. They leave Crisfield at 12:30 P.M. and depart Smith Island at 4:00. Be sure, however, to ask your captain what time he plans to leave Smith Island, since actual times of departure may vary somewhat depending on the demands of the day. The trip takes about 45 minutes each way.

There is also a large excursion boat (the *Captain Tyler II*) that runs between Somers Cove Marina in Crisfield and Ewell on Smith Island from Memorial Day weekend through October. There are, however, several disadvantages to the *Captain Tyler II*. Unlike the boats that run from Crisfield's municipal dock (and which are used by the islanders themselves), the *Captain Tyler II* is exclusively a large-scale tourist operation; it is more expensive; and it is a half-hour slower, leaving less time to explore the island. The *Captain Tyler II* departs from Somers Cove at 12:30 P.M., arrives at Ewell at 1:45, departs Ewell at 4:00, and arrives at Crisfield at 5:15. Somers Cove Marina can be reached via Seventh Street off Route 413 (Main Street) 0.3 mile inland from Crisfield's municipal dock. Tickets can be purchased ahead of time at the Paddlewheel Motel at the corner of Main Street and Seventh Street. Always call (410) 425-2771 beforehand to make a reservation. During exceptionally stormy weather or on weekdays late in October, the excursion boat may not run.

During summer and early fall, all of the Smith Island boat companies provide their passengers with a free tour of the island via school bus. Tell your captain if you are interested.

The boat operators also, of course, hope that you will eat at restaurants on the island with which they are affiliated, but there is no obligation to do so. In any case, their restaurants are open only during the tourist season. The *Island Princess* docks at the Harborside Restaurant, patronized by a mixture of islanders and tourists seated in the conventional manner at tables of different sizes, so usually you can have your own table. The other boats dock opposite the Bayside Inn, which caters exclusively to tourists seated together at uniformly large tables. At both restaurants, you may order a huge family-style meal or just a few items.

TOURING SMITH ISLAND: Map 28 shows the island and the three villages of Ewell, Rhodes Point (these two are linked by road), and Tylerton.

I have an opinion on how best to see the island, but it assumes that you would prefer to spend the few hours that you have there looking around on foot or on bicycle rather than eating a big meal at one of the restaurants. There probably isn't time for both, and after all, you can always have a leisurely seafood dinner back in Crisfield after your trip.

Take one of the boats that leave from Crisfield's municipal

MAP 28 -- Smith Island

MARTIN NATIONAL WILDLIFE REFUGE

Big Thorofare

Caleb Jones Rd.

Tyler Rd.

Smith Island Rd.

Somers Rd.

Ewell

Tyler Ditch

Big

Thorofare

SMITH

Rhodes Point

ISLAND

Tylerton

Tyler Creek

MD
VA

Shanks Creek

MD
VA

CHESAPEAKE BAY

TANGIER SOUND

0   mile   1

dock (I recommend the *Island Princess*). If you have a bicycle, by all means bring it along — for which there may be a small charge. After a quick crab sandwich at one of the island's restaurants (bring your own lunch October through May), spend your time exploring Ewell and Rhodes Point on foot or by bicycle, which necessarily involves hiking or biking back and forth (2 miles each way) between the two villages. You will see far more this way than you would from the bus. If you are walking, be alert for cars; walk on the left shoulder, facing the oncoming vehicles. There is a fair amount of traffic on this road, but drivers are used to sharing the road with pedestrians and bicyclists.

Finally, if you want to stay on Smith Island overnight, call the Smith Island Motel for information: (410) 425-4441 or (410) 425-3321. The motel is open year-round.

FROM CRISFIELD TO JANES ISLAND STATE PARK: While you are in the vicinity of Crisfield, you may want to visit the nearby Janes Island State Park.

As shown by the bold line on Map 29, follow Main Street (Route 413) away from the Crisfield municipal dock for 1.3 miles, then turn left onto Route 358. For 1.1 miles, follow the twisty road, then turn left at a large sign for Janes Island State Park. After passing the park office, go less than 0.1 mile, then turn left for Camping Area A and the boat launching ramp.

JANES ISLAND STATE PARK: The park has two distinct areas. The mainland portion (called the Hodson Area) is developed with a launching ramp, picnic grounds, camping sites, and a few rental cabins. Across the Annemessex Canal from the Hodson Area is Janes Island itself, undeveloped and consisting almost wholly of marsh bordered by a narrow ribbon of wild beach that extends for miles along the island's western shore. The island is a very attractive place, reachable only by boat. When there is enough money in the budget, the park staff operates a pontoon ferry from Memorial Day through Labor Day, leaving the Hodson Area dock every hour on the hour. It is also possible to rent skiffs and canoes May through September, but that is a rather pricey proposition if all you want to do is to navigate the mile-long channel (called Ward Creek) that leads from the mainland launching ramp to the dock behind Flat Cap Beach. Or you may use your own boat or canoe at any time of year.

MAP 29 -- Janes Island State Park

If you *do* have your own boat, the best time for a visit to the island is the off season, not only because there is less of a crowd then, but also because there are fewer biting insects. I have gone several times late in October and have found the water still warm enough for swimming, the jellyfish gone for the season, and no bugs. I also had the entire island to myself.

WALKING ON JANES ISLAND: Once you are on the island, it is possible to walk south along the shore 4 miles to the chimney and large rendering vats of an old fish factory at the island's lower end (see Map 29); however, doing so entails wading chest deep across the mouth of a small stream located at a point marked on the map. Clearly, this is something that you would only want to do during the swimming season (bring your suit) and if you are confident that you can handle the strong tidal current that you may find when you cross or recross the stream. Be conservative; only you know what the actual conditions are when you are there. Also, from Flat Cap Beach a shorter walk leads north to Rock Hole. Swimming is permitted from the beach, but there are no lifeguards, so extra caution is necessary. Finally, since there is no drinking water on the island, bring your own beverage, especially during hot weather.

13

TANGIER ISLAND

A visit to Tangier Island, which is located in Virginia's portion of Chesapeake Bay 12 miles southwest of Crisfield, Maryland, combines a pleasant cruise with a stopover at the village of Tangier, a centuries-old community of watermen. Tangier's harbor provides a quick education in the paraphernalia of commercial crabbing, oystering, and fishing. The main street is a one-lane road bordered by white frame houses, a half-dozen stores, and a few community structures, all tightly packed together. Good eating (crab cakes and oysters, of course) is found at several restaurants and good walking is had by following narrow lanes that lead from the main village across marsh and tidal channels to outlying clusters of houses.

An excursion boat operates daily (including Sunday) from May 15 through October, leaving Crisfield at 12:30 P.M., arriving at Tangier at 1:45, departing Tangier at 4:00, and arriving back at Crisfield at 5:15. Because of stormy weather or lack of passengers (especially on weekdays in October), the boat sometimes does not go, so always telephone Tangier Island Cruises beforehand: (410) 968-2338 or (804) 891-2240.

There are also excursion boats to Tangier Island that operate from Reedville, Virginia, located at the mouth of the Potomac River — call (804) 333-4656 for further information — and from Onancock, Virginia, on the Eastern Shore — telephone (804) 787-8220. The directions at the end of this chapter, however, assume that you are leaving from Crisfield, which provides the most frequent and reliable service to Tangier.

Because the various tour boats allow only a few hours at Tangier Island, you may want to stay overnight, which not only provides more time for leisurely and thorough exploration, but also enables you to see the island at periods when it is not jammed with other visitors. An overnight stay also provides time to hike along the long beach and sandy hook at the island's southern end. For lodgings, make a reservation at one of the following establishments: Located on the main north-south street, Chesapeake House is open April 15 through mid-October; telephone (804) 891-2331. As its name implies,

Chesapeake House is simply a house; its accommodations are plain but entirely adequate. There are no private bathrooms. In the realm of food, however, Chesapeake House is out of the ordinary — particularly its seafood lunches and dinners served family style at communal tables. On the western side of the island near the beach is Grace and Jim Brown's Sunset Inn, which is open year-round and provides all the usual amenities, including private baths, air-conditioning, cable TV, and even a light breakfast; telephone (804) 891-2535. If you plan to go during the colder half of the year, you may want to check first with the Browns to make sure that at least one of the island's sandwich shops will be open to provide you with lunch and dinner. Another number to call for overnight lodgings is (804) 891-2425; ask for Mrs. Dise.

For an overnight stay, you can take either the excursion boat mentioned above (going one day and returning the next day at 4:00 P.M.) or the mail boat that operates year-round Monday through Saturday, leaving Crisfield's municipal dock at 12:30 P.M. and Tangier at 8:00 A.M. During summer, the mail boat usually runs on Sunday also, although the times of departure may vary from other days of the week. Both the excursion boat from Crisfield and the mail boat are operated by the same company; if you plan to stay on Tangier Island overnight, let the people at the boat office know so that they can tell you about overnight parking and whether there is expected to be any difficulty with returning the next day.

IN 1608, the year after Jamestown was founded, Captain John Smith explored Chesapeake Bay and noted the existence of the string of islands that includes Tangier. Not until the end of the century, however, was Tangier settled by a few families from Cornwall, the region of maritime villages at the extreme southwest end of England. According to tradition, the first settler was John Crockett, who moved to Tangier Island with his sons and their families in 1686. In the early 1800s, nearly half of the island's one hundred residents were named Crockett. Even today most of the approximately 850 islanders still bear the surnames of a few early settlers: Crockett, Pruitt, Parks, Dize (or Dise), Evans, and Thomas. The local accent is still faintly reminiscent of the southwest of England, although for the most part the intervening three centuries have produced a unique accent and body of colloquialisms that are the islanders' own.

During the War of 1812, Tangier Island was used for more than a year by a British squadron as a base of operations for raids against bayshore towns and plantations. In particular, the island was the staging area for the attack on Baltimore in September, 1814 — an attack which was doomed to failure, as Joshua Thomas, the "Parson of the Islands," pointedly told the British beforehand. Thomas was a waterman and resident of Tangier who had been converted to Methodism at a camp meeting on the mainland in 1807. As an exhorter (or lay preacher), he had thereafter helped to spread Methodism throughout the islands of Tangier Sound, in part by organizing camp meetings held at the southern end of Tangier Island. Here, before the war (and afterwards too until the middle of the nineteenth century) thousands of people came annually by boat from the nearby islands and from the Chesapeake's Eastern and Western shores for a week of religious convocation and preaching by itinerant Methodist preachers.

> The place suddenly assumed an attractiveness and importance which belonged to no other mustering ground [wrote Thomas's biographer, the Reverend Adam Wallace].
> Even before the war, its fame had become wide spread, and its popularity as a place of resort for all classes of people established. But who can write its stirring history? who tell its tremendous moral results? — or enumerate the thousands who were born for glory there; and the tens of thousands who were edified, sanctified, and established in the faith of the gospel, as years rolled on, for full half a century, on the famous beach at Tangier?

On this same sandy spit the British camped and built two forts when they seized Tangier Island in the summer of 1813. For their forts they cut down most of the trees in the vicinity of the encampment, but at the request of Joshua Thomas they spared the prayer grove where the camp meetings were held. During the period of British occupation, Thomas was allowed to minister to those among the troops who wished to hold Methodist services. Apparently the officers were impressed by Thomas, for before the British embarked to attack Baltimore, "they sent me word to be ready to hold a public meeting, and exhort the soldiers, on the campground," as Thomas later recalled. But to the chagrin of the British officers, Thomas shouted at the assembled infantry that "I could not bid them God speed in what I understood they were going to do."

> I warned them of the danger and distress they would bring upon themselves and others by going to Baltimore with the object they had in view. I told them of the great wickedness of war, and that God said, *"Thou shalt not kill!"* If you do, he will judge you at the last day; or, before then, he will cause you to "perish by the sword."

187

> I told them it was given me from the Almighty that they *could not* take Baltimore, and *would not succeed in their expedition.*
>
> I exhorted them to prepare for death, for many of them would in all likelihood die soon, and I should see them no more till we met at the sound of the great trumpet before our final Judge.

With this disheartening send-off, the British embarked for Baltimore, where in the first few minutes of the first day of fighting, the commander of their land forces — Major General Robert Ross — was killed. After two days, the British gave up the attack, and when they returned to Tangier Island, some officers told Thomas that "all the time we were fighting *we thought of you,* and what you had told us. You seemed to be standing right before us, still warning us against our attempt to take Baltimore."

Such, at any rate, are Thomas's recollections, and he was by all accounts a scrupulously honest, sincere man. Because of ongoing erosion from waves, however, the site of the British encampment and of the Methodist camp meetings on Tangier Island is now under water. During the last century and a half, the sandy hook at the island's southern end has shrunk drastically and shifted eastward about half a mile, just as the entire island has diminished considerably since it was first settled.

Today Tangier Island — which actually is several islands, as shown on Map 30 — is only 3.5 miles long by 1.5 miles wide, and the habitable, or buildable, part is far smaller than that. Approximately 250 houses are clustered along three parallel "ridges," which, in fact, nowhere rise more than 7 feet above sea level. Flooding from storms and high tides is not uncommon, and hurricane-driven waves have sometimes inundated most of the island. There are about 3 miles of roadway — typically one-lane streets — used by pedestrians and bicyclists, plus a few cars and trucks and a larger number of golf carts, motorcycles, and motorbikes, on which the young men buzz around the island in the evening "scooping up" (or giving rides to) the girls. A small airport provides quick transport to and from the mainland in the event of medical emergency, and also is the means by which many recreational flyers and hunters stop by for a visit.

Most transport, of course, is by boat, as would be expected on a small island where the vast majority of male residents are watermen, making a living by crabbing, oystering, and fishing. In a November 1973 article for *National Geographic*, Harold G. Wheatley, at that time the principal of the Tangier Island School, said, "Boats hold the same place in our lives that automobiles do for mainlanders. You've just got to have one: skiffs for the little ones, outboards for the youths, and workcraft for the breadwinners. . . . The sea is our life, our highway,

MAP 30 -- Tangier Island

TANGIER SOUND

0   0.25   0.5
mile

main docks

Chesapeake House

airport

West Ridge

Big Gut Canal

Main Ridge

Canton Creek

Canton Ridge

TANGIER ISLAND

CHESAPEAKE BAY

our farm, our prison." This description is not much different than what another observer wrote in the middle of the nineteenth century: "The inhabitants of Smith's and Tangier Islands may almost be called an amphibious race, for nearly all the men and boys spend fully half their time if not *in* yet *on* the water."

Once a young man gets a workboat — probably a used one at first — he is set to embark on an independent career "following the water." As one boy told Wheatley, "This is a good place to live, and I like to work on the water. My father's been taking me with him since I was 10. I've been growed up with it. On the land it seems like you're always under somebody, but on the water you do as you please."

Of course, in actuality, doing as one pleases means doing as the seasons and the work require, not just when the prospects of daily profits are high, but even when they are low, for everyone acknowledges that the only way to make a success at this sort of life is to go at it day in and day out. During summer the watermen labor alone — or perhaps with a school-age son or hired hand — from 4 A.M. to early afternoon, tending as many as 400 crab pots made of anodized steel wire formed into rectilinear cages. During winter most watermen tong for oysters, again going out every day that they can, except Sundays. Virginia also allows winter dredging for crabs, which requires a bigger, more expensive boat than summertime crabbing. For crab dredging, the captains and their crews of two men are away from home for six days at a time, working sometimes in freezing temperatures to dredge up female crabs that migrate annually to the mouth of Chesapeake Bay, where they bury themselves at the bottom.

The existence of crews clearly indicates that not all watermen have the wherewithal or even the ambition to be their own boss. Even apart from high school students, some crew members are young men still unsettled about their path in life, and a few are people who, although they have worked on the water for many years, have through bad luck or improvidence or lack of perseverance failed to join the ranks of the better capitalized independent watermen.

Finally, in case you read earlier in Chapter 12 about Smith Island, it is important to note that Tangier Island is different in several major respects. For one thing, Tangier is governed by a major and town council, with all the usual powers of local government, making it a more cohesive, more organized, and yet more ordinary place than Smith Island, with its three unincorporated villages. Also, Tangier's one school goes all the way through twelfth grade, graduating a very small class but nonetheless supported by the community because the local school is thought to minimize the out-migration of young people, at least compared with Smith Island, whose youngsters attend high school on the mainland.

AUTOMOBILE DIRECTIONS: Tangier Island lies in
Virginia's portion of Chesapeake Bay, below Smith Island and
the mouth of the Potomac River. (See Map 1 in the Table of
Contents.) The island is reached by commercial passenger
boats from Crisfield, Maryland, which is located about 40 miles
south-southwest of Salisbury.

**To Crisfield from northern Delmarva and Interstate
95 southwest of Wilmington:** From Interstate 95 take
Route 7 south, then follow the signs for Route 1 to Route 13
toward Dover. (Please note, however, that Route 7 will not be
linked to Route 1 until the fall of 1992, so until then simply take
Route 7 south to Route 13.) Once you are on Route 13
southbound, follow it down through Delaware and into
Maryland. After passing east of Salisbury and west of Princess
Anne, turn right onto Route 413 toward Crisfield and go 14.6
miles to the end of the road at Crisfield's municipal dock.

To Crisfield from the Chesapeake Bay Bridge: After
crossing the bridge, follow Route 50/301 across Kent Island.
At the point where Route 50 and Route 301 split, fork right to
follow Route 50 past Easton, Cambridge, and Salisbury. East
of Salisbury, take Route 13 south toward Norfolk. Follow
Route 13 past Princess Anne to the junction with Route 413,
and there turn right toward Crisfield. Follow Route 413 for 14.6
miles to the end of the road at Crisfield's municipal dock.

**To Crisfield from southern Delmarva and the
Chesapeake Bay Bridge-Tunnel at Norfolk:** After
crossing the bridge-tunnel, follow Route 13 north into
Maryland. From the intersection with Route 113 near
Pocomoke City, continue on Route 13 for 3.8 miles to the
intersection with Route 667 west toward Crisfield. Turn left
onto Route 667 and follow it 11.5 miles to an intersection with
Route 413. Turn left onto Route 413 and follow it 6.0 miles to
the end of the road at Crisfield's municipal dock.

**To Crisfield from Salisbury and the Delaware and
Maryland seashore resorts:** From the vicinity of
Salisbury, follow Route 13 south past Princess Anne to the
junction with Route 413, and there turn right toward Crisfield.
Follow Route 413 for 14.6 miles to the end of the road at
Crisfield's municipal dock.

From the vicinity of Rehoboth Beach, follow Route 1 north to the intersection with Route 9 westbound, then take Route 9 west through Georgetown and across Route 113 to Route 13 southbound. Alternatively, from the vicinity of Ocean City, follow Route 50 west to Route 13 southbound. In either case, once you are on Route 13, follow it south around Salisbury and past Princess Anne to the junction with Route 413, and there turn right toward Crisfield. Follow Route 413 for 14.6 miles to the end of the road at Crisfield's municipal dock.

BOATS TO TANGIER ISLAND: Once you are at Crisfield's municipal dock, make a U-turn and go two blocks to the office of Tangier Island Cruises, located on the right at the corner of Tenth and Main Streets. A parking lot can be reached from Tenth Street behind the office. When you buy your ticket, specify whether you want to go by the Tangier mail boat, which leaves from the municipal dock and requires an overnight stay on the island, or by the excursion boat, which leaves from the bulkhead next to the parking lot and stops over at the island for only two and a half hours. For variety you can probably take the mail boat out and the excursion boat back the same day; this arrangement has the further advantage of providing more time on the island, since the mail boat is faster than the excursion boat.

WALKING ON TANGIER ISLAND: Once the boat reaches Tangier Island, use Map 30 to explore the town's narrow lanes on foot. Or, if you prefer, you can join a tour via golf cart. The golf-cart tours are quick and easy, but by walking you will have more freedom to explore and to pause where you want.

There are several eateries on the island, the most noteworthy being the **Chesapeake House.** There is time for both eating and exploring if you don't linger excessively over your meal. Of course, if you stay overnight, you will have time to explore not only the town but also the long **beach** extending down the western shore below the airport and terminating at the sandy hook at the southern end of the island.

14

SNOW HILL
POCOMOKE RIVER via canoe or
excursion boat
FURNACE TOWN
POCOMOKE CITY
SHAD LANDING

The 55-mile car tour outlined in this chapter (and shown on Map 34) explores the vicinity of Snow Hill and Pocomoke City, both located on the Pocomoke River in southern Worcester County, Maryland. In addition to its handsome streetscapes, churches, and waterfront, Snow Hill features the small but excellent Julia A. Purnell Museum, which displays clothes, tools, and artifacts from three hundred years of everyday life in Worcester County. The museum is open April through October, Monday through Friday from 10 to 4, and from 1 to 4 on Saturday and Sunday; telephone (410) 632-0515. In Pocomoke City the Victorian Italianate Costen House — home of the town's first mayor and furnished in the style of the times — is open on weekdays from noon to 1 P.M.; telephone (410) 957-0972.

Near Snow Hill is Furnace Town, a re-created nineteenth-century village centered around the old masonry stack of the Nassawango Iron Company. Furnace Town is open daily from 11 to 5 during April through October. It is managed by Furnace Town Foundation, Inc.; telephone (410) 632-2032.

For many people, however, the main attraction of this area is not its old, quiet towns along the Pocomoke, but the Pocomoke River itself, flowing from headwaters within a dozen miles of Ocean City southwest 50 miles to its muddy mouth (termed simply The Muds) at Chesapeake Bay. Like something transplanted here from the Gulf Coast, an extensive bald cypress swamp borders the Pocomoke and its tributaries in what is, in fact, the nation's northernmost stand of this quintessentially southern tree. Two trails described in this chapter provide an opportunity to penetrate the bald cypress swamp on foot — without getting your feet wet. However, a far better way to see this exotic forest is from the water. Accordingly, a section of this chapter (see page 204) is devoted to canoeing on the

Pocomoke, as is easily done because of the availability of rental canoes. Also, from mid-June until early September, a small excursion boat (*Tillie the Tug*) operates on the river, leaving from Snow Hill's Sturgis Park dock; telephone 1-800-345-6754 or (410) 632-0680 for schedule information. Charter trips may be arranged in spring and fall when there is no regular schedule.

The car tour eventually ends at the Shad Landing area of the Pocomoke River State Park, where camping and marina facilities are available. The park is managed by the Maryland Department of Natural Resources; telephone (410) 632-2566.

Finally, bicyclists may enjoy a 25-mile ride that leads from Snow Hill through farmland and forest north of the Pocomoke River, passing Furnace Town and the Pusey Branch Nature Trail along the way. The bicycle route is shown on Map 31 opposite. It starts and ends with a short leg along Route 12, where bicyclists must be prepared for cars traveling at high speeds.

LOCATED AT THE HEAD OF NAVIGATION on the Pocomoke River, **Snow Hill** was platted by order of the General Assembly in 1686 and made county seat when Worcester County (pronounced Wooster) was carved out of Somerset County in 1742. During the colonial period, the town was a prosperous port of entry whose merchants dealt directly with their counterparts in London and other centers of British commerce. From this town far up the Pocomoke, tobacco was shipped to Great Britain and salt-meat and other foodstuffs were carried to East Coast ports and to Caribbean plantations. And to this town manufactured goods from England — fabrics, paper, household utensils, notions, books, tools, and other necessities of every description — were sent for eventual sale by Snow Hill's merchants to the planters and farmers scattered throughout the hinterland.

During the nineteenth century, however, the rapid growth of Baltimore as the chief Chesapeake port relegated Snow Hill to the status of just another small Eastern Shore town sending its products to the big city for transshipment there. After the Civil War, large steamboats plied the Pocomoke once or twice weekly, carrying freight and passengers to and from Baltimore, with stops at Crisfield and Pocomoke City. A steamboat continued to make the Pocomoke run as late as the 1920s, but long before then most local products, such as potatoes, canned vegetables, livestock, hides, and large timbers, were taken from Snow Hill by railroad.

Directions for Pusey Branch Nature Trail:

From the gate behind the cemetery, follow a white oystershell road into the woods for 20 yards, then turn left onto a narrow footpath, which winds through the woods next to Pusey Branch and eventually returns to the oystershell road, where you should turn right to return to the cemetery.

NOTE: Although the names of roads are shown on the map, in reality road signs may be missing at some intersections. But if you keep track of your progress as you go along, you won't have any difficulty knowing where to turn.

Today Snow Hill remains an agricultural center. Its businesses include a feed mill, a chicken hatchery, a fertilizer plant, a lumber mill, and a plant that makes business forms. The railroad is still important to the town's economy, but as for the Pocomoke River, it is only rarely used to transport some bulk products, chiefly fuel oil brought up to Snow Hill by barge.

Five miles northwest of Snow Hill is **Furnace Town**, which was once a small company-owned village engaged in smelting iron. From our present-day perspective, the location of the furnace at this remote, swampy site bordering Nassawango Creek seems strange. The location, however, simply reflects the technology of iron-making during the early nineteenth century. The essential ingredients were iron ore, charcoal fuel, and calcium carbonate for flux to help remove impurities in the ore. The Pocomoke region had all three. Since the late 1700s, beds of iron oxide (technically termed limonite but more prosaically called bog iron) were known to exist in the vicinity of Nassawango Creek, where they had been deposited below the still waters of the swamp after the ore was leached from throughout the watershed. Charcoal could be made from the region's extensive forests by partially burning cordwood in a slow, smouldering fire. And calcium carbonate was available in the form of oyster and clam shells, dredged from Chincoteague Bay or even found ready at hand on the shore in heaps left by Indians.

The Nassawango site offered other advantages as well. By the late eighteenth century it already had been developed with a dam and millpond to provide waterpower for a sawmill and gristmill. Also, the nearby Pocomoke River could serve to transport pig iron to Chesapeake Bay and from there to foundries in Baltimore and Philadelphia.

Nassawango Furnace and village operated from 1832 to 1847 as the Maryland Iron Company. As still seen today, the furnace consisted of a fat masonry stack that was hollow and lined with firebrick. As was typical of such furnaces, it was built at the bottom of a steep bluff, so that a wooden trestlework bridge wide enough to accommodate a mule and cart could run from the top of the slope to the top of the stack.

When the furnace was in operation, charcoal, iron ore, and shells were carted across the bridge and dumped into the top of the stack, which also served as the chimney. The stack gases were nearly smokeless but occasionally streams of sparks shot out, and at night flames lit the sky and surrounding village. A water-powered bellows provided an intermittent blast of air that, with a heavy, pulsing roar, fanned the furnace fire. The rush of air was called a *hot blast*, because the air was preheated by passing through pipes exposed to the flames at the top of the stack. Hot-blast furnaces were more efficient than the earlier cold-blast smelters, and they also could burn hard coal — not that coal was available at Nassawango.

Once fired, the furnace was kept in continuous blast for many months at a time, until supplies were used up or the furnace lining deteriorated to the point where it had to be replaced. Men known as fillers labored around the clock, feeding the furnace at regular intervals as the fuel, ore, and flux were consumed and the molten iron slowly sank to the crucible at the bottom of the stack. Working in the recessed casting arch at the foot of the furnace, the founder — a man of experience and judgment — occasionally opened the higher of two taps to draw off the molten slag that floated on the heavier molten iron. And by opening a lower tap, the founder could sample the iron itself and to some extent control its quality by calling for an adjustment in the proportion of ingredients and the blast of air. Then, two or three times a day, the founder released the molten iron into molds dug in the sandy floor of the casting house, which was a barnlike structure built around the opening of the casting arch. Typically, the molds consisted of nothing more than short, parallel troughs branching from a central channel. In the early days of iron making, the main pouring channel and the row of smaller molds were noted to resemble a sow with suckling pigs; hence the term *pig iron* for crude iron.

In addition to the workmen who actually operated the furnace were others, far more numerous, who supplied the necessary raw materials. With pick and shovel, diggers extracted bog iron from the swamp. Carters transported the ore to the top of the bank — as the bluff by the furnace was called. Other men loaded and unloaded the barges that were towed by mules along a canal that linked the town with a lock and landing at Nassawango Creek, which in turn led to the Pocomoke River. The barges were used to bring in oyster and clam shells and to take out the iron pigs once they were cast. Woodcutters supplied cordwood, which was needed in immense quantities, as indicated by an advertisement in the Snow Hill *Messenger* for May 20, 1833: "Wood Choppers Wanted at Naseongo Furnace. 50 good steady hands will meet with constant employment at forty cents per cord. Apply to manager at the Works." And after the wood had been cut, colliers converted it to charcoal.

Making charcoal was a laborious and painstaking process. First the cordwood was hauled to charcoal hearths scattered throughout the forest. These hearths were nothing more than large, circular clearings where first the wood was allowed to stand and dry for a few months. After the cordwood was seasoned, the colliers arranged the logs in a circular mass 30 or 40 feet in diameter, with all the pieces standing on end and leaning toward a wooden chimney at the center. Another smaller layer of cordwood was placed on top of the first, and a third layer on top of that, until a rounded heap of wood was built. Then the colliers covered the logs with a layer of leaves and dirt. The chimney was filled with kindling and a fire set at the top.

For as long as two weeks the colliers, who lived in huts near their work in the woods, watched over the mound while the wood smouldered and turned to charcoal. Outbreaks of flame were quickly smothered with dirt. Blue smoke indicated that all was going well, but white smoke was a sign of too much combustion. The rate of charring was controlled by opening and filling air holes. The most dangerous part of the job was "jumping the pit," which entailed climbing on top of the smoking heap and stamping on it to settle the coals and fill in air spaces. Finally, when the charring appeared to be complete, the colliers uncovered the mound a little at a time. The hot charcoal was loaded into metal-lined wagons, which then were hauled to the village and parked in a shed to protect the coals from rain. After the charcoal had cooled, it was added to the supplies stored in the charcoal house at the top of the bank.

Making charcoal was so time-consuming that it was the weak link in the entire iron-smelting process for many furnaces operating during the first half of the nineteenth century, especially after the introduction of hot-blast technology made possible the use of hard coal. Coal was far cheaper than charcoal, and labor costs for iron produced with anthracite were about 20 percent of labor costs for iron made with charcoal.

Although Nassawango Furnace suffered from a competitive disadvantage compared to furnaces located near coal fields, it continued in business during most of the 1840s, and, indeed, the furnace and village became a substantial operation. For married men and their families, there were about fifteen company-owned houses, plus several smaller cottages. Single men lived in a large and crowded boarding house. There were a general store with post office, a bank, a school, a Methodist meeting house, and the ironmaster's house called "the mansion," where for a period Furnace Town's owner lived. Other structures included several barns for draft animals, a blacksmith shop, a shoemaker's shop, and a shop for making patterns for iron castings. Assets included not only the furnace village but also 7,000 acres of land.

The enterprise, however, was at best barely profitable, and became altogether unprofitable as time past. About 700 tons of pig iron were produced annually — somewhat less than at comparable furnaces of the period. Costs were high and by some accounts the iron was marketable only at a low price because it was tainted with phosphorous. About 1840 the iron company was bought by Thomas A. Spence, who proceeded to pour the fortune of his wealthy, Baltimore-bred wife into the venture, but without good result.

By 1847 iron making at Nassawango Furnace had stopped, and during the following decades the village decayed and disappeared. By 1908 only the furnace, the ironmaster's house, and three cottages remained, and by 1978, when Furnace Town, Inc. was organized, the lone structure still standing was the massive masonry furnace stack. Since then Furnace Town has been the scene of ongoing restoration. Various buildings, including a company store, a museum, a blacksmith shop, a smoke house, and a church, have been moved here in recent years in order to show the appearance and ancillary activities of a working iron village. (See Map 35 on page 208.)

AUTOMOBILE DIRECTIONS: For the various activities described in this chapter, go first to Snow Hill, which is located 17 miles southeast of Salisbury, where Route 12 crosses the Pocomoke River. (See Map 1 in the Table of Contents.)

To Snow Hill from northern Delmarva and Interstate 95 southwest of Wilmington: From Interstate 95 take Route 7 south, then follow the signs for Route 1 to Route 13 toward Dover. (Please note, however, that Route 7 will not be linked to Route 1 until the fall of 1992, so until then simply take Route 7 south to Route 13.) Once you are on Route 13 southbound, follow it down through Delaware and into Maryland. After passing the exit for Route 50 toward Ocean City, continue south on Route 13 to the next exit for Route 12 toward Snow Hill. At the bottom of the exit ramp, turn left onto Route 12 southbound and go slightly more than 15 miles to Snow Hill on the Pocomoke River.

To Snow Hill from the Chesapeake Bay Bridge: After crossing the bridge, follow Route 50/301 across Kent Island. At the point where Route 50 and Route 301 split, fork right to follow Route 50 past Easton, Cambridge, and Salisbury. East of Salisbury, take Route 13 south toward Norfolk, but go only to the first exit for Route 12 toward Snow Hill. At the bottom of the exit ramp, turn left onto Route 12 southbound and go slightly more than 15 miles to Snow Hill on the Pocomoke River.

To Snow Hill from southern Delmarva and the Chesapeake Bay Bridge-Tunnel at Norfolk: After crossing the bridge-tunnel, follow Route 13 north about 73

MAP 32 -- Car tour of Snow Hill

miles to the intersection (near Pocomoke City, Maryland) with Route 113, and there turn right onto Route 113 north toward Berlin and Ocean City. Follow Route 113 for 9.4 miles, then turn left onto Route 394 north toward Snow Hill. Follow Route 394 for 2.8 miles to the center of Snow Hill.

To Snow Hill from Salisbury and the Delmarva and Maryland seashore resorts: From the intersection of Route 13 and Route 12 southeast of Salisbury, take Route 12 south slightly more than 15 miles to Snow Hill on the Pocomoke River.

From the Delaware and Maryland seashore resorts, first go west to Route 113, then follow it south. From the interchange at Route 113 and Route 50, follow Route 113 south about 15.0 miles, then fork right onto Route 394 toward Snow Hill. Follow Route 394 for 1.4 miles to the center of Snow Hill.

TOURING SNOW HILL: The bold line on Map 32 shows the route of a car tour that provides a quick overview of Snow Hill, where there are more than a hundred century-old dwellings. The tour starts on Green Street, near the clock at the intersection with Washington Street (Route 12). Lined with brick stores, many of which were rebuilt after a fire in 1893, Green Street is Snow Hill's main business street. Follow Green Street to a five-way intersection and then, in quick succession, turn right onto Church Street, left onto Pettit Street, and left again onto Water Street, which will bring you alongside the **Julia A. Purnell Museum.**

From the Purnell Museum follow Market Street past Gunby and Morris streets, then turn left onto Ross Street and left again onto Federal Street, where there are a succession of handsome, mostly nineteenth-century houses. At Washington Street, turn right , then (after two blocks) turn right again onto Ironshire Street, which leads past the **Mt. Zion One-Room School Museum**.

Just beyond the school museum, turn right onto Church Street, then (after three blocks) turn right onto Market Street. **All Hallows Episcopal Church** at the corner of Market and Church streets was built over a period of seven years between 1748 and 1755; the interior was redone in the late 1800s. **Makemie Memorial Presbyterian Church** was started in 1887 and finished three years later. Prior Presbyterian churches stood in the old churchyard burial ground to the rear of the present-day church, which serves a congregation that has existed in this part of Maryland since the late 1600s. Dissenters from the prevailing Anglican orthodoxy of the time, many Presbyterians settled in the region just to the north of the border with Virginia, which they had left for the more tolerant atmosphere of Maryland. Lacking a minister, they petitioned for aid from a Presbytery in Great Britain, which sent out the Reverend Francis Makemie. This energetic Ulsterman arrived in 1683 and organized several Presbyterian congregations throughout Maryland's Eastern Shore.

Just beyond the 1894 **Worcester County Courthouse**, turn left onto Washington Street, then (after passing Green Street and Willow Street) turn left onto River Street, which borders **Sturgis Park**. During the summer an excursion boat operates from Sturgis Park and offers sightseeing trips downstream and back. There is also the possibility of canoeing on the Pocomoke River, as discussed below.

CANOEING ON THE POCOMOKE RIVER: Although the car tour and foot trails described later in this chapter provide a look at the swampy bald cypress forest that borders the Pocomoke River and Nassawango Creek, a far better way to see this unusual environment is by canoe. The meandering stretch of river shown on Map 33 provides the best canoeing that Maryland's Eastern Shore has to offer.

If you own a canoe, by all means bring it with you. However, if you want to rent a canoe and gear, the Pocomoke River Canoe Company is centrally located by the Route 12 bridge in Snow Hill. This canoe livery is open weekends in spring and fall. From Memorial Day through Labor Day, it is open daily. For information telephone (410) 632-3971 or write to the Pocomoke River Canoe Company, Snow Hill, Maryland 21863. Canoes can also be rented at the Shad Landing area of the Pocomoke River State Park; telephone (410) 632-2566. However, the river at Shad Landing is less interesting than farther upstream.

Canoes can be launched at Snow Hill's Byrd Park (shown along the left edge of Map 32 and again by a dot on Map 33) or at one of the other four locations marked by a dot on Map 33. Whether you bring your own canoe or rent one, the Pocomoke River Canoe Company can be hired to take you and your canoe upstream to Porters Crossing Road or Whiton Crossing Road, both on the Pocomoke River, or to Red House Road on

MAP 33 -- Canoeing on the Pocomoke River and Nassawango Creek

Nassawango Creek, thus enabling you to paddle one way back to Snow Hill. Unless your interest is simply to paddle for an hour or two immediately upstream from Snow Hill (recommended for beginners), I suggest that you start at one of the places mentioned above. The trip from Whiton Crossing to Snow Hill is an all-day outing; from Porters Crossing or Red House Road to Snow Hill takes half a day. Even for a short outing, bring something to drink.

Finally, if you intend to explore the river's swampy, narrow sections, you will need insect repellent (although on the many occasions when I have been there during autumn, mosquitoes have not been a problem).

CAR TOUR OF SOUTHERN WORCESTER COUNTY:
This 55-mile car tour is shown by the bold line on Map 34.

The tour starts at Snow Hill and goes first to Nassawango Iron Furnace. However, the furnace site is closed November through March, so during that period you should simply skip the next paragraph and head north out of town on Route 12 for 2.8 miles to Red House Road intersecting from the left.

For the furnace, follow Route 12 north out of town 3.9 miles, then turn left onto Furnace Road and go 1.1 miles to **Furnace Town**, which is discussed in the commentary for this chapter starting on Page 198. Furnace Town includes not only many exhibits and old structures, but also access to The Nature Conservancy's mile-long **Paul Leifer Memorial Trail**, shown on Map 35. The trail starts behind the furnace stack and penetrates, via boardwalk, a swampy bald cypress forest bordering the old canal that used to link Furnace Town with a landing on Nassawango Creek.

Whether or not you first go to Furnace Town, the car tour continues from the intersection of Route 12 and Red House Road, as shown on Map 33. Follow Red House Road 1.3 miles. Bear left onto Creek Road, then (after only 0.2 mile) bear right onto Scotty Road. Follow Scotty Road 5.2 miles to an intersection where it joins River Road, and there bear right to follow the main trend of the road, which soon becomes Route 364 south. Follow Route 364 south 5.5 miles to and across Route 13. Turn left at a T-intersection and go 1.9 miles across the Pocomoke River and through Pocomoke City on Market Street.

MAP 34 -- Car tour of southern Worcester County

MAP 35 -- Furnace Town

Like Snow Hill, **Pocomoke City** owes its existence and development to the Pocomoke River. Since 1670 there has been a landing here, known at first as Stevens Ferry, for Colonel William Stevens, who also helped to found Snow Hill and Berlin. In about 1683 or '84, the place was called Meeting House Landing, after a Presbyterian house of worship in the vicinity. In about 1700 a public tobacco warehouse was built, and for 120 years it stood at what then became known as Warehouse Landing. In 1780 the place was platted as Newtown and finally was incorporated as Pocomoke City in 1878, when both the river and the new railroad (which had arrived in 1872) seemed to guarantee a bustling future for the town.

Exploitation of the region's extensive bald cypress forests was a powerful stimulus to the village's economy. A steam-powered shingle mill — the town's first — was established in 1839. In 1845 two entrepreneurs from New Jersey arrived, purchased large tracts in the cypress swamps downstream from the town, and established a sawmill and shipyard. Writing nearly forty years later, the Reverend James Murray recounted that these men "aroused the citizens of New Town and the entire surrounding country to the idea of business which has never died out. They infused a spirit of industry and enterprise in all, from the day laborer to the merchant behind the counter and the farmer at the plow. They . . . produced an entire revolution in business life." At the time Murray wrote, Pocomoke City and the surrounding countryside had five sawmills, two flour and gristmills, three shipyards, and two marine railways. Among the ships built at Pocomoke City was the four-masted schooner *Lillian E. Kerr* and numerous coastal and bay craft.

The Reverend Murray's 1883 *History of Pocomoke City* is a veritable paean to local commerce:

> We have now eight large vessels sailing from Pocomoke City which are engaged exclusively in the bay trade. One and sometimes two steamboats plying between here and . . . [Baltimore] city and the railroad running daily to all parts north, by which facilities we have daily access to all the cities, doing an annual shipping business aggregating probably the round sum of $500,000. . . .
>
> [The] steamers are superseding, in a great measure, the sail vessels in carrying the produce of the Eastern Shore to Baltimore. . . [T]hey have first-class accommodation for passengers in their saloons, staterooms and cabins, and the viands upon their tables are selected from the best city markets. The writer having traveled on all of these steamers can say that the officers are polite and obliging, and passengers may be sure of being treated as ladies and gentlemen.
>
> Our youthful readers cannot realize the advantages of steamboat

travel to the same extent that some of us can, whose memory goes back to the time when there was no steamboat plying between Pocomoke City and Baltimore, and when it would require, at certain seasons of the year, two weeks or more for a sail vessel to make a trip from Pocomoke City to Baltimore and return.

Whereas with the present facilities of travel the trip can be made in thirty-nine hours, and give you eleven hours of that time to attend to business in the city. With these facts before us we can see clearly that progress is marching onward.

Indeed it has. Now, of course, the river carries very little commercial traffic, and the railroad too carries no passengers and relatively little freight compared to the past. Timber and timber products no longer play a significant part in Pocomoke City's economy. Instead, the oldest major business is Robertson Bros. foundry and machine works, established in 1907. There is also a plant making clam chowder and other clam products, a gun manufacturer making police pistols (Beretta USA), a factory producing scuba and deep-sea diving suits, and a new and somewhat experimental fish farm.

In 1983 Pocomoke City received a Certificate of National Merit from the federal Department of Housing and Urban Development for restoring Market Street to its appearance in the 1920s, when the central part of town was rebuilt "in the latest style" after a fire in 1922 destroyed 250 houses and businesses. Built in 1927, the Art Deco **Mar-Va Theater** (telephone (410) 957-0252) still operates on Market Street, showing movies Friday, Saturday, and Sunday evenings. The Victorian Italianate **Costen House** is located on Market Street just east of the business district and across from the post office; built in 1870 and now furnished with late Victorian pieces, it was the home of Dr. Isaac T. Costen, mayor of Pocomoke City from 1888 to 1892 and again from 1908 to 1912.

In 1985 Pocomoke City was named an All-American City for redeveloping its waterfront, previously the site of shipyards, warehouses, and commercial docks, with a park, walkway, and facilities for recreational boating. More recently the town was named a Maryland Main Street Community for its efforts to preserve the vitality and architecture of its central business district.

CAR TOUR (Map 34): After passing through Pocomoke City on Market Street, turn left to follow Route 366 east. Cross Route 13 almost immediately and continue on Route 366 for 8.2 miles to a crossroads with Route 12 in **Stockton** (formerly Stock Town, where in the middle of the nineteenth century cattle were gathered before being herded north to the nearest railhead).

Turn left in Stockton onto Route 12 and follow it 2.9 miles to a crossroads by the post office in the town of **Girdletree**, thought to be named for a farm called Girdle Tree Hill, whose owner removed a large beech tree by girdling it. As you approach Girdletree, you will pass the obscure entrance to the State of Maryland's **E. A. Vaughn Wildlife Management Area** on the right, located 2.2 miles north of Stockton.

WALKING AT THE VAUGHN WILDLIFE MANAGEMENT AREA: During the colder months when mosquitoes are not a problem, this area provides a very pleasant walk of about 3 miles round-trip to the marshes bordering Chincoteague Bay and back. The route is shown by the dashed line near the bottom of Map 34. Because this is a public hunting area, you should wear orange during the hunting season and stick to the main track, which starts by the gate next to the parking lot at the end of the entrance road. A worn track leads more or less straight through fields, woods, and marsh to the water's edge.

CAR TOUR (Map 34): At the post office in Girdletree, turn right and follow the main trend of the road 2.4 miles to the boat ramp at **Taylor Landing**, one of a dozen or more such Worcester County landings long used by oystermen and fishermen on Chincoteague Bay.

From Taylor Landing, return 0.8 mile, then turn sharply right onto Bayview Road. Follow Bayview Road 2.0 miles, then turn right at a T-intersection. Go 0.3 mile, then again turn right at a T-intersection. Continue 0.5 mile, then turn right at yet another T-intersection in the hamlet of **Boxiron** (a corruption of bog iron, after nearby Bog Iron Creek). At the next intersection, which is a skewed crossroads, bear slightly right and continue 0.3 mile, then turn right and go 3.6 miles to a T-intersection in the village of **Public Landing** (also called Snow Hill Landing). The distance from here to the head of navigation on the Pocomoke River at Snow Hill is only 6 miles. Before the advent of railroads and steamboats, some products of the lower Eastern Shore were shipped up the Pocomoke to Snow Hill, carried from there by wagon to Public Landing, then reshipped north by coastal schooners small enough to navigate the shallow channel at Chincoteague Inlet.

From Public Landing, follow Route 365 west 5.2 miles, then turn left onto Route 113 and continue 4.8 miles to the

MAP 36 -- Shad Landing Area of Pocomoke River State Park

POCOMOKE RIVER

Hardship Branch

Trail of Change

parking

picnic area

parking

trailhead

camping

Corkers Creek

marina

parking

restrooms and
marina services

camping

youth group camping

swimming pool

parking

camping

nature center

parking

camping

park headquarters

Rte. 113

N

entrance

0   mile   0.25

entrance to **Pocomoke River State Park — Shad Landing Area**. Follow the entrance road 0.5 mile, then turn right at a T-intersection and go 0.2 mile to the marina, where the car tour ends.

WALKING AT SHAD LANDING: Although this section of Pocomoke River State Park caters primarily to campers and boaters, there is also the mile-long **Trail of Change**, which provides a glimpse of a bald cypress forest. If you have not by now seen these trees, here is your chance.

The trail is shown at the upper-right corner of Map 36. To reach the trailhead from the parking lot at the marina, follow the circle road clockwise about 200 yards to the Trail of Change on the left.

The "bald" in bald cypress derives from the fact that this conifer sheds its needles in autumn. Other distinguishing characteristics are the swollen, fluted base of the trunk, which helps provide stability in the sodden soil, and the woody "knees," which protrude from the ground or water and supply oxygen to the wide-spreading root system.

During the nineteenth century, logging for bald cypress was a major industry in Worcester County. Because bald cypress wood resists decay, it was particularly valued for shipbuilding, siding, and shingles — hence, Shingle Landing on the Saint Martin River west of Ocean City, where shingles were shipped to Philadelphia and New York.

Virtually all stands of bald cypress seen today in the Pocomoke region are second growth. As the bald cypress forest reestablishes itself, the large size of the mature trees (100 to 125 feet tall) should eventually enable them to shade out competing species, principally red maple, and once again become the dominant swamp tree.

15

ASSATEAGUE ISLAND NATIONAL SEASHORE (northern section) ASSATEAGUE STATE PARK

This chapter describes the northern two-thirds of Assateague Island — the part, that is, in Maryland, which includes most of Assateague Island National Seashore and all of Assateague State Park. The southern (or Virginia) section of Assateague Island is described in Chapter 16. Treating the northern and southern sections separately reflects not only the considerable differences between the two, but also the admirable fact that no public road on the island connects the two ends. As a result, the long midsection of Assateague is quite wild, especially in Virginia, where no vehicles are allowed on the beach between the state line and the Toms Cove Visitor Center.

The national seashore's northern section and Maryland's Assateague State Park have something for everyone. Most people come to swim at the two lifeguarded beaches. For walkers, there are three short trails at the national seashore, plus the opportunity to hike all day along the edge of the surf. North of the state park are 6 miles of beach accessible only on foot; south of the state park are 12 miles of beach open to off-road vehicles with permits. Most of the 5 miles of paved roads at the northern end of the national seashore either are bordered by a bicycle path or at least have a bicycle lane.

Both the national seashore and the state park have facilities for car camping; in addition the national seashore has several remote campsites for backpackers and canoeists. Together the national seashore and state park also provide opportunities for surf fishing, surf boarding, crabbing, boat launching, and hunting. During summer, and to a lesser extent in spring and fall, the national seashore offers a variety of nature programs, such as slide shows and guided walks. For information about any of these activities, call the visitor center.

Although the northern section of the national seashore is not as rich in wildlife as the southern section, it is still a good place for observing the many species of birds that frequent the beach and offshore waters, the dunes and marsh, and Sinepuxent and

Chincoteague bays. There are also, of course, the wild ponies, which you should never forget really are wild. Accordingly, please do not approach the horses closely or feed them; they can bite and kick, inflicting severe injuries.

The national seashore is open every day, all day, year-round. The admission fee entitles you to enter as often as you want for one week. Annual passes are also available. The state park is open daily from early morning to dusk. During summer the parking lots fill early in the day, especially on weekends.

At the national seashore, pets must be on leashes no more than 6 feet long, and are prohibited at backcountry campsites and in the primitive area north of the state park, so by bringing a pet you are immediately barring yourself from the best place for beach walking. During summer the sand, sun, and insects can be very hard on dogs and other domestic animals, so the wisest thing to do is to leave your pet at home. And at the state park, pets are prohibited altogether, even on a leash and even in your car.

Assateague Island National Seashore is managed by the National Park Service; telephone (410) 641-1441 for general information and interpretive services at the Barrier Island Visitor Center or (410) 641-3030 for the campground office. Assateague State Park is administered by the Maryland Department of Natural Resources; telephone (410) 641-2120.

AUTHORIZED IN 1965 and now one of the most visited public recreation areas on the East Coast, Assateague Island National Seashore is an outstanding park that very nearly never came to be. Its creation and management philosophy help to illustrate the evolution of national park policy over a period of more than a century.

Until the early 1960s, Congress had never authorized spending more than trivial amounts to buy land for national parks. Rather, our great national parks, starting with Yellowstone in 1872, were at first created from land already federally owned, with the minor exception of private inholdings (such as homesteads and mining claims) that existed when the parks were established, and some of which were bought by the government. (Many inholdings still exist today, and at least 25 national parks contain valid mining claims. Congress even permitted the establishment of *new* mining claims in some national parks until 1976.)

When the National Park Service eventually was established within the Department of Interior in 1916, it was put in charge of a dozen parks that had already been created. Most of the parks were huge (taken together, they were more than three times bigger than the state of Delaware) and all were in the West, where, of course, the overwhelming bulk of federal land was — and still is. According to standards formulated by the new park service, future national parks would be modeled on those already in existence. In brief, they were supposed to be vast, spectacular examples of unspoiled natural grandeur, like the Grand Canyon, designated a national park in 1919. As new parks were established, very few were near major cities, nor was the use of the parks intended to include more than low-keyed forms of nature appreciation, such as sightseeing, camping, horse trekking, and hiking.

Because all the early federal parks were in the West, the newly-established National Park Service recommended — and Congress authorized — a series of large national parks in the eastern United States. Here, however, the federal government owned little land, and for each new park that it authorized, a frugal and conservative Congress allocated no federal funds to buy land. Rather, the land had to be donated or bought with donated money. The states where the proposed parks were to be located served as intermediaries to assemble the land from gifts and from their own holdings, with the goal of eventually presenting the land to the federal government. In this way, Arcadia National Park was established in Maine in 1919, Great Smoky Mountains in 1930, Shenandoah in 1935, Mammoth Cave in 1936, and Isle Royale in Lake Superior in 1940.

Meanwhile, the responsibilities of the National Park Service were expanding rapidly, sometimes in directions that had little to do with its original mission. During the 1930s the park service was assigned — by transfer from other federal agencies — responsibility for managing many small historic sites (chiefly battlefields) scattered throughout the eastern states. In the decades that followed, the park service acquired numerous houses and other structures and even whole hamlets of historic value, such as Hopewell Furnace National Historic Site in Pennsylvania and Colonial National Historic Park, which includes Yorktown, Virginia. This growth was in addition to the stewardship the National Park Service already exercised over a lengthening list of "national monuments," consisting mainly of outstanding natural landmarks, like Devil's Tower in Wyoming, and areas of scientific interest, such as Dinosaur National Monument in Colorado and Utah. (Whereas national parks may be established only by Congress, the president has authority to designate national monuments, but, of course, no power to allocate funds for their acquisition if they are not already federally owned.) Thus during the second quarter of this century, the National Park Service became what might be described as a Smithsonian Institution of American land, charged with acquiring, preserving, and presenting to the public a diversified roster of scenically, historically, and scientifically important places.

Starting in the 1930s, a broader concept of recreation — beyond the National Park Service's traditional emphasis on nature appreciation — was also promoted by federal planners. In 1936 the first "national recreation area" was established to take advantage of the obvious opportunity for swimming and boating at Lake Mead, the reservoir created by the construction of Hoover Dam. During the 1940s and '50s, similar recreation areas, all administered by the National Park Service, were established incidental to other federal dam projects.

The nation's seashores, combining as they do striking scenery with vast potential for intensive recreation, also received attention from the National Park Service. After inventorying all the unspoiled beaches along the Atlantic and Gulf coasts, the park service in 1935 recommended twelve areas (including Assateague Island) for acquisition. Congress, however, approved only one such coastal park — the Cape Hatteras National Seashore in 1937 — and as usual authorized no funds for land. Over a period of decades, tracts totaling thousands of acres were assembled by the state of North Carolina, which in installments donated the land to the federal government. The federal government did, however, spend large sums at Cape Hatteras in an attempt to stabilize the shoreline — efforts which, with the benefit of hindsight, appear to have been futile and have provided a lesson for the management of other oceanfront parks that were established much later.

After authorization of the Cape Hatteras National Seashore, the possibility of creating a similar national seashore on Assateague Island gradually faded. During the late 1930s and throughout the '40s, legislation to create a seashore park at Assateague was repeatedly introduced in Congress, but without favorable result. Instead, a variety of other projects were implemented. Using funds derived from the annual sale of duck stamps to hunters, the federal government's Bureau of Sports Fisheries and Wildlife (now the Fish and Wildlife Service) purchased the southern third of Assateague Island — the part, that is, in Virginia — to create Chincoteague National Wildlife Refuge in 1943. (See Chapter 16). In 1940 and again in 1952, the Maryland State Planning Commission recommended that a state park be established on Assateague. Noting this interest, a developer who had bought most of the Maryland section of the island in the late 1940s gave the state a piece 2 miles long for an oceanfront park in 1961 in the hope that the state would then build a bridge to Assateague, as eventually was done. Meanwhile, the National Park Service stopped recommending Assateague for national seashore status after concluding in 1956 that the 60 percent of the island that was privately owned had been consigned irrevocably to resort development.

Assateague was, in fact, ripe for commercialization. The increase in national prosperity, urbanization, automobile ownership, and leisure time that followed World War II sparked booming development activity on the barrier islands of the mid-Atlantic coast. "Millions of Americans hungry for salt-air gratify their craving for ocean bathing and seashore recreation by patronizing the Nation's overcrowded beaches," declared a sales brochure for the nascent community of Ocean Beach on Assateague Island, and the brochure went on to tout the 15 miles of pristine beach at the doorstep of Ocean Beach residents. More than 5850 lots were actually sold on Assateague Island during the 1950s and early '60s as the developer of Ocean Beach embarked on a plan that included a dense grid of paved roads 130 blocks long, with shopping centers and hotel districts spaced at intervals. A paved road — Baltimore Boulevard — was built as far south as the state line, and many side streets were cleared as houses started to go up.

In March 1962, however, a nor'easter lasting three days literally swept over Assateague Island. Immense quantities of sand were shifted from the ocean front to the bay side of the island. For 2 or 3 miles south of Ocean City Inlet, the shoreline was moved more than 400 feet westward. Much of Baltimore Boulevard was torn out. (Part of what remains can be seen at the Life of the Dunes Trail.) Of about 50 houses that had been built, all but 18 were total losses. To protect the island against future storms, the developer of Ocean Beach sought assistance from the Army Corps of Engineers, but the government concluded that measures for erosion control would be excessively expensive and probably futile, so nothing was done.

Meanwhile, in 1961 Congress finally broke with the precedent that frowned on the use of federal funds to buy land for national parks. Elected in 1960, President John F. Kennedy successfully pushed for creation, in his home state of Massachusetts, of the Cape Cod National Seashore, to be pieced together almost entirely from private land purchased with federal tax dollars, plus inholdings that would be subject to various restrictions but not purchased. Similar authorization for Point Reyes National Seashore in California and Padre Island National Seashore in Texas followed in 1962.

Also in 1962, the Outdoors Recreation Resources Review Commission issued, after three years' study, its influential report *Outdoor Recreation for America*, which documented a lack of outdoor recreation areas — particularly waterfront areas — that were convenient to major cities. The report was embraced enthusiastically by Stewart

Udall, Kennedy's secretary of interior, who initiated a policy of acquiring parkland in or near the nation's largest metropolitan regions, even if the sites did not entirely meet traditional National Park Service standards for large size, spectacular scenery, or lack of previous development.

To pay for the new acquisitions, Udall persuaded Congress to establish the Land and Water Conservation Fund, effective at the beginning of 1965 and presently scheduled to continue in existence until the year 2015. Revenue from the fund, which is used for a wide variety of park and conservation purposes (including grants to state and local governments), comes from national park user fees and a share of payments from offshore oil-drilling leases. Although Congress must still annually authorize allocations from the fund to the National Park Service and other agencies of the Department of Interior (and money not so allocated goes into the government's general account), the Land and Water Conservation Fund nonetheless has helped to institutionalize the federal practice of buying land as a necessary and appropriate means to create some national parks.

Assateague is one of those parks. As a result of the recommendations embodied in *Outdoor Recreation for America*, the Department of Interior undertook to re-evaluate the island, where development had been temporarily thwarted and even in part eradicated by the 1962 storm. The result was a proposal to create the Assateague Island National Seashore, submitted to Congress in 1963 but not approved until 1965, the year after Maryland completed the Route 611 bridge and opened Assateague State Park.

As authorized, the new national seashore was to include construction of a road running along the island from one end to the other, plus other facilities for "maximum public recreation use," such as fishing piers, a marina, and a 600-acre concession area with a restaurant, a gift shop, and a motel with 500 units in twenty buildings. However, as tourist accommodations multiplied at nearby Ocean City and Chincoteague Island, a reaction set in. Not only did those resorts remove the necessity of providing similar tourist facilities at the national seashore, but also (it became apparent) visitors to Assateague wanted to see something different: a relatively wild barrier island and beach. In response to the burgeoning environmental movement and the renewed value placed by the public on undeveloped natural areas, Congress in 1976 amended the National Seashore Act to delete provisions for commercial development at Assateague, thus to some extent vindicating traditional National Park Service emphasis on conservation and nature appreciation. At Assateague today, the park service promotes the same low-keyed activities — camping, hiking, and wildlife observation —

that have always been associated with our great national parks, while at the same time, of course, operating an intensively used bathing beach, plus accommodating the interests of hunters, surf fishermen, and those who simply want to drive on the beach for fun.

AUTOMOBILE DIRECTIONS: Assateague Island is the long barrier island that stretches south of Ocean City, Maryland for 37 miles. (See Map 1 in the Table of Contents.) The island's upper end, discussed in this chapter, is reached by the Route 611 bridge from the mainland and is not accessible directly from Ocean City to the north or Chincoteague in the south.

To Assateague from northern Delmarva and Interstate 95 southwest of Wilmington: From Interstate 95 take Route 7 south, then follow the signs for Route 1 to Route 13 toward Dover. (Please note, however, that Route 7 will not be linked to Route 1 until the fall of 1992, so until then simply take Route 7 south to Route 13). Once you are on Route 13 southbound, follow it past Smyrna to Dover, and there fork left onto Route 113 south toward Milford and the beaches. (Starting in 1994, you will be able to take Route 1 south from the vicinity of Smyrna to Route 113 below Dover.) Follow Route 113 south through Delaware and into Maryland. After passing over Route 50, continue south on Route 113 for 1.3 miles, then turn left onto Route 376 east toward Assateague. Go 4.1 miles to a T-intersection, and there turn right onto Route 611 south toward Assateague Island. Follow Route 611 for 3.1 miles to the national seashore's Barrier Island Visitor Center on the right.

To Assateague from the Chesapeake Bay Bridge: After crossing the bridge, follow Route 50/301 across Kent Island. At the point where Route 50 and Route 301 split, fork right to follow Route 50 past Easton, Cambridge, and Salisbury toward Ocean City. Stay on Route 50 past the exit for Route 90, then exit onto Route 113 south toward Snow Hill. From the end of the exit ramp, follow Route 113 south only 1.0 mile, then turn left onto Route 376 east toward Assateague. Go 4.1 miles to a T-intersection, and there turn right onto Route 611 south toward Assateague Island. Follow Route 611 for 3.1 miles to the national seashore's Barrier Island Visitor Center on the right.

To Assateague from southern Delmarva and the Chesapeake Bay Bridge-Tunnel at Norfolk: After crossing the bridge-tunnel, follow Route 13 north about 73 miles to the intersection (near Pocomoke City, Maryland) with Route 113, and there turn right onto Route 113 north toward Berlin and Ocean City. Follow Route 113 for about 28 miles to an intersection with Route 376, then turn right (east) toward Assateague. Go 4.1 miles to a T-intersection, and there turn right onto Route 611 south toward Assateague Island. Follow Route 611 for 3.1 miles to the national seashore's Barrier Island Visitor Center on the right.

To Assateague from Salisbury: Follow Route 50 east toward Ocean City. Stay on Route 50 past the exit for Route 90, then exit onto Route 113 south toward Snow Hill. From the end of the exit ramp, follow Route 113 south only 1.0 mile, then turn left onto Route 376 east toward Assateague. Go 4.1 miles to a T-intersection, and there turn right onto Route 611 south toward Assateague Island. Follow Route 611 for 3.1 miles to the national seashore's Barrier Island Visitor Center on the right.

To Assateague from the Delaware and Maryland seashore resorts: From the southern end of Ocean City, take Route 50 east only 1.3 miles to the intersection with Route 611 at a traffic light, and there turn left (south) toward the Assateague parks. Follow Route 611 for 7.2 miles to the national seashore's Barrier Island Visitor Center on the right.

From the more northerly seashore resorts (and even from the upper end of Ocean City), the fastest route is first to go west to Route 113, then follow it south. After passing over Route 50, continue south on Route 113 for 1.3 miles, then turn left onto Route 376 east toward Assateague. Go 4.1 miles to a T-intersection, and there turn right onto Route 611 south toward Assateague Island. Follow Route 611 for 3.1 miles to the national seashore's Barrier Island Visitor Center on the right.

BARRIER ISLAND VISITOR CENTER: Here you can orient yourself, see a film and various exhibits, and learn about the naturalist programs that are offered by the National Park Service at different seasons. You may also want to rent or buy a tape cassette for a **Driving Tape Tour** of the Maryland portion of the national seashore. The tape runs about an

MAP 37 -- Northern Assateague Island: main visitor areas

SINEPUXENT BAY

Rte. 611 →

Barrier Island Visitor Center

boat ramp

Verrazano Bridge

ASSATEAGUE ISLAND

wild beach (foot access only)

state park entrance

state park ranger station

bathhouse

parking

camping

Assateague State Park

CHINCOTEAGUE BAY

Bayberry Dr.

camping

ATLANTIC OCEAN

Bayside camping

Life of the Marsh Nature Trail

Bayside Dr.

national seashore entrance

parking: North Ocean Beach

bathhouse

national seashore ranger station

group camping

Old Ferry Landing Rd.

Oceanside camping

history exhibit

Life of the Forest Nature Trail

walk-in tent sites

Life of the Dunes Nature Trail

parking: South Ocean Beach

0   mile   1

hour, but you should allow more time in view of the likelihood that you will want to get out of your car at various exhibits and other points of interest. Exploring the three **Life of Assateague walking trails** passed by the car tour may occupy another hour or more. And then there is the **beach**, where the car tour ends, and where you can easily spend the better part of a day.

NORTHERN ASSATEAGUE ISLAND (Maps 37 and 38): From the national seashore's Barrier Island Visitor Center on the mainland, continue east on Route 611 for 1.1 miles to an intersection beyond the bridge. For the state park, continue straight another 0.1 mile. For the national seashore, bear right and go 2.2 miles to the entrance station and North Ocean Beach parking lot, where a ranger station is located.

For **swimming** during the period from late June through Labor Day, there are lifeguarded beaches with bathhouses at the national seashore's North Ocean Beach and at the state park. Swimmers at the state park should leave their cars in the day-use lot (open until sunset) unless they are also camping.

WALKING AT NORTHERN ASSATEAGUE ISLAND: The northern section of the national seashore provides excellent opportunities for walking. However, to avoid areas where hunting is permitted from late autumn through January, hikers should stay on the trails or on the beach.

Life of the Dunes, Life of the Forest, and **Life of the Marsh** are the names of three short interpretive trails at the national seashore, each about 0.5 mile round-trip. (See Map 37.) A booklet called *The Life of Assateague* provides commentary on these trails and is sold at the Barrier Island Visitor Center. The marsh trail is accessible by wheelchair, and eventually the forest trail will be too.

The beach north to Ocean City Inlet provides an outstanding round-trip walk of 12 miles, although, of course, you can turn round at any point in order to shorten your walk. (See Map 38.) Here, off-road vehicles are not permitted, whereas south of the state park, vehicular traffic on the beach can be heavy and detracts from a walk along the shore.

For a walk north toward Ocean City, leave your car in the state's day-use parking lot (which closes at sunset) and cross to the beach. During winter, when the state lot is usually closed, you will have to park 2 miles farther south at the national

MAP 38 -- Northern Assateague Island

N

0 1 2 3 4 5
miles

Rte. 113
Rte. 376
Rte. 611

Ocean City Inlet

SINEPUXENT BAY

(foot access only)

Sinepuxent campsite

wild beach

Barrier Island
Visitor Center

state park entrance

Assateague State Park

national seashore entrance

North Ocean Beach

ranger station

South Ocean Beach

Tingles campsite

Little Levels campsite

Pine Tree campsite

ASSATEAGUE ISLAND

CHINCOTEAGUE BAY

ATLANTIC OCEAN

Jims Gut campsite

jeep trail

Pope Bay campsite

State Line campsite

MD
VA

seashore. With the ocean on your right, walk north along the beach, which extends 6 miles from the state park to a boulder jetty at Ocean City Inlet. Please observe signs indicating that hikers should stay on the low beach so as not to disturb nesting birds.

CAR CAMPING: There are campgrounds at both the national seashore and the state park. During summer there is a strong demand for campsites, so call long ahead of time to reserve a spot. Only some of the sites can be reserved; the rest are available on a first-come, first-served basis.

At the national seashore, there are two campgrounds — Oceanside and Bayside — as shown on Map 37. Oceanside is open year-round; Bayside operates from spring through fall. Both campgrounds offer drive-in pads that can accommodate trailers, motorhomes, and tents. Both have drinking water, chemical toilets, and showers (cold water only), but no hookups for electricity or water. Some Oceanside tent sites are located a few hundred feet from parking spaces. For information telephone (410) 641-3030 or write to the Superintendent, Assateague Island National Seashore, Route 611, 7206 National Seashore Lane, Berlin, MD 21811.

The campground at the state park is open during the warmer half of the year and is equipped with drinking water, hot showers, bathhouses, and flush toilets. The campsites can accommodate trailers, motorhomes, and, of course, tents. For information on opening and closing dates and reservations, telephone (410) 641-2120.

BACKCOUNTRY CAMPING: An alternative to car camping is backpacking to designated remote campsites where there are picnic tables and chemical toilets but no water. The national seashore's pamphlet on "Assateague Island Backcountry Camping" will help with your planning. To obtain a copy, call (410) 641-3030, or write to the address noted two paragraphs above.

The various backcountry campsites are shown on Map 38. The campsites at Sinepuxent, Little Levels, and State Line are oceanside sites, open year-round and consisting simply of a bare expanse of sand behind the first ridge of dunes. Tingles, Pine Tree, Jims Gut, and Pope Bay are bayside campsites, open February through October. They are located among pine trees and are accessible by canoeists as well as by hikers. I prefer the oceanside sites, since there are fewer biting insects. I especially recommend camping during a warm spell in late fall, winter, or early spring, when there are no mosquitoes, flies, or ticks and when the sun and heat are not oppressive. Of course, even if the forecast is for pleasant weather, you should be prepared for storms and cold.

Before setting out for backcountry camping, you must obtain a free backcountry use permit at the national seashore ranger station at the North Ocean Beach parking lot on the day that you want to start. In order to allow enough daylight during which to reach your campsite, you are required to pick up your permit by specified times depending on the season and the destination. From February through March, the deadline for most sites is 5 P.M., but if you are going to the distant State Line or Pope Bay sites, the deadline is 2 P.M. From November through January, the deadline for the oceanside sites is 4 P.M., except for State Line, for which the deadline is noon.

For backcountry camping, you must carry in your own water (allow a half-gallon per day absolute minimum for drinking) and carry out your own trash. If you plan to cook, bring a stove. Also, bring sunscreen, sunglasses, a hat, insect repellent, and extra-long, sturdy tent stakes, since ordinary pegs will not hold in the sand.

OFF-ROAD VEHICLES: If you have a car or truck suitable for off-road use, you may enjoy driving along the beach. The stretch of beach open to ORVs is about 12 miles long, extending from the vicinity of the national seashore's South Ocean Beach parking lot to the Maryland/Virginia line. (See Map 38.) An annual permit is required and may be obtained at the ranger station. Information about off-road vehicle permits, vehicle specifications, required equipment, and other regulations are set forth in a leaflet called "Assateague Island Off-Road Vehicles," available from the national seashore.

BOATING AND CANOEING: Trailered boats can be launched from the state park's ramp at the west end of the Route 611 bridge. (See Map 37.) Canoes can be launched at the end of Ferry Landing Road in the national seashore. This is a good spot from which to set out for the four bayside backcountry campsites or from which simply to explore the marsh. Be aware, however, that strong winds can sometimes make canoeing here very difficult.

CHINCOTEAGUE NATIONAL WILDLIFE REFUGE
ASSATEAGUE ISLAND NATIONAL SEASHORE (southern section)

Despite its name, Chincoteague National Wildlife Refuge is located almost entirely on the Virginia portion of Assateague Island and is situated within the boundaries of Assateague Island National Seashore. Together, the federal refuge and seashore are among Delmarva's greatest natural areas. During fall and winter many thousands of waterfowl congregate on the refuge ponds, marshes, coves, and offshore waters, and some species are year-round residents, making southern Assateague a Mecca for bird watchers. (Seasonal fluctuations in waterfowl and wading birds more or less follow the same timetable as set forth in Chapter 3 on Bombay Hook National Wildlife Refuge.) Woods and scrubby brush provide habitat for other birds and wildlife, including sika deer (actually diminutive elk). And, yes, there are the wild ponies. (I enjoy these animals as much as anybody, but still, in my opinion, they are among the least of the reasons to come to Chincoteague.) Please do not approach the horses closely or feed them; they can bite and kick, inflicting severe injuries. The nationally-famous pony penning occurs the last Wednesday, Thursday, and Friday in July.

For those who want to watch birds from their car, Wildlife Loop is open daily from 3 P.M. to dusk. For walkers there are trails of all lengths, from less than a mile to an overnight trek of two dozen miles. For bicyclists there are paved paths that are closed to motor vehicles, although as just noted, bicyclists must share Wildlife Loop with cars after 3 P.M. And for beach lovers, there are many miles of seashore, including a bathing beach with bathhouses and lifeguards during summer. The refuge and seashore also offer a variety of interpretive programs and opportunities for clamming, crabbing, surf fishing, hunting, and driving off-road vehicles.

Chincoteague refuge is open every day year-round. The times at which the entrance gates are opened and closed change with the seasons and correspond roughly with pre-dawn twilight and nightfall. The admission fee entitles you to enter as often as you want for one week. Annual passes are also available. During summer the parking lots at the beach fill early in the day, especially on weekends. All pets are prohibited, even in your car.

Chincoteague National Wildlife Refuge is administered by the U.S. Fish and Wildlife Service; telephone (804) 336-6122. The National Park Service provides recreational services and management in the Toms Cove area, which includes the lifeguarded beach; telephone (804) 336-6577.

BARRIER ISLANDS SUCH AS ASSATEAGUE occupy much of the Atlantic coast of the United States south of New England. These long, thin, changeable islands are a product of waves, longshore currents, tides, and wind acting on the unconsolidated sediments of the coastal plain and continental shelf, which really are one continuous apron of sand, silt, and clay eroded from the Appalachian and Piedmont highlands to the west. Also contributing to the mile-thick mantle of deposits along the mid-Atlantic coast are immense quantities of gravel, sand, and rock flour scoured by continental glaciers from regions farther north and carried to the sea by huge rivers of meltwater that today survive in the relatively trivial trickle of the Hudson, Delaware, and Susquehanna rivers.

Together the coastal plain and continental shelf slope slightly eastward, and across this surface the shoreline has advanced and receded repeatedly as the ocean has risen and fallen, depending on how much of the planet's water has been amassed in the polar ice caps and in continental ice sheets. Since onset of the Pleistocene Epoch — or Ice Age — about two million year ago, there have been four episodes of continental glaciation in North America. The most recent incursion of northern ice to reach what are now New York, New Jersey, and Pennsylvania lasted from about 70,000 to 12,000 years ago, and during that period sea level was as much as 300 feet lower than at present. Even today the Ice Age continues at higher latitudes, where enough ice remains in the polar ice caps and the Greenland ice sheet to raise the ocean another 130 feet if the ice were to melt, as no doubt some of it will.

The rising sea level of our present geologic time has helped to create barrier islands in several different ways. For one thing, the rising ocean has resulted in massive and relentless erosion of the shore, and in this environment barrier islands have often originated as long spits of silt, sand, and pebbles trailing downcurrent from an eroding headland. Because the longshore current is simply the result of wind-driven waves striking the shore at an angle, the direction in which a spit grows reflects the region's dominant onshore winds interacting with the general orientation of the coastline. For example, the vicinity of Bethany Beach, Delaware, is an eroding headland — a visibly truncated peninsula bound by Indian River Bay to the north, Assawoman Bay to the south, and the open ocean to the east. (See Map 1 in the Table of Contents.) Both above and below Bethany, the coast angles slightly westward, like a boomerang or chevron pointing toward the ocean. Arriving from the east, incoming waves that strike above Bethany Beach produce a longshore current that washes sand along the coast toward the northwest, ultimately producing the spit at Cape Henlopen. Striking the shore below Bethany Beach, waves from the east wash material along the coast toward the southwest, producing the long coastal barrier consisting of Fenwick Island, Ocean City, and Assateague, which together trail downcurrent from the eroding Bethany headland.

Such spits can eventually grow so long that they may reach another headland or curve inland, thus nearly impounding the water behind them, as has occurred at Chincoteague Bay. When this happens, storm-driven waves and tide may rise so fast on the ocean side of the sandy barrier that the sea breaks through, creating an inlet and turning the spit into a narrow island or string of islands. Similarly, after a storm surge has partly inundated a low barrier island and has overfilled the bay behind it, the outgoing rush of water as the tide ebbs and the wind slackens may quickly carve a gap across the barrier. During the first third of this century, Assateague was linked to Ocean City, but a hurricane in 1933 blew so much water into Chincoteague, Sinepuxent, and Assawoman bays that the water broke out just south of the city, carving a channel across the spit and turning Assateague into an island. Normally, such gaps eventually fill in with sand swept laterally along the beachfront by the longshore current, but the inlet at Ocean City proved to be so convenient for boats that long jetties were constructed in order to keep the gap open.

Other forces are also at work. Because the coastal plain and continental shelf slope eastward at such a low gradient, the water offshore is shallow. In these shallows waves break, dissipating their energy and depositing their load of churned-up sand. As a shoal or bar develops, more and more sand is deposited behind the bar where the waves break. Eventually, the shoal may merge with an existing island or it may even by itself build upward above sea level, at which point vertical growth is augmented by wind-blown sand that is captured and anchored by grasses and other plants that colonize the new land to form dunes rising 5 or 10 or even as much as 30 feet above the ocean. At the same time, a very gradual rise in sea level — about a foot a century, geologists say — floods the shallows behind the sandy barrier, resulting in a bay of considerable width and depth separating the island from the mainland. Such a scenario can by itself lead to the creation of small barrier islands in areas where there is a substantial and continuous input of sand, as near a river mouth. Some of these processes appear to be at work in the vicinity of Chincoteague Inlet, where there is considerable shoal formation and where a few low islands have developed opposite the tip of Toms Cove Hook at the southern end of Assateague.

The growth of spits and shoals and their transformation into barrier islands are processes that have actually been observed over long periods of time. A third way for barrier islands to originate is more speculative. It is possible that some long, narrow barrier islands started simply as rows of high dunes along the coast of the mainland. Over time these sandy ridges may have been isolated by the rising sea, which flooded the low areas behind the dunes to create wide lagoons and bays. This process could explain, for example, the Outer Banks of North Carolina in the vicinity of Cape Hatteras, where the narrow barrier islands, now spectacularly far offshore, may once have been high dunes along the mainland coast when sea level was 300 feet lower than at present.

Even a cursory glance at old (and not so old) maps shows that barrier islands such as Assateague are constantly changing. Inlets form and heal or move under the influence of the longshore current. For example, Martinet's 1885 Map of Maryland — which includes also the bordering areas of Virginia — shows only a rudimentary spit at the southern end of Assateague, but during the last hundred years this spit has grown about 3 miles to form Toms Cove Hook (see Map 39).

Over the longer term — at least during the period of rising sea level that has been under way since the retreat of the last continental glacier — the barrier islands of the mid-Atlantic region have been migrating westward under the influence of occasional major storms. The biggest storms may wash entirely over some of the low islands, such as those of the Delmarva Peninsula, eroding the side that faces the sea and at the same time burying in sand the marshes along the islands' western margins. In fact, long, low, narrow islands such as Assateague are sometimes termed washover barriers, and there are large parts of Chincoteague National Wildlife Refuge at southern Assateague that occupy areas that are called wash flats.

Evidence that much of Assateague Island is retreating westward toward the mainland is plain to see. At some places on Assateague, beds of peat that were formed in what was once marsh along the island's back shore have been exposed by waves on what is now the ocean front. Similarly, stumps from forests of cedar and pine that once grew on the western side of the islands have on occasion been revealed by erosion at what is now the beach. The fact that Assateague and similar barrier island are retreating westward does not necessarily mean, however, that the bays behind the islands are shrinking or that the islands will one day merge with the mainland. Rather, in most places the mainland shore is also retreating westward as the sea rises, so that an expanse of water between the mainland and barrier islands is maintained.

Although washover has historically been a common phenomenon at Assateague, the formation of inlets is a more usual process by which sand from the ocean front is transported to the back shore of a barrier, resulting in westward movement of an island or spit. When a storm carves a new inlet, that event alone often involves the displacement of an immense quantity of sand, some of which may be swept into the bay behind the barrier. And as long as the gap remains open — which could be merely for a season or for a period of years — the inlet intercepts sand carried by the longshore current. Waves and tide wash the sand into the bay, where it settles in the relatively still waters and forms a delta-like complex of shoals and channels that persist even after the inlet heals at the beachfront. At Assateague, ample evidence of former inlets is readily apparent along the back side of the island. For example, Map 37 on page 223 in Chapter 15 shows various channels and delta-like formations of old inlets along the western side of the island. Such bayside shoals provide the foundation for the growth of marshes and ultimately of dry land as wind and overwash bury the marsh in yet more sand. In this way the island grows on the west side as it erodes on the east, resulting in retreat toward the mainland, which is itself retreating as the sea rises.

When the first European settlers arrived at Assateague in the mid-1600s, they found waterfowl "in millionous multitudes," according to one colonist's account. At that time, nobody lived year-round on Assateague, but the testimony of the Europeans shows that Indians from the mainland regularly hunted and gathered shellfish on the island.

By the last quarter of the seventeenth century, English settlers were using Chincoteague and Assateague islands for grazing livestock, and it is probably from some of their horses that the wild ponies seen on Assateague today are descended. The islands were considered to be good places for grazing cattle and horses because no fences were needed and the marsh and dune grasses provided ample fodder. Several small settlements were established by stockmen and by those who fished or hunted for a livelihood. This pattern continued through the eighteenth and nineteenth centuries.

The largest settlement on Assateague Island was Assateague Village, located in the vicinity of the lighthouse built in 1867 near what was then the southernmost tip of the island. At the beginning of the twentieth century, Assateague Village had a population of about 200 people, engaged in commercial fishing, clamming, and oystering, as well as grazing sheep, horses, and cattle. From 1912 until it burned in 1916, there was a fish factory where as many as fifty workers were employed processing menhaden into oil and fertilizer. (The foundations of this factory are still visible on the southeast shore of Toms Cove.) Another fish factory operated from 1919 to 1929. However, as the hook grew in length and the cove filled with sand, large boats could no longer land there, so the factory was closed and the houses of the village — or at least most of them — were moved by barge to neighboring Chincoteague Island. The abandonment of Assateague Village prepared the way for the creation in 1943 of Chincoteague National Wildlife Refuge, occupying the southern third of Assateague Island.

Please keep in mind, when you visit Chincoteague National Wildlife Refuge, that the priorities here mandated by law are first to protect endangered species, then to promote waterfowl and other native animals, and only lastly to accommodate visitors. If we cannot behave responsibly during our visits, in the future we will simply be barred from many activities and areas within the refuge that we presently enjoy.

AUTOMOBILE DIRECTIONS: Chincoteague National Wildlife Refuge occupies the Atlantic coast in Virginia immediately south of the boundary with Maryland. Only a very small part of the Chincoteague refuge is on Chincoteague Island. Most of the refuge occupies the southern third of Assateague Island, which is the long barrier island that stretches south of Ocean City Inlet for 37 miles. (See Map 1 in the Table of Contents.)

To Chincoteague Refuge from northern Delmarva and Interstate 95 southwest of Wilmington: From Interstate 95 take Route 7 south, then follow the signs for Route 1 to Route 13 toward Dover. (Please note, however, that Route 7 will not be linked to Route 1 until the fall of 1992, so until then simply take Route 7 south to Route 13.) Once you are on Route 13 southbound, follow it down through Delaware and into Maryland. Continue south on Route 13 past Salisbury, Princess Anne, Pocomoke City, and the junction with Route 113 (which provides an alternative approach from the north). After crossing the state line into Virginia, continue south on Route 13 for 4.0 miles to the intersection with Route 175, and there turn left (east) toward Wallops Island, Chincoteague, and Assateague. Go 10.4 miles, although along the way you may want to stop at the visitor center for NASA's Wallops Flight Facility. At a T-intersection in the town of Chincoteague, turn left to follow Route 175-Y north toward Assateague. Continue 0.4 mile, then turn right onto Maddox Boulevard toward Assateague. Go 2.1 miles — at one point passing almost half-way around a traffic circle, beyond which are the Oyster and Maritime Museum and Refuge Waterfowl Museum. Continue to the entrance station for Chincoteague National Wildlife Refuge and Assateague Island National Seashore.

To Chincoteague Refuge from the Chesapeake Bay Bridge: After crossing the bridge, follow Route 50/301 across Kent Island. At the point where Route 50 and Route 301 split, fork right to follow Route 50 past Easton, Cambridge, and Salisbury. East of Salisbury, take Route 13 south toward Norfolk. Follow Route 13 past Princess Anne and Pocomoke City. After crossing the state line into Virginia, continue south on Route 13 for 4.0 miles to the intersection with Route 175 and there turn left (east) toward Wallops Island, Chincoteague, and Assateague. Go 10.4 miles, although along the way you may want to stop at the visitor center for NASA's Wallops Flight Facility. At a T-intersection in the town of Chincoteague, turn left to follow Route 175-Y north toward Assateague. Go 2.1 miles — at one point passing almost half-way around a traffic circle, beyond which are the Oyster and Maritime Museum and Refuge Waterfowl Museum. Continue to the entrance station for Chincoteague National Wildlife Refuge and Assateague Island National Seashore.

To Chincoteague Refuge from southernmost Delmarva and the Chesapeake Bay Bridge-Tunnel at Norfolk: After crossing the bridge-tunnel, follow Route 13 north from the toll plaza for about 64 miles, passing (toward the end) through Temperanceville and Oak Hall. Continue to the intersection with Route 175, and there turn right (east) toward Wallops Island, Chincoteague, and Assateague. Go 10.4 miles, although along the way you may want to stop at the visitor center for NASA's Wallops Flight Facility. At a T-intersection in the town of Chincoteague, turn left to follow Route 175-Y north toward Assateague. Continue 0.4 mile, then turn right onto Maddox Boulevard toward Assateague. Go 2.1 miles — at one point passing almost half-way around a traffic circle, beyond which are the Oyster and Maritime Museum and Refuge Waterfowl Museum. Continue to the entrance station for Chincoteague National Wildlife Refuge and Assateague Island National Seashore.

To Chincoteague refuge from Salisbury and the Delaware and Maryland seashore resorts: From Salisbury follow Route 13 south. From the Delaware and Maryland beach resorts, go west to Route 113 and follow it south. In either case, go to the junction of Route 13 and Route 113 near Pocomoke City, and from there continue south on Route 13. After crossing the state line into Virginia, continue south on Route 13 for 4.0 miles to the intersection with Route 175, and there turn left (east) toward Wallops Island, Chincoteague, and Assateague. Go 10.4 miles, although along the way you may want to stop at the visitor center for NASA's Wallops Flight Facility. At a T-intersection in the town of Chincoteague, turn left to follow Route 175-Y north toward Assateague. Continue 0.4 mile, then turn right onto Maddox Boulevard toward Assateague. Go 2.1 miles — at one point passing almost half-way around a traffic circle, beyond which are the Oyster and Maritime Museum and Refuge Waterfowl Museum. Continue to the entrance station for Chincoteague National Wildlife Refuge and Assateague Island National Seashore.

CHINCOTEAGUE REFUGE AND ASSATEAGUE SEASHORE: Map 39 shows the roads, visitor centers, parking lots, bicycle paths, foot trails, and other facilities at the southern end of Assateague Island.

The main refuge road leads 2.7 miles to the beach, where there are several large parking lots, some bathhouses, and the **Toms Cove Visitor Center** (administered by the National Park Service). Along the road are places to pull over for viewing waterfowl from your car.

MAP 39 -- Southern Assateague Island: main visitor areas

The **Chincoteague Refuge Visitor Center** (administered by the Fish and Wildlife Service) is located next to the parking lot at the entrance to Wildlife Loop, which is open to cars from 3 P.M. to dusk. Wildlife Loop is also a popular walkway and bicycle path, so drive very slowly.

Swimming draws large crowds to the national seashore during summer and early fall. From mid-June through Labor Day, lifeguards are on duty from 9:30 A.M. to 5:30 P.M. daily at the beach by the Toms Cove Visitor Center. Although you may swim elsewhere or at other hours if you wish, it is clearly safer to swim at the lifeguarded beach.

A wide range of **wildlife tours and programs** are offered at Chincoteague National Wildlife Refuge. A concessionaire provides a 1.5-hour Wildlife Safari via a large, bus-like trailer. This tour explores the back roads of the refuge, including the service road that stretches north from Wildlife Drive. There is also a 1.5-hour evening cruise through Assateague Channel via tour boat. For information and reservations call (804) 336-5593 or (804) 336-5511, or write to Island Cruises, Inc., P.O. Box 83, Chincoteague, VA 23336. Schedules change with the seasons. If you have not secured a reservation before you arrive, you can inquire in person at the tour booth located at the Chincoteague Refuge Visitor Center. Refuge and park service staff also provide a variety of naturalist activities, including auditorium programs and guided nature walks. Information about these activities is available at the refuge visitor center or at the park service's Toms Cove Visitor Center.

WALKING AT CHINCOTEAGUE REFUGE AND ASSATEAGUE SEASHORE:

Assateague Island provides some of the best walking on the East Coast.

Wildlife Loop (see Map 39) is a paved road 3.0 miles long around Snow Goose Pool. It is open to pedestrians, bicyclists, and — from 3 P.M. to dusk — to cars also. Park at the refuge visitor center just west of Snow Goose Pool.

The Marsh Trail leads 1.0 mile round-trip from the parking lot at the refuge visitor center to an overlook at Snow Goose Pool.

The Lighthouse Trail is a pedestrian loop only a few hundred yards long. On weekends during the warmer months, there are exhibits of wildlife art at the lighthouse oil shed.

The Toms Cove Nature Trail is another short loop; it starts opposite the southern beach parking lots.

The Woodland Trail is a paved loop 1.6 miles long. It is open to pedestrians and bicyclists. The loblolly pine forest through which the trail passes is the best area to see the endangered Delmarva Peninsula fox squirrel. The trail also has an observation deck that overlooks a marsh where you might see wild ponies or deer.

Toms Cove Hook provides an opportunity to walk for as much as 8 miles, first along the exposed ocean beach, then along the sheltered shore of Toms Cove, where waterfowl congregate during fall and winter. Off-road vehicles also have access to the hook's southern and westernmost beaches. In order to allow tern's and plovers (particularly the endangered Piping Plover) to nest undisturbed, the hook is closed to hikers and vehicles from March 15 through August 31.

To reach Toms Cove Hook from the large parking lots at the beach, cross the dunes at one of the established crossovers, then hike along the beach with the ocean on your left. Pass the old Assateague Beach Coast Guard Station, now used as a seasonal residence for park staff. Follow the beach to the tip of the hook (Fishing Point), where the shore curves sharply right. Return the way you came, or, if you prefer, return by continuing along the shore of Toms Cove, where vehicles are not permitted. You can cross back to the beach at the old Coast Guard station.

The wild beach that stretches north 11 miles from the Toms Cove Visitor Center to the Virginia-Maryland boundary is a hiker's paradise. (See Map 40.) Vehicles are not permitted here. As you walk north, you will see fewer and fewer people, and if you go during winter, you can have the beach virtually to yourself. In gauging how far you want to walk, simply remember that you must return the way you came.

D Dike Crossover provides the opportunity for a circuit of 7 miles, as shown by the bold line on Map 41. This is one of my favorite walks, passing through most of the different habitats present at Chincoteague National Wildlife Refuge. However, because the route in part follows the service road for a mile, please read also the paragraph on hunting and other hazards starting at the bottom of page 242.

For D Dike Crossover, park in the lot by the refuge visitor center just west of Wildlife Loop. Enter the drive and turn left in order to follow the paved road north, with woods on your left and — after a few hundred yards — the marsh and Snow Goose Pool on your right. (Watch for cars after 3 P.M.) Where

MAP 40 -- Southern Assateague Island

the paved road veers right across the water, continue straight past a gate and go about 1 mile on the dirt service road through piny woods. Bear half-right at the second dirt road intersecting from the right. (This is the D Dike road, and sometimes it is marked as such, but signs have a way of falling down in the sand or being vandalized.) Follow the D Dike road to and across the dunes; then — with the ocean on your left — follow the beach south about 3 miles. When you reach stairs over the foredunes, cross to a large parking lot within sight of Toms Cove Visitor Center.

To return to the parking lot west of Wildlife Loop, locate the paved hiker/biker path at the northwest corner of the parking lot — that is, at the corner farthest from Toms Cove Visitor Center. Follow the trail along a backdune and to the left through the woods. Merge with Wildlife Loop and continue straight. (Watch for oncoming cars) Pass a bicycle trail intersecting from the left. About 75 yards after passing a dirt road that intersects from the left, bear left to the parking lot where you started.

The service road, which is open to pedestrians but closed to all but authorized vehicles, extends along the western side of Assateague Island. (See Map 40.) For the most part, the service road is a well-graded dirt road terminating at a turn-around 7.5 miles north of the Chincoteague Refuge Visitor Center. From the turn-around, the service road continues half-left as a rutted jeep trail, leading another 3 miles to the Old Fields Crossover, which is the only place — other than D Dike — where it is permissible to cross from the service road to the beach.

With certain caveats mentioned in the next paragraph, the service road provides outstanding walking. Of course, you do not have to hike all the way to the Old Fields Crossover. In gauging how far you want to go, simply remember that you must return the way you came.

In planning a walk along the service road, bear in mind that hunting in this area is allowed on weekdays during certain periods in fall and winter, and on those occasions you must wear a blaze-orange coat or vest. Call (804) 336-6122 for information about dates when hunters — with their vehicles — are permitted on the service road. If you do not want to bother to call, simply wear orange or go on Saturday or Sunday, when hunting is prohibited. Also, avoid walking on the service road during the two weekends and intervening week that embrace

MAP 41 -- Southern Assateague Island: D Dike walking tour

Thanksgiving. During this period, the service road is open to general traffic for people who want to see the area from their cars. Finally, from mid-April through November, bring insect repellent.

To start your walk on the service road, park in the lot for the refuge visitor center just west of Wildlife Loop. Enter the drive and turn left in order to follow the paved road north, with woods on your left and — after a few hundred yards — the marsh and Snow Goose Pool on your right. (Watch for cars after 3 P.M.) Where the paved road veers right across the water, continue straight past a gate on the dirt service road.

BACKPACKING AND CAMPING: These activities are permitted, but only if you are willing to hike 12.5 miles to the State Line backcountry campsite, located a mile north of the boundary with Maryland. (See Map 40.) The State Line campsite consists of nothing more than an expanse of sand behind the foredunes, a picnic table, and a chemical toilet. There is no nearer campsite, and camping at undesignated points is prohibited. The national seashore's pamphlet on "Assateague Island Backcountry Camping" will help with your planning. To obtain a copy, call (804) 336-6577 or (410) 641-3030, or write to the Superintendent, Assateague Island National Seashore, Route 611, 7206 National Seashore Lane, Berlin, MD 21811.

If you are in reasonably good physical condition, hiking north to the State Line campsite makes a memorable overnight excursion, allowing ample time to enjoy the bleak and pleasant ambiance of the surf, beach, and low dunes. But remember, hiking in soft sand with a heavy pack is hard work, requiring more time and effort than walking on firm ground. I especially recommend camping during a warm spell in late fall, winter, or early spring, when there are no mosquitoes, flies, or ticks and when the sun and heat are not oppressive. Of course, even if the forecast is for pleasant weather, you should be prepared for storms and cold.

For backcountry camping, you must obtain a free backcountry use permit at the Toms Cove Visitor Center before 2 P.M. (or before noon from November through January) on the day that you want to start. You must also carry in your own water (allow a half-gallon per day absolute minimum for drinking) and carry out your own trash. If you plan to cook, bring a stove. Also, bring sunscreen, sunglasses, a hat, insect repellent, and extra-long, sturdy tent stakes, since ordinary pegs will not hold in the sand.

When you set out for the State Line campsite from the Toms Cove Visitor Center, the ocean, of course, will be on your right. The State Line campsite is located about a mile north of a fence that marks the boundary between Maryland and Virginia. A small sign showing a hiker marks the campsite.

For your return walk from the State Line campsite, you may want to hike along the service road. (See Map 40 and the discussion starting on page 242). The area through which the road passes is very scenic, and I strongly recommend it. From the beach, the service road can be reached via the Old Fields Crossover, located 1.7 miles south of the fence at the state line and marked (maybe) by tire tracks issuing from the dunes and also (maybe) by a post bearing the letters OF. Of course, at its southern end, the service road terminates at Wildlife Loop, so from there you must follow Wildlife Loop left to the paved bicycle path that leads to the Toms Cove Visitor Center. Or you can cross over to the beach at D Dike. Either way, the distance from the state line to Toms Cove Visitor Center is 13 miles — slightly greater than along the beach, but from the service road you will see far more birds and also deer and horses.

Finally, long-distance hikers may be tempted by the prospect of **walking along the beach from one end of Assateague Island to the other**, camping along the way. I have done this, and it was a disappointment. Between the state line and the North Ocean Beach access point (see Map 38 on page 225 in Chapter 15) all but the last mile of beach is open to off-road vehicles, so that progress for the hiker is measured by marching from one fisherman's motor vehicle to the next parked at intervals of a few hundred yards along the heavily rutted beach, while yet other cars and pickup trucks zoom by at fairly frequent intervals. This goes on for 13 miles. Even if the fish are not running, there can be a lot of traffic on this section of the beach, making it unattractive to hikers, especially compared to the marvelous wild beach south of the state line or at the northern end of Assateague Island.

17

ACCOMACK and NORTHAMPTON COUNTIES

This chapter explores the -va in Delmarva, or that is, the small piece of Virginia occupying the extreme southern end of Chesapeake Bay's Eastern Shore. So long and narrow are Virginia's Accomack and Northampton counties (see Map 1 in the Table of Contents) that in themselves they form a peninsula appended to the lower end of the larger Delmarva Peninsula.

For many people, this is an utterly blank place on their mental map of the Atlantic seaboard. Although Assateague Island National Seashore and the resort town of Chincoteague are well known, they occupy the extreme northeastern corner of this part of Virginia and are described separately in Chapter 16. As for the rest of Virginia's Eastern Shore, it is an agricultural region characterized by numerous farm hamlets, many dating from the colonial period, as well as a few larger Victorian towns created by the railroad. More recently, some commercial strips have been spawned by Route 13, the main north-south highway. At the ends of the roads that extend east to the marshes and channels behind the barrier islands of the Atlantic coast, there are a series of wharf-villages devoted to commercial and sport fishing. And at places on or near the navigable tidal creeks that penetrate inland from Chesapeake Bay are various faded villages and a few larger towns going back hundreds of years, in some cases derived from this or that tavern, general store, tobacco warehouse, court, or church built in the seventeenth century.

The 95-mile car tour outlined on Map 43 starts at the town of Accomac (seat of Accomack County), where there is an attractive historic district best seen on foot. From Accomac the route leads past Wachapreague and Willis Wharf (two fishing towns) to Brownsville Farm, which offers outstanding walking through woods, past cultivated fields, and across marsh bordering Hog Island Bay. Brownsville Farm is part of The Nature Conservancy's Virginia Coast Reserve; telephone (804) 442-3049. The Nature Conservancy allows walkers who do not make a nuisance of themselves to enter the property between dawn and dusk. Because hunting is sometimes permitted at Brownsville Farm, please see page 263 for a note on safety.

Still trending south, the car tour eventually reaches Eastville (seat of Northampton County), where a museum consisting of the colonial courthouse, the early nineteenth-century clerk's office, and the debtor's prison is open on weekdays from 9 to 5. Almost next door is the colonial Eastville Inn, open for dining from 11 to 3 on weekdays, plus Friday and Saturday evenings during summer; telephone (804) 678-9034.

From Eastville the car tour heads north along the bayside stage road, passing through such ancient villages as Bridgetown and Pungoteague, sites of the two oldest churches on Virginia's Eastern Shore. At Onancock the sumptuous mansion at Kerr Place is open Tuesday through Saturday from 10 to 4. Kerr Place is managed by the Eastern Shore of Virginia Historical Society; telephone (804) 787-8012.

The car tour ends at the Victorian railroad town of Parksley, where the Eastern Shore Railway Museum is open Tuesday through Saturday from 10 to 4 and on Sunday from 1 to 4. During winter the museum may be closed on Tuesday.

Finally, the Eastern Shore of Virginia has an annual Garden Week Tour on the last Friday and Saturday of April, when many private houses are open to view. For information telephone the Chamber of Commerce in Accomac: (804) 787-2460.

ENGLISH SETTLEMENT on the Eastern Shore of Virginia started in 1614, when seventeen men were sent from Jamestown to operate a salt works on a tract of land facing Cherrystone Creek just north of the present-day town of Cape Charles — which in turn is a dozen miles above the actual Cape Charles at the mouth of Chesapeake Bay. Periodically a ship from Jamestown brought supplies to sustain the outpost and took away the barrels of salt produced by evaporating sea water in large kettles over wood fires. By 1617, however, the outpost had been abandoned.

For strategic reasons the colony's leaders at Jamestown were anxious to control both sides of Chesapeake Bay, and accordingly in 1620 another settlement was established at Cherrystone Creek when seventy-five men were sent out under contract with the Virginia Company to work company-owned land. The Virginia Company (originally called the London Company) was the commercial venture that sponsored and governed the colony from the time Jamestown was founded in 1607 until 1624, when the company's charter was annulled because of mismanagement and lack of profits. Thereafter Virginia was a royal colony, subject to an ill-defined balance of power between the governor, who was appointed by the king and answerable only to him, and the locally elected House of Burgesses, which had been established in 1619.

In 1624 the English population of Accomack Plantation — as the settled area of Virginia's Eastern Shore was called — was only 79 people, and the following year it dropped to 51 after the employees on the Virginia Company's land were transferred to the Western Shore of the Chesapeake. The land books sent to England that year listed only three owners of private tracts east of the bay. Presumably the rest of the adult population of Accomack Plantation were tenants on the company land (which had been subdivided and leased after removal of the company's men), settlers in the process of perfecting title to land, and indentured laborers.

Land policy was intended to promote rapid yet orderly settlement. Under the headright system, a settler received 50 acres of land for each person (including himself) whom he transported to Virginia at his own expense to live and work on his land for a stipulated period. The colony's various local courts — meeting monthly at private houses or taverns — had authority to issue certificates allowing a settler to move onto unclaimed land with his workers. After the claimant had improved the property with a house, garden, and orchard and had cleared and planted some fields, and after he had the land surveyed (which was sometimes delayed for years because of the shortage of qualified surveyors), he could exchange the certificate for a patent granting him title to the land. To prevent settlers from scattering far and wide in search of the most fertile land, the courts could — and sometimes did — refuse to issue certificates for sites that were considered to be too distant for collective defense and convenient government.

Part and parcel of the land system was the practice of indentured servitude, by which immigrants without money bound themselves to work for a master for a term of years in exchange for being transported to the New World and provided with food, lodging, clothing, and tools during the period of servitude, plus a modest premium at the end of their term. By 1641, when the population of Virginia was about 7,500, three-fourths of the settlers had come from England as indentured servants, most of whom worked as field hands. After about 1670, however, the influx of indentured immigrants declined, and instead labor was increasingly performed by African slaves. At first slaves were imported primarily from Caribbean plantations, but after the beginning of the eighteenth century, they were brought in large numbers directly from Africa.

The population of Virginia's Eastern Shore in 1641 was about 700 people. The entire region was one county, established in 1634 and termed Accomack County, but the population was confined to the southern half below Occahannock Creek, or what is now Northampton County. The county had its own court, whose commissioners (typically the leading citizens) not only adjudicated minor civil and criminal cases but also issued local laws and regulations. By the end of 1642, the region had two churches, each with its own minister, who like every other man was also a tobacco planter, supported in part by his glebe or farm owned by the parish. There was also a commander of the militia, in which all men served without pay. The county was divided into six military districts, and drills and target practice were held regularly. Occasionally the militiamen were alerted in response to perceived threats from Indians, conflicts with foreign powers (mainly the Dutch), or the appearance of pirates in Chesapeake Bay. Compared, however, to the area along the upper James River, where there were major massacres by the Indians and bloody reprisals by the settlers, the Eastern Shore was peaceful.

Every Virginia planter grew tobacco, which was used as a substitute for money (debts, for example, being expressed in pounds of tobacco). Raising cattle, pigs, and sheep was also common. Marked by brands or by various ways of slashing and cropping the ears, the livestock were allowed to wander freely in the woods. Each planter was responsible for erecting a fence conforming to legal standards in order to keep livestock out of his fields; if the animals broke through such a fence, their owner was accountable for the damage they did. Salt-meat, cheese, hides, and wool were exported to England and also to other colonies; some food was sold to reprovision ships. For the most part, however, effort was so concentrated on growing and exporting tobacco that in 1647 the Burgesses enacted a law requiring that every planter also grow, as a precaution against famine, 3 acres of corn for each of his tithables — or that is, people on whom taxes were paid.

By 1663 settlement of Virginia's Eastern Shore had spread over such a large area that the region was divided into two counties — Accomack and Northampton — although the dividing line was placed somewhat south of the present-day boundary that runs from the vicinity of Belle Haven on the west side of the peninsula to Willis Wharf on the east. Three years later, the pace at which vacant land was patented increased greatly when the headright system was replaced by a new set of requirements for acquiring title. Large tracts could be patented merely by building a tiny house (12 by 12 feet minimum), putting someone in it for a year, and fencing 1 acre for an orchard and garden. However, such patents were subject to a rent, payable to the king, of two shillings per year for each 50 acres. The new land system favored those who had the capital to pay the rent while the land was brought into production, or who could possibly make the land immediately profitable by putting herds of cattle on it. Under the new land system, immense tracts were patented in the northern part of Accomack County, including the coastal marshes and Atlantic barrier islands. These remote and isolated areas were used for grazing livestock because the animals could not easily wander away or damage farm fields.

During Bacon's Rebellion in 1676, William Berkeley, the royal governor at the time, fled from Jamestown to Virginia's Eastern Shore, where he established a stronghold and temporary capitol at the residence of John Custis II on Old Plantation Creek, south of the present-day town of Cape Charles. The Eastern Shore militia remained loyal to the governor, who retained the sympathies of the tidewater planters against Bacon's frontiersmen. Bacon sent a ship with soldiers to seize Berkeley, but it was boarded and captured by the governor's forces. From the Eastern Shore Berkeley led an expedition to reinstall himself at Jamestown, but Bacon attacked and burned the town, and Berkeley again fled. After Bacon died of malaria, the rebellion collapsed, and early in 1677 Berkeley returned from the Eastern Shore to the region along the James River. There he executed many of Bacon's followers before being recalled to England by King Charles II, who is said to have remarked of Berkeley, "The old fool has put to death more people in that naked country than I did here for the murder of my father."

By the beginning of the eighteenth century, the settlement of Virginia's Eastern Shore was as far advanced as any other part of the colony's tidewater region. Virginia's Eastern Shore had a population of 6,000 people, as compared with 70,000 for all of Virginia. Almost 90 percent of Northampton County and 80 percent of Accomack County were patented. Ferries sailed twice weekly from Kings Creek to the ports of York and Hampton on the Western Shore. Although most of the creeks of Virginia's Eastern Shore were too shallow to accommodate large ships, many smaller vessels came and went. A few major ports, through which all goods shipped into or out of the colony were supposed to pass, had collectors of customs, and even minor ports had ballast overseers to supervise the unloading of stone, gravel, and sand ballast onto land, rather than allowing it to be dumped overboard where it might hinder navigation.

Virginia's Eastern Shore in 1700 had two roads, one bayside and the other seaside, each running from Cape Charles to the Maryland line, plus in Accomack County a middle north-south road. There was also a network of cross roads, leading to churches, meeting places of the courts, public wharves, tobacco warehouses, and mills. Along these roads tobacco was either hauled in carts or rolled in large barrels called hogsheads, through which an axle was run like a lawn roller. To construct and maintain roads, every freeman was required to supply laborers in proportion to the number of tithables he had, and owners of land adjacent to roads were responsible for keeping the way free from fallen trees.

During the years leading up to the Revolutionary War, the Eastern Shore of Virginia participated in the widespread opposition to England's attempts to raise more revenue from the American colonies. Resolutions denouncing the Stamp Act were adopted by the courts of Accomack and Northampton counties, and people who chose to ignore the Stamp Act were not prosecuted. When actual fighting broke out, the two counties supplied seven companies of soldiers to the Continental Army. Because the British blockaded the mouth of Chesapeake Bay, supplies from France and from neutral countries were landed at Metompkin and Chincoteague creeks on the Atlantic coast, then brought overland and reloaded onto small craft that evaded the British barges operating in the bay. Occasionally during the war, British raiding parties seized flour, livestock, and poultry to replenish the supplies of their warships. Operating from remote outposts along the Chesapeake shore, bands of loyalists — or in some cases merely piratical opportunists called picaroons — ransacked and burned the plantations of known patriots and seized their slaves and ships. Except for this nasty guerilla war, however, the Eastern Shore was relatively peaceful compared to the Western Shore, where Portsmouth was burned and the war eventually reached its climax at Yorktown.

Throughout the eighteenth century, tobacco and livestock were the principal sources of wealth, but by the beginning of the nineteenth century, when the population of Virginia's Eastern Shore was more than 22,000, cotton began to be grown, and for a few decades it replaced tobacco as the chief money crop. Cotton, in turn, gave way to vegetables shipped to rapidly expanding urban markets, especially after 1829, when completion of the Chesapeake and Delaware Canal across the isthmus at the northern end of the Delmarva Peninsula greatly reduced the distance from Chesapeake Bay ports to northern cities. Sailing vessels carried farm products and also seafood from Delmarva to Norfolk, Washington, Baltimore, Philadelphia, and New York. On Virginia's Eastern Shore, the transition to producing and shipping perishable foodstuffs accelerated when steamboats went into service in the early 1840s.

By the beginning of the Civil War in 1860, the Eastern Shore of Virginia was growing mainly sweet potatoes, Irish potatoes, corn, oats, and some cotton. The fact that Union forces completely controlled the region and all of Chesapeake Bay throughout the war reinforced the orientation of local markets toward northern cities. Extension of the railroad southward from Maryland in 1884 to a terminus at the new town of Cape Charles provided further stimulus to an economy based on shipping vegetables, strawberries, and seafood.

The twentieth century has seen yet other shifts in the Eastern Shore's agricultural economy. As has occurred nationally, farm population and the number of farms has steadily decreased since the early 1900s, while the size and efficiency of farms has increased. During the first third of the century, potatoes were the main cash crop, but as with all agricultural commodities, overproduction caused prices to plummet during the Great Depression of the 1930s, just as the price of tobacco had periodically collapsed during the colonial period. During the Depression, soybeans were introduced as a new crop, and by 1960 led in acreage, followed by a variety of vegetables harvested by migrant laborers.

Probably the most important development on Virginia's Eastern Shore in the latter half of the twentieth century has been construction of the 17.6-mile Chesapeake Bay Bridge-Tunnel at the southern tip of the peninsula. Completed in 1964, it has greatly increased traffic passing up and down the peninsula and has stimulated tourism and light industry, although the economy of the region remains primarily agricultural. Linking Cape Charles and Norfolk, the bridge-tunnel caused immediate abandonment of the automobile ferries that used to serve Virginia's Eastern Shore. Just as building the railroad in the nineteenth century stole business from the old towns on the stage roads and created a new locus of commercial activity, so the advent of motor vehicles, the building of Route 13 (finished in 1931), and construction of the bridge-tunnel have caused a relocation of business away from the railroad towns to the vicinity of the highway. The tour outlined below, however, largely ignores Route 13 and follows instead some of the region's oldest roads through areas unseen by most visitors.

AUTOMOBILE DIRECTIONS: Accomack and Northampton counties in Virginia occupy the extreme southern end of the Delmarva Peninsula. (See Map 1 in the Table of Contents.) Together, they comprise all of the portion of Virginia that is located east of Chesapeake Bay. The car tour shown on Map 43 starts at the town of Accomac, so you should go there first.

To Accomac from northern Delmarva and Interstate 95 southwest of Wilmington: From Interstate 95 take

Route 7 south, then follow the signs for Route 1 to Route 13 toward Dover. (Please note, however, that Route 7 will not be linked to Route 1 until the fall of 1992, so until then simply take Route 7 south to Route 13.) Once you are on Route 13 southbound, follow it down through Delaware and into Maryland. Continue south on Route 13 past Salisbury, Princess Anne, Pocomoke City, and the junction with Route 113 (which provides an alternative approach from the north). After crossing the state line into Virginia, continue south on Route 13 for nearly 22.0 miles. Pass an exit for Business Route 13 toward Accomac, then (after 1.5 miles) turn left toward Accomac at a crossroads with Route 764. Park in the center of town next to the courthouse green.

To Accomac from the Chesapeake Bay Bridge: After crossing the bridge, follow Route 50/301 across Kent Island. At the point where Route 50 and Route 301 split, fork right to follow Route 50 past Easton, Cambridge, and Salisbury. East of Salisbury, take Route 13 south toward Norfolk. Follow Route 13 past Princess Anne and Pocomoke City. After crossing the state line into Virginia, continue south on Route 13 for nearly 22.0 miles. Pass an exit for Business Route 13 toward Accomac, then (after 1.5 miles) turn left toward Accomac at a crossroads with Route 764. Park in the center of town next to the courthouse green.

To Accomac from the Chesapeake Bay Bridge-Tunnel at Norfolk: After crossing the bridge-tunnel, follow Route 13 north from the toll plaza for more than 46.0 miles. Pass an exit for Business Route 13 toward Accomac, then (after 1.1 miles) turn right toward Accomac at a crossroads with Route 764. Park in the center of town next to the courthouse green.

To Accomac from Salisbury and the Delaware and Maryland seashore resorts: Follow Route 13 south from the vicinity of Salisbury, or Route 113 south from the vicinity of the Delaware and Maryland beach resorts. In either case, go to the junction of Route 13 and Route 113 near Pocomoke City, and from there continue south on Route 13. After crossing the state line into Virginia, continue south on Route 13 for nearly 22.0 miles. Pass an exit for Business Route 13 toward Accomac, then (after 1.5 miles) turn left toward Accomac at a crossroads with Route 764. Park in the center of town next to the courthouse green.

Accomac, spelled without a k at the end, is the seat of Accomack County. Although Accomack County was established in 1663, the area that had been settled by the English did not at that time reach as far north or as far inland as the present-day town of Accomac. So for fifteen years the county court met at Pungoteague, farther south and closer to Chesapeake Bay; then for a few more years court sessions alternated between Onancock, which was the county's chief port and center of commerce, and Metompkin (now Accomac), which was selected for its central location. Travel distance to court was an important consideration because county residents had many reasons for going. Court was not only where litigants resolved disputes, but also where all freemen voted (and were fined if they failed to vote), where residents petitioned for this or that government act or improvement, where wills were probated, where land transactions and sales of important chattels were recorded, and even where divine services were sometimes held.

In 1693 the court of Accomack County was established permanently at Metompkin, meeting at first in a tavern. In 1710 a wooden courthouse was built (and for ten years was used also as a place of worship). But not until 1786 did the Virginia General Assembly, in response to a petition by residents of Metompkin, pass legislation providing that "ten acres of land, the property of Richard Drummond, adjoining Accomack Courthouse, shall be laid out into lots of half an acre each, with convenient streets, and together with twenty other half acre lots already improved shall form a town by the name of Drummond." Trustees were empowered to sell the lots in order to pay Richard Drummond. The purchaser of each lot was required to build a house at least 16 feet on each side within two years. In addition to its two dozen houses, Drummondtown at that time also had a tavern, a saddle shop, at least one store, a courthouse that had been rebuilt in brick in 1756, a wooden jail, and a brick house for the jailor.

During the late eighteenth century and the first half of the nineteenth century, Drummondtown prospered, as is readily apparent from the handsome churches and houses that were built during this period (and which are detailed in the walking tour described below). In 1835 the town was described as follows in *A New and Comprehensive Gazetteer of Virginia and the District of Columbia*:

> Accomack Court House, or Drummondtown, besides a brick court-house and jail, contains a Methodist house of worship, 39 dwelling houses, 1 common school, 3 mercantile stores, 1 tannery, 2 saddle and

harness makers, 3 tailors, 3 cabinet makers, 1 watch and clock maker, 1 carriage maker, and 2 boot and shoe factories. There are 3 grist mills in the vicinity The population is 240, including 4 attorneys and 2 physicians. County courts are held on the last Monday of every month. . . .

In 1893 the name of Drummondtown was changed to Accomac. By then the village, which had been bypassed by the railroad in 1884, was threatened with relocation of the county seat to the new town of Parksley on the railroad. Although the county's voters rejected the move in 1895, Accomac again suffered economic loss when the town was bypassed by Route 13 in the 1920s.

Today Accomac is a small and quiet place. Although the town's commercial main street is somewhat decayed, the courthouse green (with its clustered lawyer's offices) and the nearby residential streets possess an air of prosperity and historic continuity derived in large part from the ongoing business of county government.

WALKING TOUR OF ACCOMAC: This short tour, which entails little more than a walk around the town's oldest block, is shown by the bold line on Map 42.

Start at the county office building, which is located on Route 764 a few hundred yards from the intersection with Business Route 13. Across the street from the county office building is the **Debtor's Prison**, built in 1783 as a home for the county jailor and converted in 1842 to use as a place where insolvent debtors were confined separately from criminal prisoners. As small as it is, this structure — which has two lower rooms and a loft — is substantially larger than the minimum 16 by 16 feet required for houses when the town was laid out in 1786. A sign on the door explains current arrangements for gaining entry to the prison, where there is a small museum.

From the intersection of Business Route 13 and Route 764, follow a relatively narrow local street (Road 1502) away from the courthouse, as shown by the bold line on Map 42. The large brick structure at the corner on Business Route 13 is the former **Accomac Hotel**, built in 1922 to replace a colonial tavern that had burned the previous year. As noted on the historic marker in front of the hotel, the tavern that previously stood here was the birthplace of Henry A. Wise, governor of Virginia immediately before the Civil War.

At the corner of Road 1502 and Road 1503 (Back Street) is the **Makemie Presbyterian Church**, built in 1837 and

MAP 42 -- Accomac walking tour

named for Francis Makemie, the first Presbyterian minister in America. Behind the church is a statue of Makemie. During his life (1658-1708), Makemie organized Presbyterian churches at Snow Hill and Rehobeth, Maryland, and preached from the Carolinas to New York. When he was not traveling, he lived in Accomack County, where he had substantial property and various business interests.

On the corner across Road 1502 from Makemie Presbyterian Church is a house called **Seven Gables**, the oldest part of which was built near the end of the eighteenth century. The one-room structure next to the house and fronting on Road 1502 was once used as the office of a doctor who lived at Seven Gables in the 1840s.

At the T-intersection where Road 1502 meets Road 1503, turn left. The first house on the right is the **Fletcher House**, built about 1817. Continue along Road 1503 for several hundred yards to a long house on the left called **The Haven** and consisting of eight sections strung out in a row, of which the oldest part was built about 1794.

Turn around and return past the front of Makemie Presbyterian Church. Half way down the block on the right is the small clapboard **office of St. James Episcopal Church**, and next beyond it is the brick **rectory**, built about 1811. The office, like that next to Seven Gables, was originally used by a doctor. Throughout the Civil War, when Virginia's Eastern Shore was occupied by Union forces, their commander made the rectory his headquarters; what is now the church office was his telegraph office. Although the Episcopal church was unscathed by the war, the town's Methodist and Presbyterian churches were damaged by federal troops who used them for barracks and stables.

Turn right at the corner with Route 605, past **Bloodsworth Cottage**, built in the late 1700s. Next on the right is **St. James Episcopal Church**, constructed in 1838 in the Greek Revival style and containing inside, on the altar wall, *trompe d'oeil* architectural effects first painted about 1855 and recently restored.

Turn right at the T-intersection with Business Route 13. The second house on the right (set back only a dozen feet from the road) is the **Seymour House**, of which the oldest part was built in 1791. The arrangement of distinct sections, commonly described as "big house, little house, colonnade, and kitchen," was fairly common on Virginia's Eastern Shore in the early

1800s. Also popular at that time was the more modest double house, featuring a passage joining two somewhat larger but nearly identical sections. (There is a double house about 0.3 mile farther north along the road, on the right-hand side.) Still other houses, termed step or telescope houses, have sections that are progressively bigger or smaller.

In the yard just beyond Seymour House, notice the round **ice house**, set low in the ground and with a conical roof.

Leaving behind Seymour House on the right, continue straight ahead to the courthouse green, where the walking tour ends.

CAR TOUR OF ACCOMACK AND NORTHAMPTON COUNTIES: The bold line on Map 43 shows the route followed by this 95-mile car tour.

From the courthouse green at the center of Accomac, follow Business Route 13 southwest. (That is, start with the courthouse green on your right.) Go only a few hundred yards, then turn left onto Route 605, which is part of the old stage road along the ocean side of Virginia's Eastern Shore. After 4.4 miles you will enter the hamlet of **Locustville**.

At the northern edge of Locustville is the **Locustville United Methodist Church** (built in 1923) and across the road is **Locustville Academy**, which operated as a private school from 1859 until 1879, when it was acquired by the county school board. Girls used the first floor and boys occupied the second floor. Locustville Academy prepared its male students for business careers or college. Subjects included not only the usual reading, writing, and arithmetic, but also Greek and Latin and, for girls, such accomplishments as piano and drawing.

Locustville proper is located another 0.3 mile beyond the academy on Route 605. This hamlet is typical of many small Eastern Shore villages of the nineteenth century. By all means find an excuse to stop in at the **general store**, even if only to buy a snack. Across Route 605 are two double houses, and about 70 yards farther along the road from the general store is the old **Locustville Hotel**.

CAR TOUR (Map 43): From Locustville continue south on Route 605 about 4.0 miles to a T-intersection with Route 180, and there turn left. Go 0.8 mile to the waterfront village of Wachapreague.

Although a wharf, shipping firm, and village were established at **Wachapreague** in 1872, it was not until construction of the 30-room Hotel Wachapreague in 1902 that the town became a resort for water-fowl hunters and sport fishermen attracted by advertisements in northern newspapers and national outdoor journals. From the nearest railroad station at Keller, visitors were conveyed to Wachapreague by the hotel's carriages. In the 1920s the town's attractions included a dance hall, a poolroom, a drugstore with soda fountain, and a movie theater. Although the resort business gradually tapered off and the hotel itself burned in 1978, the town is still a base for charter boats and recreational fishermen.

CAR TOUR (Map 43): From the waterfront in Wachapreague, follow Route 180 for only 0.4 mile out of town, then turn left onto Route 605. Follow Route 605 for 4.0 miles to the intersection with Route 182 on the outskirts of the town of Quinby, with occasional glimpses to the left of wooded Parramore Island in the distance. Turn right onto Route 182 and go 2.3 miles to a crossroads with Route 600, and there turn left. Follow Route 600 (again part of the old seaside stage road) for 5.0 miles to a crossroads with Route 603, and there turn left toward Willis Wharf. Go 1.1 mile; after crossing a bridge, turn left into a parking lot for a boat basin, where there is a good view back toward the village's waterfront.

In contrast to Wachapreague, which caters to recreational fishermen, **Willis Wharf** is a base for commercial oystering and clamming and seafood processing. When they are in operation, the waterfront packing houses fill the air with steam and fishy odors, giving the place an aura of economic dynamism that it altogether lacks when the ramshackle processing plants are closed.

Called Downings Wharf in the early 1800s, the village was renamed for Edward Willis, who moved here in 1850 and built the **Willis Store**, which still stands at the corner where Route 603 meets the waterfront. The store also includes a restaurant open only on weekends.

CAR TOUR (Map 43): From Willis Wharf return on Route 603 by the way you came to the crossroads with Route 600, and there turn left to continue south on Route 600. Go 4.2 miles, then turn left on Route 608 in order to visit The Nature Conservancy's Brownsville Farm. After 1.1 miles, turn sharply right into a white oystershell driveway that leads to a parking area for the office of The Nature Conservancy's Virginia Coast Reserve.

MAP 43 -- Car tour of Northampton and Accomack counties

The Nature Conservancy is an international, nonprofit organization devoted to preserving ecologically important areas, which also, of course, often have great scenic and recreational value. Among The Nature Conservancy's largest and most spectacular holdings is the **Virginia Coast Reserve**, which has its headquarters at **Brownsville**, a 2,400-acre working farm named for John Brown, who patented this land in 1652.

Brownsville Farm is merely a small part of the Virginia Coast Reserve, which extends for 60 miles along the Atlantic coast and consists of 14 islands, vast saltmarsh tracts, and adjacent mainland sites altogether totaling 40,000 acres. With funding from the Mary Flagler Cary Charitable Trust of New York and other donors, The Nature Conservancy has since 1969 acquired most of the barrier islands of Virginia's Eastern Shore, and those that it does not own are (with the lone exception of Cedar Island) the property of the state and federal governments. In addition to buying land outright, The Nature Conservancy tries to protect its core holdings by working with nearby landowners to devise acceptable conservation easements and with local governments to help formulate zoning ordinances that balance conservation and development.

Except for Parramore, Shipshoal, and Revel islands, the barrier islands of the Virginia Coast Reserve are open to the the public during daytime for such uses as hiking, birding, fishing, and nature study. However, since they are accessible only by boat, the barrier islands are not discussed further here except to note that The Nature Conservancy itself offers occasional field trips to the islands. For information call the Virginia Coast Reserve at (804) 442-3049 or stop by the office. Trips fill early, so make reservations well in advance. The office also has information for people who wish to provide support by becoming members of The Nature Conservancy or Friends of the Virginia Coast Reserve, as is well worthwhile.

WALKING AT BROWNSVILLE FARM: First, a few words of caution. Brownsville is private property; walkers are welcome only to the extent that they do not hinder ongoing research and farm operations, so stick to the farm roads and trails. Because Brownsville is a working farm, farm vehicles are sometimes present, so be alert. Also, with the permission of the Virginia Coast Reserve, deer hunting occurs at Brownsville during fall and early winter. In the past hunters have been barred from the area through which the route described below passes, but policy may change, so it is wise to wear orange. Even during the deer season, you can avoid hunters by walking on Sunday, when hunting is prohibited.

Map 44 shows Brownsville Farm, where shell roads and foot trails pass through woods and skirt cultivated fields that in turn occupy a peninsula jutting into the marsh. A dike enables walkers to cross the marsh to some timber islands — **the Hammocks** — fronting on Hog Island Bay. A round-trip walk to the Hammocks, as shown by the bold line on Map 44, totals 4.0 miles.

Starting at the office parking lot, cross the large grassy area diagonally toward the left (away from the office). Pass through the woods on a boardwalk, then turn right onto a rutted farm road, which leads nearly a mile to a screened shed.

After passing behind the screened shed, the path becomes rougher. Go several hundred yards as the path bends left, then right. As you continue along the rutted farm track with a field on the right, watch for an obscure gap in the hedgerow to the left, where a small footbridge and a dike lead across the marsh to the Hammocks. Follow the path across the marsh, then across one timber island to another island. There the trail peters out — although you can continue along the shore several hundred yards for a view out across Hog Island Bay. Hog Island itself is 8 miles distant and has such a low profile that it is barely visible.

As shown on Map 44, Brownsville Farm also includes **Brownsville House**, built in 1806 by a member of the locally prominent Upshur family, into which John Brown's granddaughter married about 1690. Brownsville House has been restored by The Nature Conservancy and serves as the residence of the director of the Virginia Coast Reserve. If you want to tour this handsome house, inquire at the office for information about the infrequent occasions when it is open to the public.

CAR TOUR (Map 43): From the Brownsville Farm office and parking lot, return on Route 608 by the way you came to the intersection with Route 600. Turn left onto Route 600 and follow it south 10.8 miles to a crossroads with Route 631 (Indiantown Drive) and there turn right. Follow Route 631 past the old Eastville Station and across Route 13 to a T-intersection with Business Route 13 in Eastville. Visible to the right is the courthouse green; to the left is the Eastville Inn. Turn left, then immediately right in order to park and explore on foot the center of this historic village.

Map 44 -- Walking at Brownsville Farm

Eastville is the seat of Northampton County. After a courthouse had been erected farther south at Kings Creek in 1664, residents from the north end of the county complained that they were inconvenienced and in 1677 requested that the court meet at a more central location. Later that year the court convened for the first time at "the Hornes," as the vicinity of Eastville was then called, supposedly because several creeks penetrate the area like the prongs of antlers.

Gradually the Hornes evolved into the permanent seat of county government. At first court was held in a "victualling house" or tavern — a precursor of the 1724 **Eastville Inn** — but beginning in 1690 the justices gathered in a new courthouse erected by the tavern keeper at his own expense in order to induce the court to continue to meet at the Hornes. In 1732 a brick courthouse was built; termed the **Old Courthouse**, it still stands on one side of the courthouse green, where it was moved in 1913 to make room for the Confederate monument. Another, larger courthouse was built in 1795, and the Old Courthouse was sold for use as a store. Now the Old Courthouse, the adjacent **Old Clerk's Office** (perhaps built as early as 1750 but certainly by the 1830s) and the **Debtor's Prison** (located behind the Old Clerk's Office) are maintained as a museum to which keys may be obtained on weekdays during business hours from the current clerk's office in the 1899 courthouse, which also faces the courthouse green.

In 1773 the owner of 20 acres adjacent to the courthouse divided his tract into 40 half-acre lots and offered them for sale. During the following half-century, the courthouse village acquired considerable commercial importance, as described in 1835 in *A New and Comprehensive Gazetteer of Virginia and the District of Columbia*:

> Eastville P.V. [Post Village] and seat of justice is in about the middle of the county and two miles from the Chesapeake Bay and the Atlantic Ocean. Eastville has 2 principal streets running at right angles to each other. Besides the usual county buildings it contains 21 dwelling houses, 4 mercantile stores, 2 taverns, 1 new and handsome Episcopal church, and 1 common school and 1 Bible society. The mechanical pursuits are : 1 coach factory, which completes about $6,000 worth of work annually; 1 harness maker, 1 cabinet maker, 2 blacksmiths, 2 boot and shoe manufacturers, 3 tailors, 1 house and sign painter and 1 hatter.
>
> There are in Eastville 3 castor oil manufactories and 2 others in the county. The county exports about 20,000 gallons of oil annually. The principal commerce is with Baltimore, Philadelphia, and New York.

The "new and handsome Episcopal church" mentioned in the gazetteer is **Christ Episcopal Church**, built in 1828 and containing stained glass windows from Germany. It is located on the north edge of town, where you may want to stop briefly as you drive out.

In 1884 the railroad was constructed a mile east of Eastville, prompting residential and commercial development in the area between the village and its station. The new railroad towns of Exmore and Cape Charles, however, grew far more rapidly than Eastville, which in the second half of the twentieth century has declined as a commercial center. Today this attractive and historic village is sustained entirely by the presence of the county government.

CAR TOUR (Map 43): From the intersection of Business Route 13 and Route 631 in Eastville, follow Business Route 13 north 1.3 miles to an intersection with the main Route 13, and there turn left. Follow Route 13 north only 2.4 miles, then turn left onto Route 628 and immediately turn right onto Route 618, which is part of the old bayside stage road. After 1.9 miles, continue straight ahead on Route 622 (Bayside Road) where Route 618 turns right. Follow Route 622 for 1.6 miles to the very old and now nearly non-existent hamlet of **Bridgetown** (where there was a settlement as early as 1660) and there bear right onto Route 619. After only a few hundred yards, turn right into the driveway of Hungars Episcopal Church.

Hungars Episcopal Church was built in 1742 on the site of an earlier church dating from about 1680. Its furnishings are supposed to have been very rich; it even had an organ, one of the earliest in the colonies. Yet following the American Revolution, the church was abandoned as many Anglican clergymen refused to affiliate themselves with the new American Episcopal hierarchy and also as much of the population turned to Methodism. The church eventually was reopened in 1819. In serious need of repair, the structure was slightly shortened in 1851, when the front was rebuilt in the same Flemish bond pattern as the original. At the same time, side doors were eliminated.

CAR TOUR (Map 43): From Hungars Episcopal Church, turn right out the driveway and continue north on Route 619, which after a while becomes Route 618. Continue as straight as possible for 2.6 miles to **Franktown**, which in the 1800s was considered an important village, with a post office and tavern on the main bayside stage road.

From the center of Franktown, continue north on Route 618. After 3.8 miles, turn left (north) onto Route 13, but follow it only 1.7 miles, then turn left onto Route 178. Go 1.0 mile, then turn

left in Belle Haven to continue on Route 178 northbound.
Follow Route 178 for 8.0 miles to the hamlet of Pungoteague.
For a bit of local color and perhaps a snack, take the time to
stop in at the old general store located at the intersection of
Route 178 and Route 180.

With its old frame houses and stores, sleepy **Pungoteague** is a
quintessential nineteenth-century crossroads village. But its history
goes back much further, as evidenced by the presence here of **St.
George's Episcopal Church**, the oldest church building on Virginia's Eastern Shore. (The church is located on the left side of Route
178 as you leave town going north; be sure to stop by.) Started in
1638, St. George's was constructed nearly in the shape of a Greek Cross
— or that is, with arms almost equal. This is not what is seen today,
however, because during the Civil War the building was badly damaged
by Union soldiers, who used it to stable their horses. All interior wood
was ripped out and even one wing of the brick shell was torn down.
What survives is a rectangular structure patched together from the opposing arms or transept of the original church.

St. George's was built on the site of a still earlier church erected in
1678, but even before that Pungoteague was a place of note, where in
1664 the court of the newly-formed Accomack County met in the house
of the area's first English settler. The court continued at or near Pungoteague for fourteen years.

An historic marker on the northern outskirts of Pungoteague marks
the site of **Coles Tavern** (also called **Folkes Tavern**), where the
county court met in 1667. That same year there was presented at the
tavern a play called "The Bear and the Cub" (said to be the first dramatic
performance in England's American colonies). The play turned out to
be grist for the court's mill after a member of the audience (a certain
John Martin) complained under oath that the presentation was indecent.
In response the court ordered "that Cornelius Watkinson, Phillip
Howard and William Darby do appear in those habiliments that they
then acted in, and give a draught of the speeches and passages they
used." Darby, the author, was even held without bail until the play was
acted before the court, whose justices decided that there was no inde-
cency and assessed against Martin the court costs, including board for
Darby while in jail.

In 1835 *A New and Comprehensive Gazetteer of Virginia and the
District of Columbia* described Pungoteague as having "20 dwelling
houses, 1 Methodist house of worship, 1 Episcopal house of worship,
1 common school, 1 tavern, 1 mercantile store, 1 tannery, 1 boot and
shoe maker and 1 blacksmith shop. The trade from Pungoteague Creek

employs 5 regular coasting vessels. The population is 100 including 1 physician." In all likelihood, this summary is apt for Pungoteague throughout most of the nineteenth century — until, that is, construction of the railroad down the middle of the peninsula in 1884 demoted Pungoteague to the status of a back-roads residential village.

CAR TOUR (Map 43): From Pungoteague continue north on Route 178 for 6.1 miles to a T-intersection, and there turn right toward Onancock. Go 1.1 miles, then turn left at a T-intersection with Market Street in Onancock. After only 0.4 mile, turn right into the driveway of **Kerr Place**, which is marked by a sign, or perhaps more noticeably by a white fence with large pointed posts. Built by John S. Kerr (pronounced Carr) at the end of the eighteenth century on what was then the outskirts of Onancock, the brick mansion now houses a collection of period furniture, paintings, and costumes that altogether make Kerr Place a "must see."

From Kerr Place turn right out the driveway and continue along Market Street, eventually passing the old town square on the right, followed by several old houses on the left. Continue as Market Street reaches the waterfront and curves right past the **Hopkins & Bros. Store**, which is worth a visit. An excursion boat for Tangier Island leaves from here June through September or early October; ask for a brochure or call (804) 787-8220 for information. (See also Chapter 13.) In addition to an assortment of miscellaneous merchandise, the store has a restaurant.

Onancock is the result of legislation, passed in 1680 by the Virginia House of Burgesses, calling for the establishment of a port of entry in every county to facilitate trade and the collection of export and import duties, as required by the authorities in England. At each port, 50 acres of land were to be purchased by the Virginia government and laid out in half-acre lots. For the port of Accomack County, a site at the head of navigation of Onancock Creek was selected, and the land was purchased from Charles Scarburgh in 1681. The purchasers of lots were required to pay 100 pounds of tobacco and to build a house at least 20 feet long within four months. At first the place was named Port Scarburgh, but within ten years the settlement was being called Onancock Town. All tobacco shipped from Accomack County was supposed to be loaded at Onancock Town, and all goods imported for sale in the county were to be unloaded there.

For three centuries Onancock (now more or less amalgamated with

Onley and the large shopping center on Route 13) has been Accomack County's chief commercial center. Between 1681 and 1693 the county court met here on and off in a courthouse that presumably stood on the present-day town square. By 1800 Onancock was spreading eastward from its original boundaries. During the nineteenth century, ships built and owned locally by such merchants as Stephen Hopkins sailed regularly to other Chesapeake ports and even the West Indies. Toward the end of the century, when Onancock was at the height of its prosperity, steamboats took on huge quantities of potatoes, onions, strawberries, and other Eastern Shore produce at the town wharf, and even as late as the 1920s there was daily steamer service from Onancock to Baltimore.

CAR TOUR (Map 43): As Market Street curves past the front of the Hopkins & Bros. Store, it turns into King Street. Follow King Street away from the waterfront and past more old houses built before the Civil War. Again pass the town square on the right. At a T-intersection with North Street, turn left and continue out of town. Go 1.8 miles, then turn right at a T-intersection. After 2.1 miles, turn left at a crossroads with Route 316. Follow Route 316 north 5.5 miles. After entering Parksley, turn right onto Route 176, but immediately after crossing the railroad, turn left into the large parking lot that occupies several acres next to the tracks in front of Parksley's main commercial street. With the railroad on your left, continue through the parking lot for several hundred yards to the Eastern Shore Railway Museum on the left.

The **Eastern Shore Railway Museum** includes a small station containing a clerk's office and two racially segregated waiting rooms. Adjacent to the station (which was actually moved to Parksley from Hopeton) is an interesting collection of railroad cars.

It is fitting that there be a train museum in **Parksley**, since the town was created entirely in response to the railroad. While the tracks were being laid in 1884, Henry R. Bennett, a traveling salesman, saw the possibility of an entirely new town here on the farm of Benjamin Parks. With his friends and relatives, Bennett organized the Parksley Land Improvement Company, which bought 160 acres from Parks and laid out streets in a grid pattern on both sides of the tracks. Bennett's planned community featured legal provisions for concentrating commercial establishments near the railroad in the center of town, for setting aside the sites of parks, schools, and churches, for barring the sale of liquor, and for segregating blacks in a separate district to the southwest, which later was placed outside the town limits. Parksley grew rapidly, with the result that there is more Victorian residential architecture here than in most other towns of Virginia's Eastern Shore, as can be seen by touring Parksley's residential streets, particularly west of the railroad.

CAR TOUR (Map 43): From the large parking lot at the center of Parksley, turn left onto Route 176 (Bennett Street) and follow it east out of town for 2.5 miles to the intersection with Route 13, where the car tour ends.

ORDER FORM

You can photocopy this form, or you can just send the necessary information to the address below.

Rambler Books
1430 Park Avenue
Baltimore, MD 21217

Please send me _____ copies of *Day Trips in Delmarva* at $9.95 apiece ($7.95 apiece if ordering five or more) plus $2.00 per total order for shipping. My payment in the amount of _____ is enclosed.

Please send me a list and order form for your Country Walks books describing excursions near major cities: Yes _____. No _____.

Send books and/or information to:

Name:

_____

Address:

_____

_____Zip: _____

COUNTRY WALKS NEAR BALTIMORE: "A model of pith and practicality. . . . The maps excel." — *Baltimore Sun* • **COUNTRY WALKS NEAR BOSTON**: "An invaluable paperback." — *Boston Sunday Globe*. "This is my favorite trail guide. . . . Unlike the others, it features a lot of social, cultural, and natural history." — *Boston Phoenix* • **COUNTRY WALKS NEAR CHICAGO**: "A handy guide. . . . The general information sections range in content from geology, birding, and the politics of an area, to tree identification and history. Most of these sections — which, if combined, constitute three-fourths of the book — are excellent." — *Chicago Tribune* • **COUNTRY WALKS NEAR PHILADELPHIA**: "Here is food for thought and good walking." — *Walkways* • **COUNTRY WALKS NEAR WASHINGTON** and **MORE COUNTRY WALKS NEAR WASHINGTON**: "Cream of the local outdoors-guide crop. . . . [The author] starts each trip/chapter with history, perspective and a map, and ends it with meticulous step-by-step directions." — *Washington Post*. "The happy union between a utilitarian and historically informative guide." — *The Washington Times Magazine*